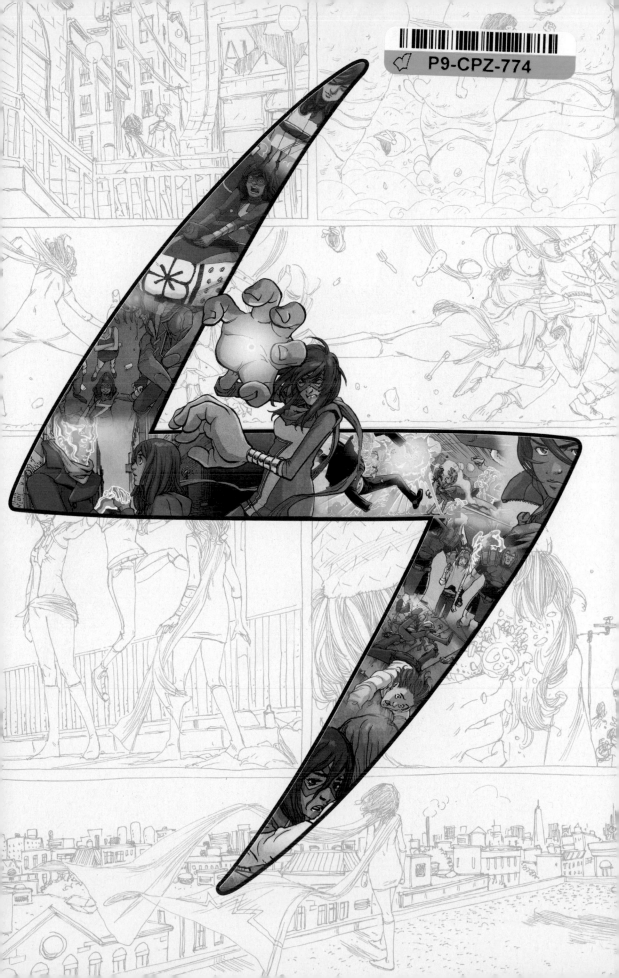

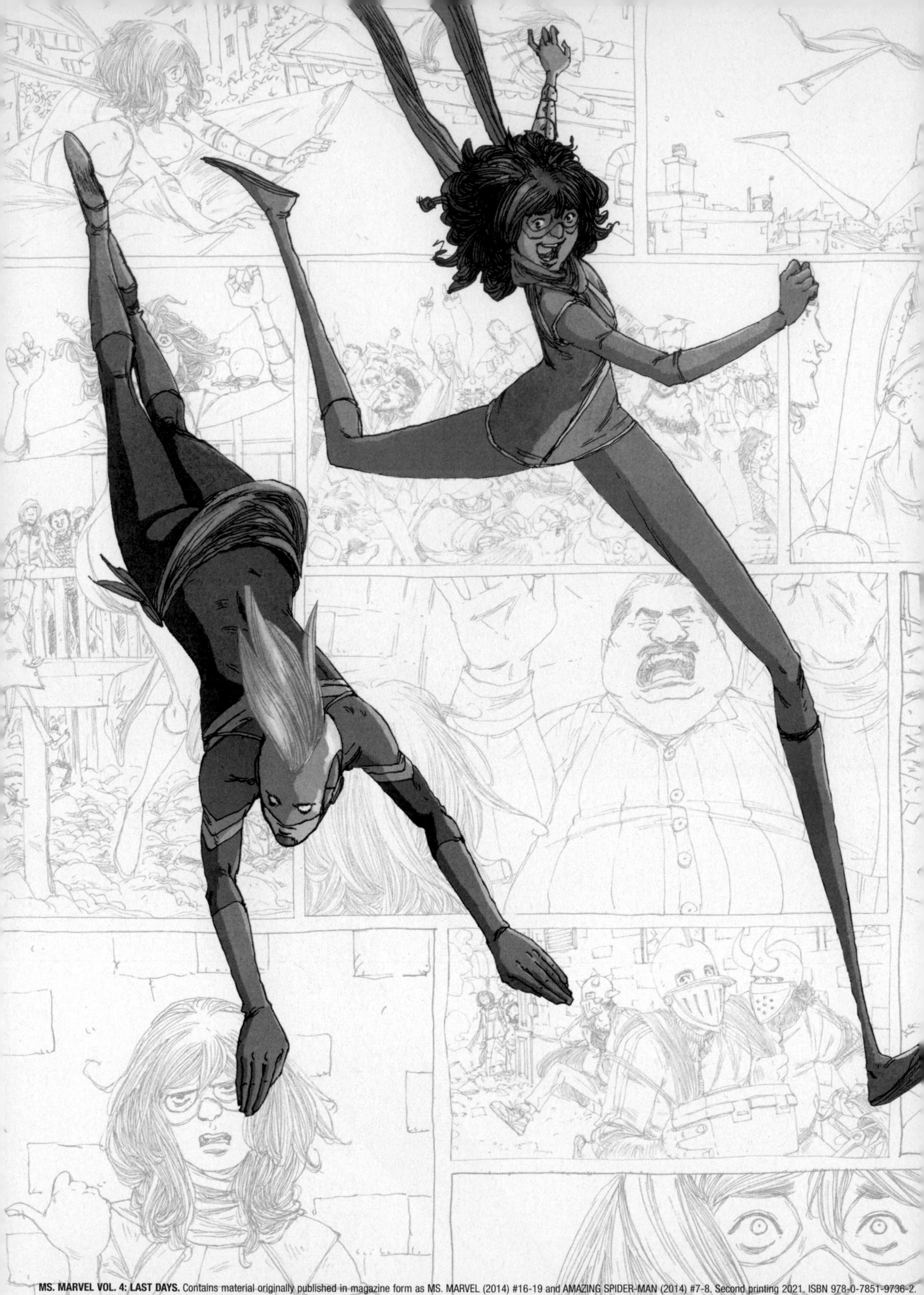

MS. MARVEL VOL. 4: LAST DAYS. Contains material originally published in magazine form as MS. MARVEL (2014) #16-19 and AMAZING SPIDER-MAN (2014) #7-8. Second printing 2021. ISBN 978-0-7851-9736-2. Published by MARVEL WORLDWIDE, INC., a subsidiary of MARVEL ENTERTAINMENT, LLC. OFFICE OF PUBLICATION: 1290 Avenue of the Americas, New York, NY 10104. **Printed in Canada.** KEVIN FEIGE, Chief Creative Officer; DAN BUCKLEY, President, Marvel Entertainment; JOE QUESADA, EVP & Creative Director; DAVID BOGART, Associate Publisher & SVP of Talent Affairs; TOM BREVOORT, VP, Executive Editor; NICK LOWE, Executive Editor, VP of Content, Digital Publishing; DAVID GABRIEL, VP of Print & Digital Publishing; JEFF YOUNGQUIST, VP of Production & Special Projects; ALEX MORALES, Director of Publishing Operations; DAN EDINGTON, Managing Editor; RICKEY PURDIN, Director of Talent Relations; JENNIFER GRÜNWALD, Senior Editor, Special Projects; SUSAN CRESPI, Production Manager; STAN LEE, Chairman Emeritus. For information regarding advertising in Marvel Comics or on Marvel.com, please contact Vit DeBellis, Custom Solutions & Integrated Advertising Manager, at vdebellis@marvel.com. For Marvel subscription inquiries, please call 888-511-5480. **Manufactured between 11/26/2021 and 12/28/2021 by SOLISCO PRINTERS, SCOTT, QC, CANADA.**

10 9 8 7 6 5 4 3 2

MS. MARVEL

writer
G. WILLOW WILSON
artist
ADRIAN ALPHONA
color artist
IAN HERRING
letterer
VC'S JOE CARAMAGNA
cover art
KRIS ANKA
assistant editor
CHARLES BEACHAM
editor
SANA AMANAT

AMAZING SPIDER-MAN #7-8

"MS. MARVEL TEAM-UP" & "ADVENTURES IN BABYSITTING"
plot DAN SLOTT
script CHRISTOS GAGE
penciler GIUSEPPE CAMUNCOLI
inker CAM SMITH
colorist ANTONIO FABELA
letterer CHRIS ELIOPOULOS
cover art GIUSEPPE CAMUNCOLI,
CAM SMITH & ANTONIO FABELA
associate editor ELLIE PYLE
editor NICK LOWE

collection editor
JENNIFER GRÜNWALD
assistant editor
DANIEL KIRCHHOFFER
assistant managing editor
MAIA LOY
assistant managing editor
LISA MONTALBANO
vp production & special projects
JEFF YOUNGQUIST
svp print, sales & marketing
DAVID GABRIEL

editor in chief
C.B. CEBULSKI

PREVIOUSLY

AFTER A STRANGE TERRIGEN MIST DESCENDED UPON JERSEY CITY, KAMALA KHAN GOT POLYMORPH POWERS AND BECAME THE ALL-NEW...

WITH STRICT PARENTS ON HER CASE, HER BEST FRIEND BRUNO BY HER SIDE AND A WHOLE LOT OF WEIRD (LIKE "LOKI-TO-THE-SCHOOL-DANCE" WEIRD) ENSNARING JERSEY CITY, KAMALA SOON REALIZED THAT BEING A SUPER HERO IS...COMPLICATED.

BUT WHEN HER CRUSH, AN INHUMAN NAMED KAMRAN, TURNED OUT TO BE A KIDNAPPING LIAR, KAMALA LEARNED THAT BALANCING IT ALL WITH A BROKEN HEART...WELL, THAT'S JUST DOWNRIGHT HARD.

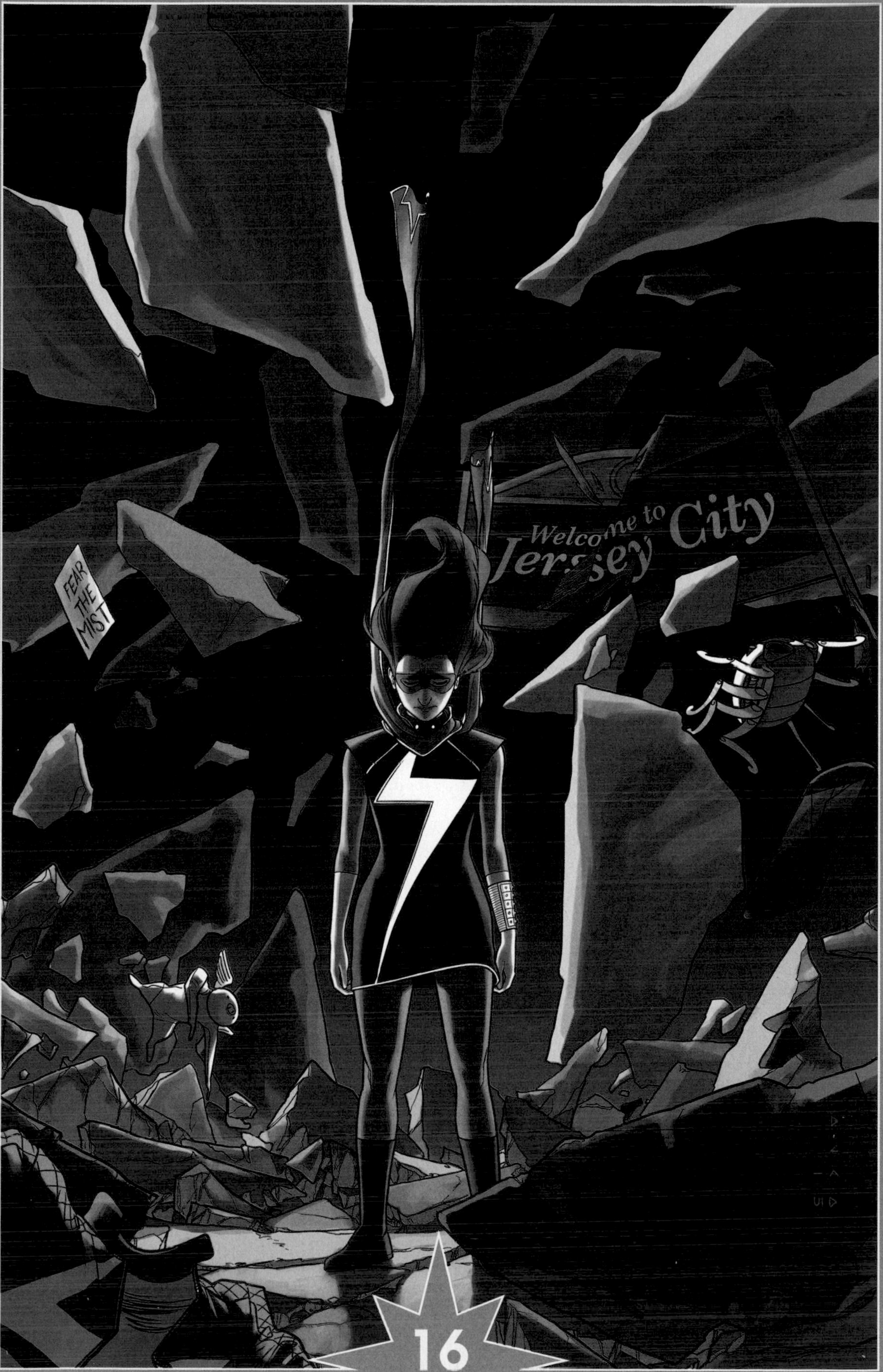
FEAR THE MIST
Welcome to Jersey City

JERSEY CITY WATERFRONT.

THREE WEEKS, TWO DAYS AND SEVENTEEN HOURS.

THAT'S HOW LONG I'VE SUCCESSFULLY *NOT* CALLED, TEXTED OR EMAILED KAMRAN.

SOULSONIC FRANKS

K SOULS
KOSHER

HOT DOG...
HOT SAU...
PRETZELS
PANDA...
SODA
WATER

IT'S GOTTEN SO BAD THAT I'VE STARTED PROCESSING MY FEELINGS WITH RANDOM STRANGERS.

Have you ever had your heart broken?

Sure.

Is it supposed to feel like the world is coming to an end?

I think that's pretty standard, yeah.

AND HOT DOGS.

Vat really shucks.

You get tougher. Eventually. I think.

Sh' too hard. I don' wanna.

Every day I wake up, and for a second, I forget. And for that second, it's fine. I feel normal.

Then I remember. After that comes the panic attack.

Rough stuff, kid.

LOTS OF HOT DOGS.

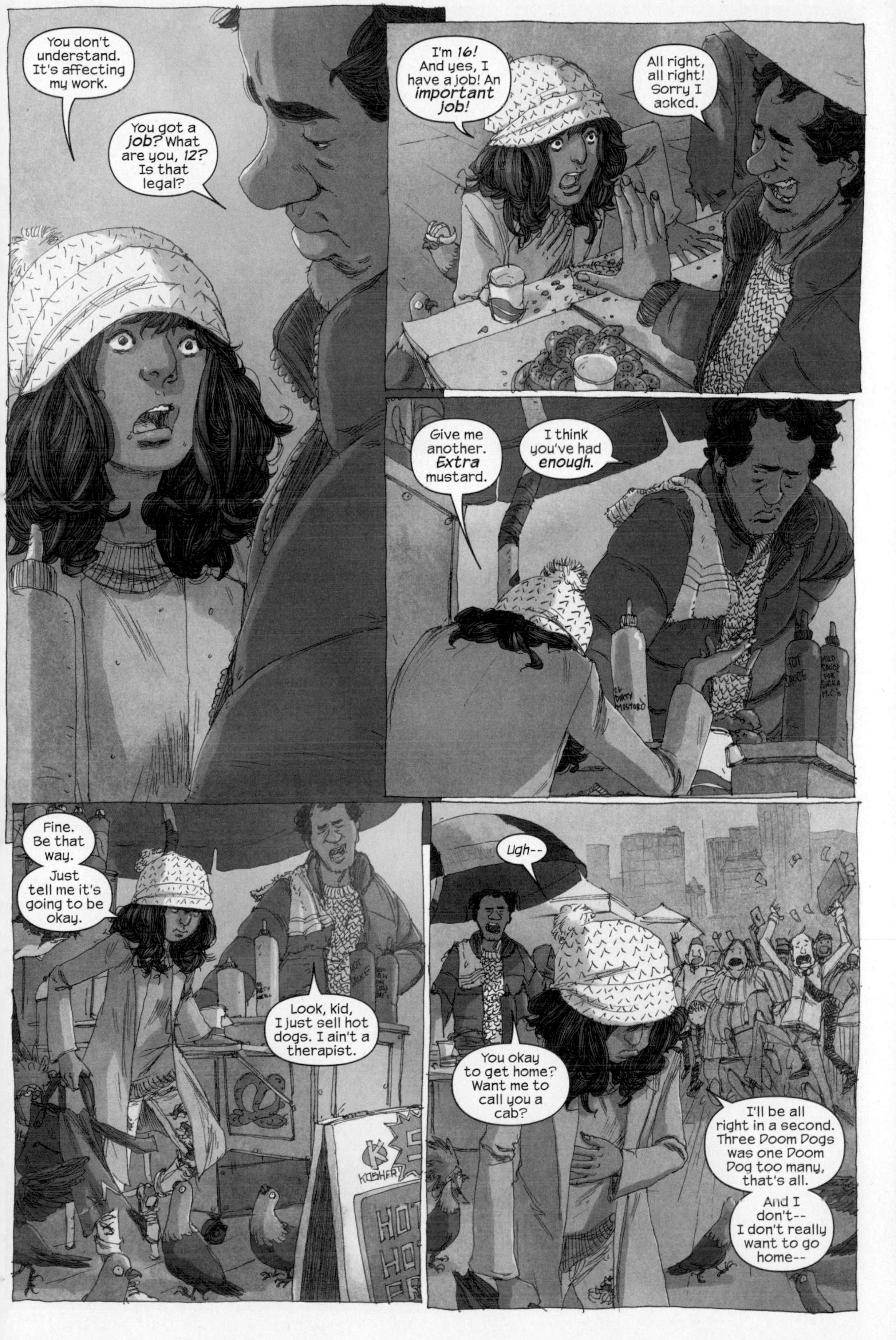
You don't understand. It's affecting my work.
You got a *job?* What are you, *12?* Is that legal?
I'm *16!* And yes, I have a job! An ***important*** ***job!***
All right, all right! Sorry I asked.
Give me another. ***Extra*** mustard.
I think you've had ***enough.***
Fine. Be that way.
Just tell me it's going to be okay.
Look, kid, I just sell hot dogs. I ain't a therapist.
KOSHER
Ugh--
You okay to get home? Want me to call you a cab?
I'll be all right in a second. Three Doom Dogs was one Doom Dog too many, that's all.
And I don't-- I don't really want to go home--

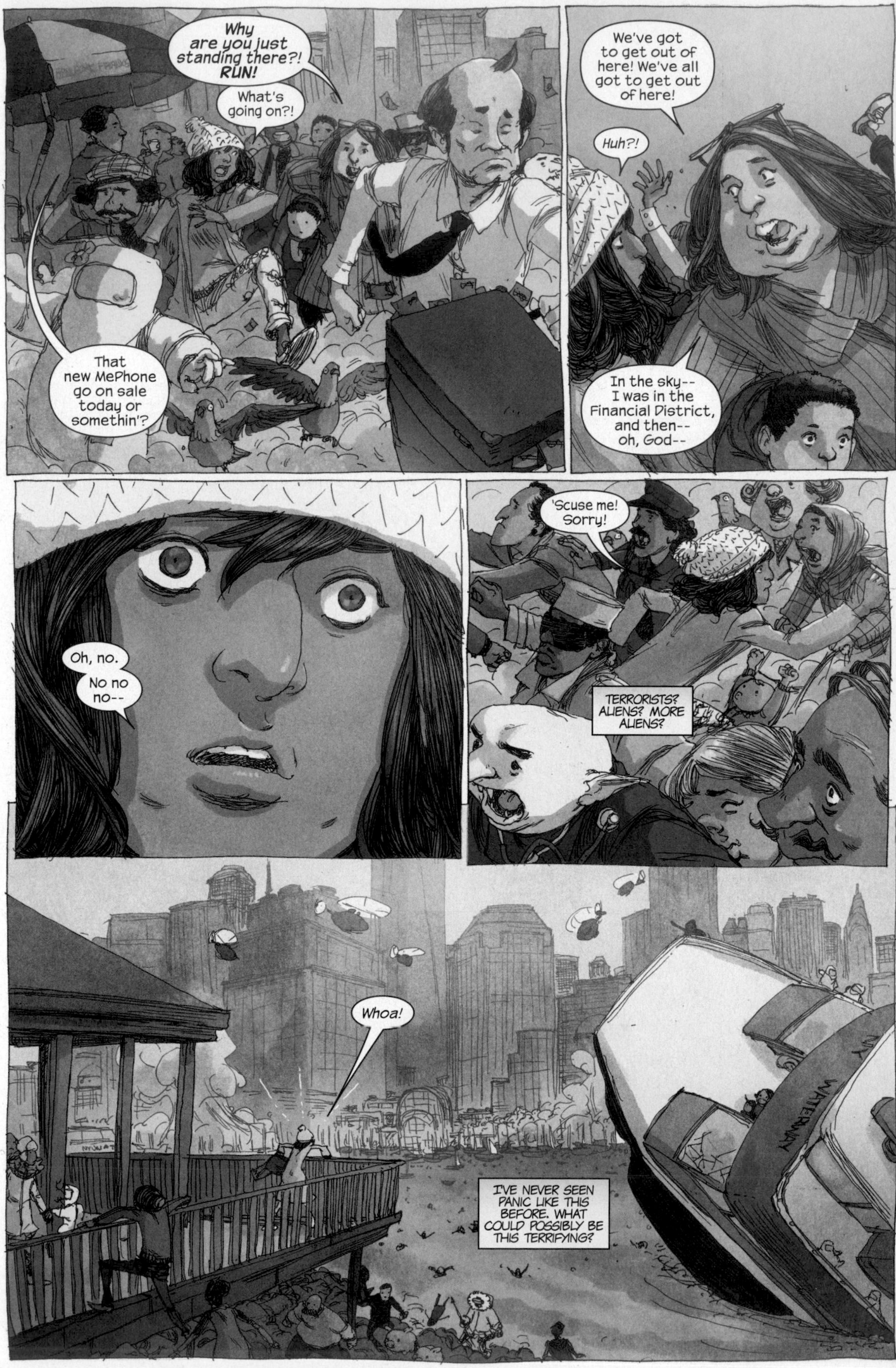
Why are you just standing there?! RUN!
What's going on?!
That new MePhone go on sale today or somethin'?
We've got to get out of here! We've all got to get out of here!
Huh?!
In the sky-- I was in the Financial District, and then-- oh, God--
Oh, no.
No no no--
'Scuse me! Sorry!
TERRORISTS? ALIENS? MORE ALIENS?
Whoa!
I'VE NEVER SEEN PANIC LIKE THIS BEFORE. WHAT COULD POSSIBLY BE THIS TERRIFYING?

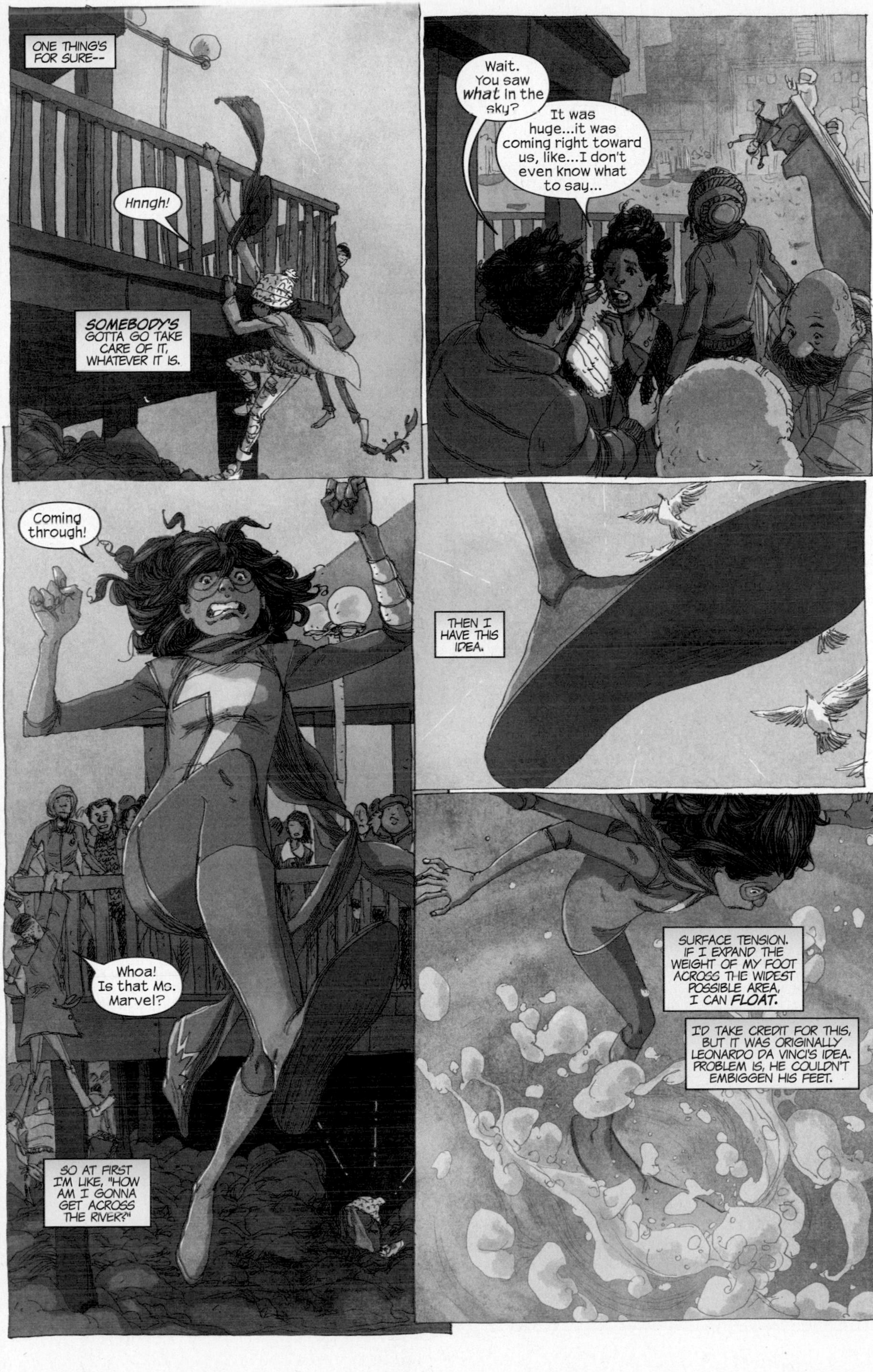
ONE THING'S FOR SURE--
Hnngh!
SOMEBODY'S GOTTA GO TAKE CARE OF IT, WHATEVER IT IS.
Wait. You saw what in the sky?
It was huge...it was coming right toward us, like...I don't even know what to say...
Coming through!
Whoa! Is that Ms. Marvel?
SO AT FIRST I'M LIKE, "HOW AM I GONNA GET ACROSS THE RIVER?"
THEN I HAVE THIS IDEA.
SURFACE TENSION. IF I EXPAND THE WEIGHT OF MY FOOT ACROSS THE WIDEST POSSIBLE AREA, I CAN FLOAT.
I'D TAKE CREDIT FOR THIS, BUT IT WAS ORIGINALLY LEONARDO DA VINCI'S IDEA. PROBLEM IS, HE COULDN'T EMBIGGEN HIS FEET.

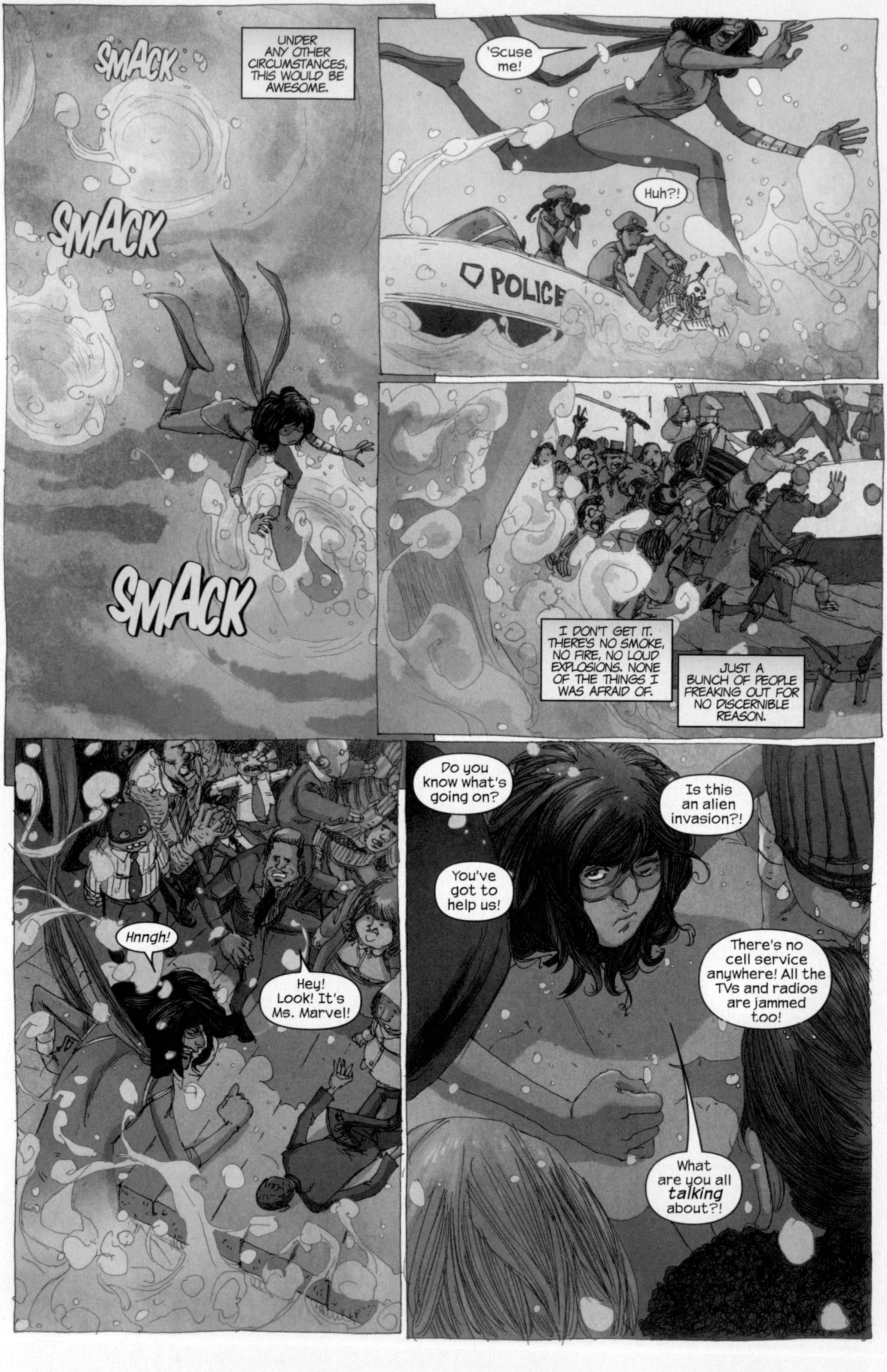
SMACK
UNDER ANY OTHER CIRCUMSTANCES, THIS WOULD BE AWESOME.
SMACK
SMACK
'Scuse me!
Huh?!
POLICE
I DON'T GET IT. THERE'S NO SMOKE, NO FIRE, NO LOUD EXPLOSIONS. NONE OF THE THINGS I WAS AFRAID OF.
JUST A BUNCH OF PEOPLE FREAKING OUT FOR NO DISCERNIBLE REASON.
Hnngh!
Hey! Look! It's Ms. Marvel!
Do you know what's going on?
Is this an alien invasion?!
You've got to help us!
There's no cell service anywhere! All the TVs and radios are jammed too!
What are you all *talking* about?!

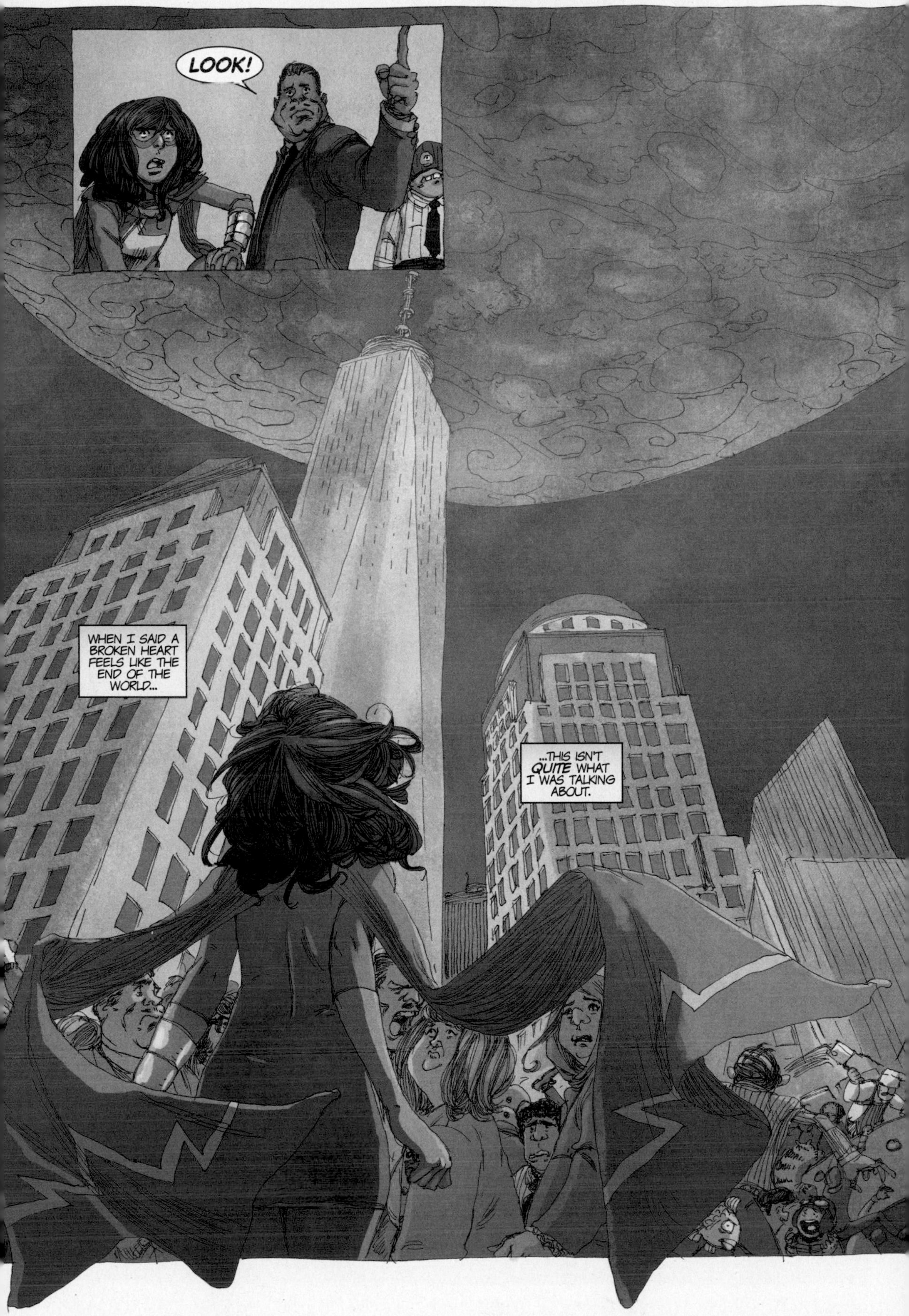
LOOK!
WHEN I SAID A BROKEN HEART FEELS LIKE THE END OF THE WORLD...
...THIS ISN'T QUITE WHAT I WAS TALKING ABOUT.

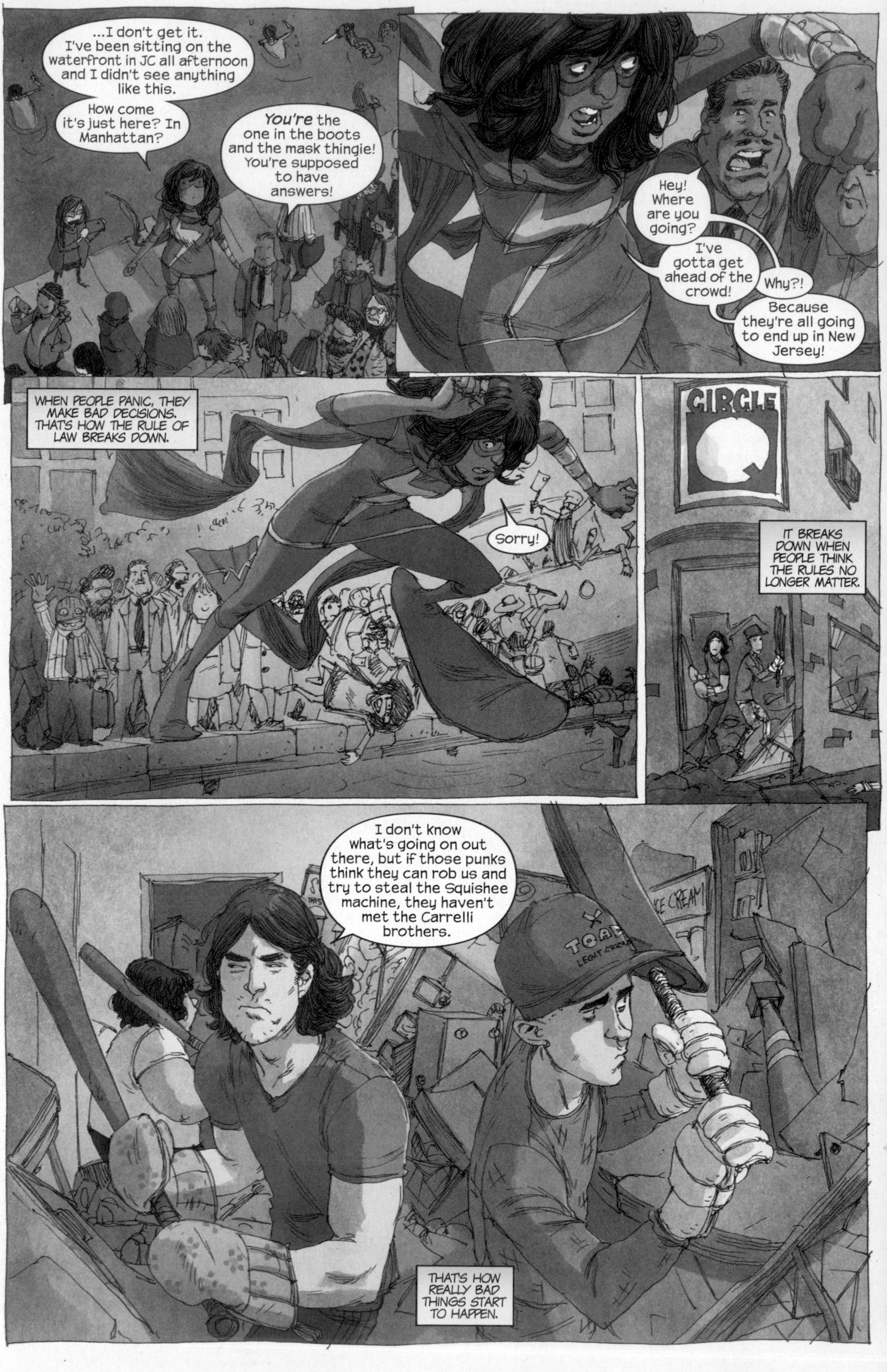
...I don't get it. I've been sitting on the waterfront in JC all afternoon and I didn't see anything like this.
How come it's just here? In Manhattan?
You're the one in the boots and the mask thingie! You're supposed to have answers!
Hey! Where are you going?
I've gotta get ahead of the crowd!
Why?!
Because they're all going to end up in New Jersey!
WHEN PEOPLE PANIC, THEY MAKE BAD DECISIONS. THAT'S HOW THE RULE OF LAW BREAKS DOWN.
Sorry!
CIRCLE Q
IT BREAKS DOWN WHEN PEOPLE THINK THE RULES NO LONGER MATTER.
I don't know what's going on out there, but if those punks think they can rob us and try to steal the Squishee machine, they haven't met the Carrelli brothers.
THAT'S HOW REALLY BAD THINGS START TO HAPPEN.

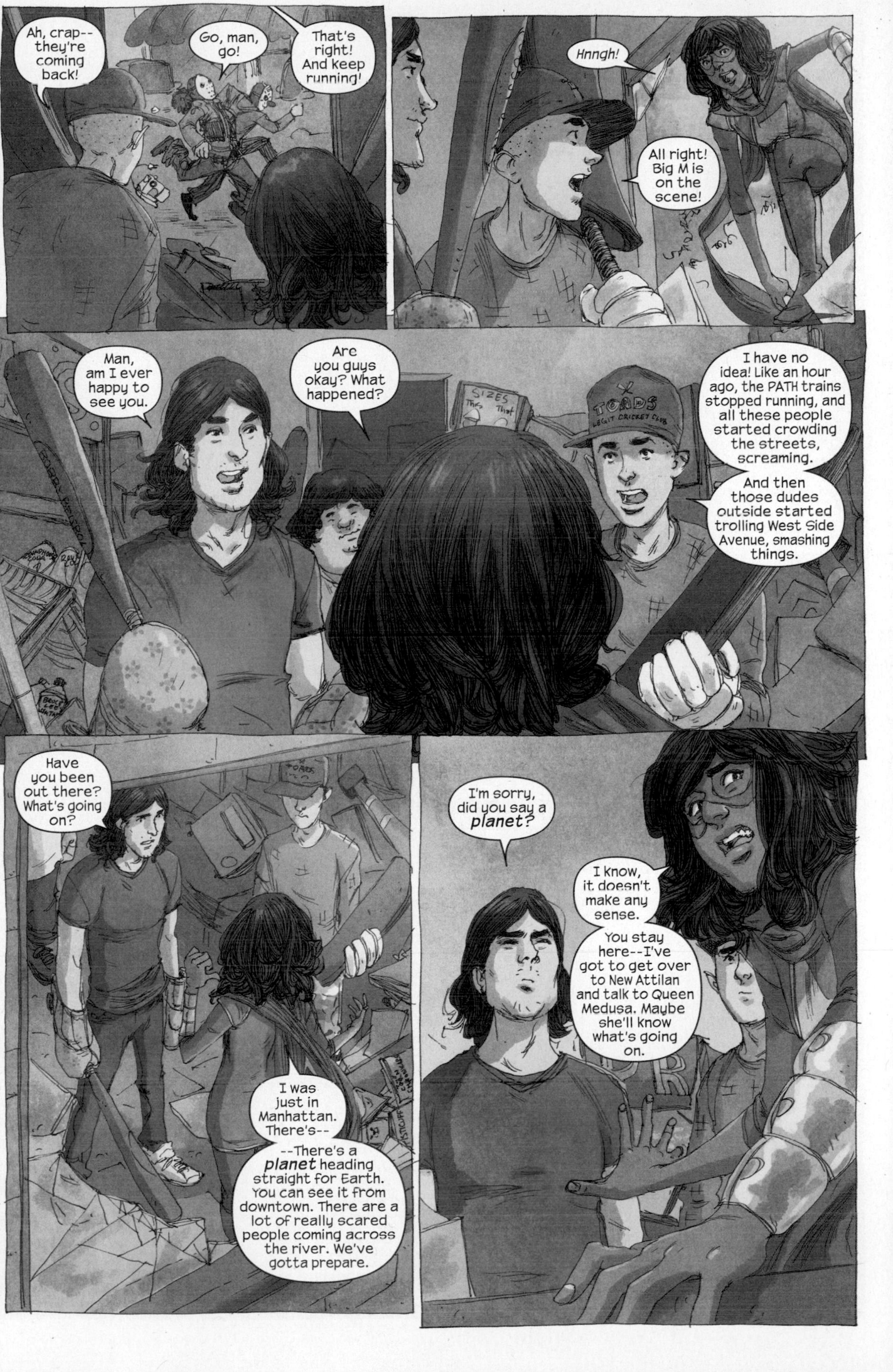
Ah, crap-- they're coming back!
Go, man, go!
That's right! And keep running!
Hnngh!
All right! Big M is on the scene!
Man, am I ever happy to see you.
Are you guys okay? What happened?
I have no idea! Like an hour ago, the PATH trains stopped running, and all these people started crowding the streets, screaming.
And then those dudes outside started trolling West Side Avenue, smashing things.
TOADS
LEGIT CRICKET CLUB
SIZES
Have you been out there? What's going on?
I was just in Manhattan. There's--
--There's a *planet* heading straight for Earth. You can see it from downtown. There are a lot of really scared people coming across the river. We've gotta prepare.
I'm sorry, did you say a *planet?*
I know, it doesn't make any sense.
You stay here--I've got to get over to New Attilan and talk to Queen Medusa. Maybe she'll know what's going on.

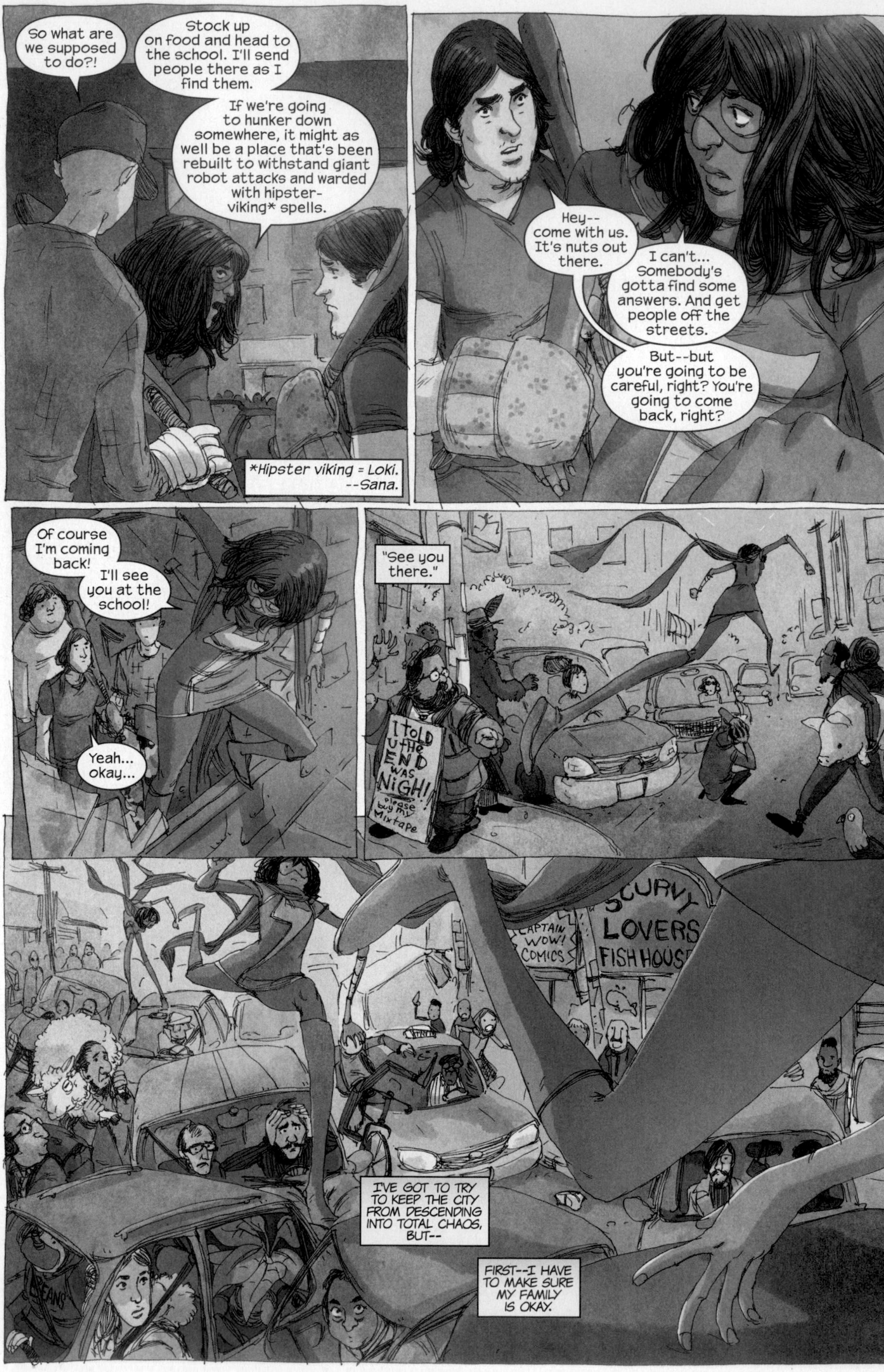

So what are we supposed to do?!
Stock up on food and head to the school. I'll send people there as I find them.
If we're going to hunker down somewhere, it might as well be a place that's been rebuilt to withstand giant robot attacks and warded with hipster-viking* spells.
*Hipster viking = Loki. --Sana.
Hey-- come with us. It's nuts out there.
I can't... Somebody's gotta find some answers. And get people off the streets.
But--but you're going to be careful, right? You're going to come back, right?
Of course I'm coming back!
I'll see you at the school!
Yeah... okay...
"See you there."
I TOLD U THE END WAS NIGH! please buy my Mixtape
SCURVY LOVERS FISH HOUSE
CAPTAIN WOW! COMICS
I'VE GOT TO TRY TO KEEP THE CITY FROM DESCENDING INTO TOTAL CHAOS, BUT--
FIRST--I HAVE TO MAKE SURE MY FAMILY IS OKAY.

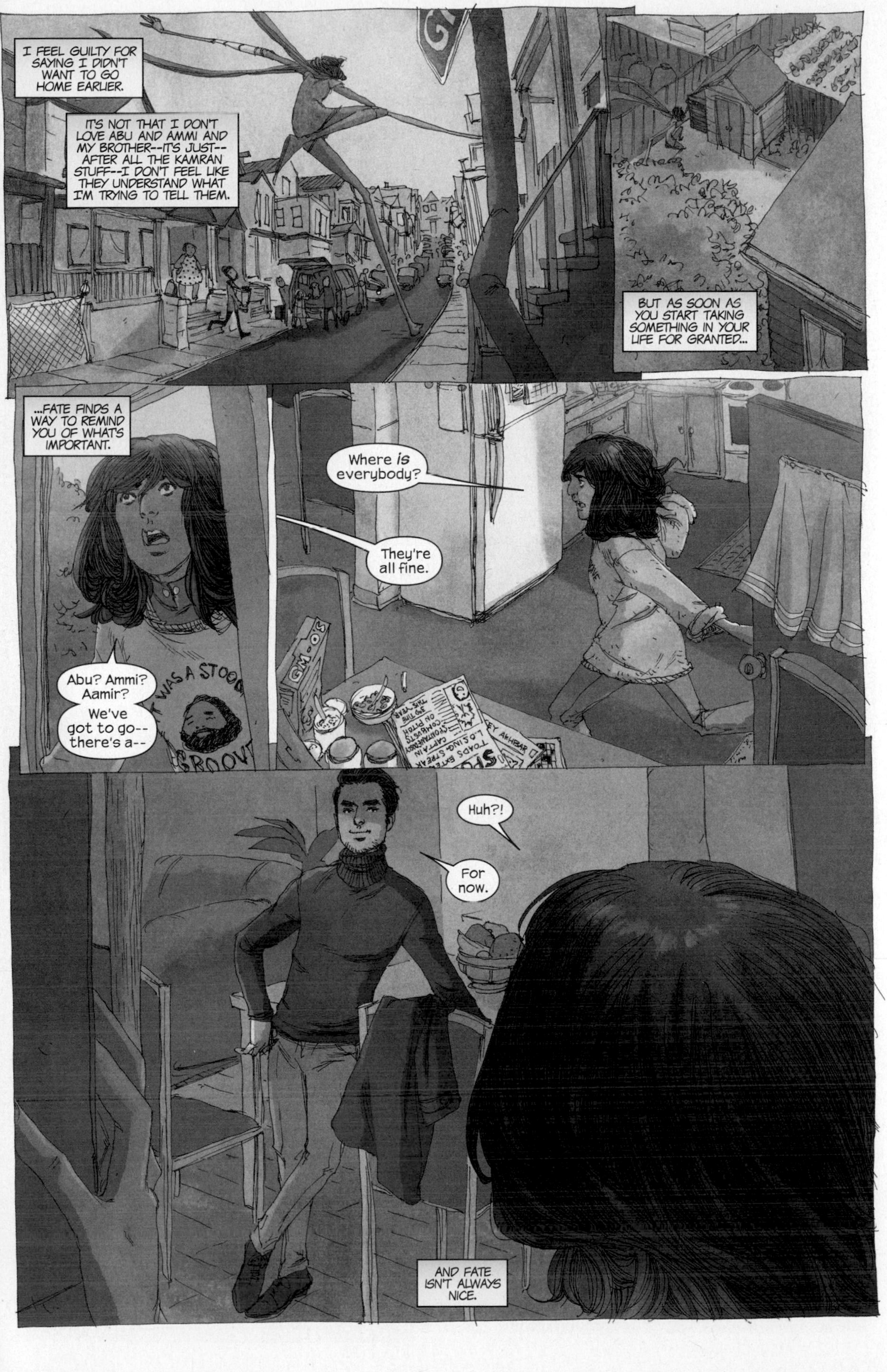

I FEEL GUILTY FOR SAYING I DIDN'T WANT TO GO HOME EARLIER.
IT'S NOT THAT I DON'T LOVE ABU AND AMMI AND MY BROTHER--IT'S JUST--AFTER ALL THE KAMRAN STUFF--I DON'T FEEL LIKE THEY UNDERSTAND WHAT I'M TRYING TO TELL THEM.
BUT AS SOON AS YOU START TAKING SOMETHING IN YOUR LIFE FOR GRANTED...
...FATE FINDS A WAY TO REMIND YOU OF WHAT'S IMPORTANT.
Where *is* everybody?
They're all fine.
Abu? Ammi? Aamir?
We've got to go-- there's a--
Huh?!
For now.
AND FATE ISN'T ALWAYS NICE.

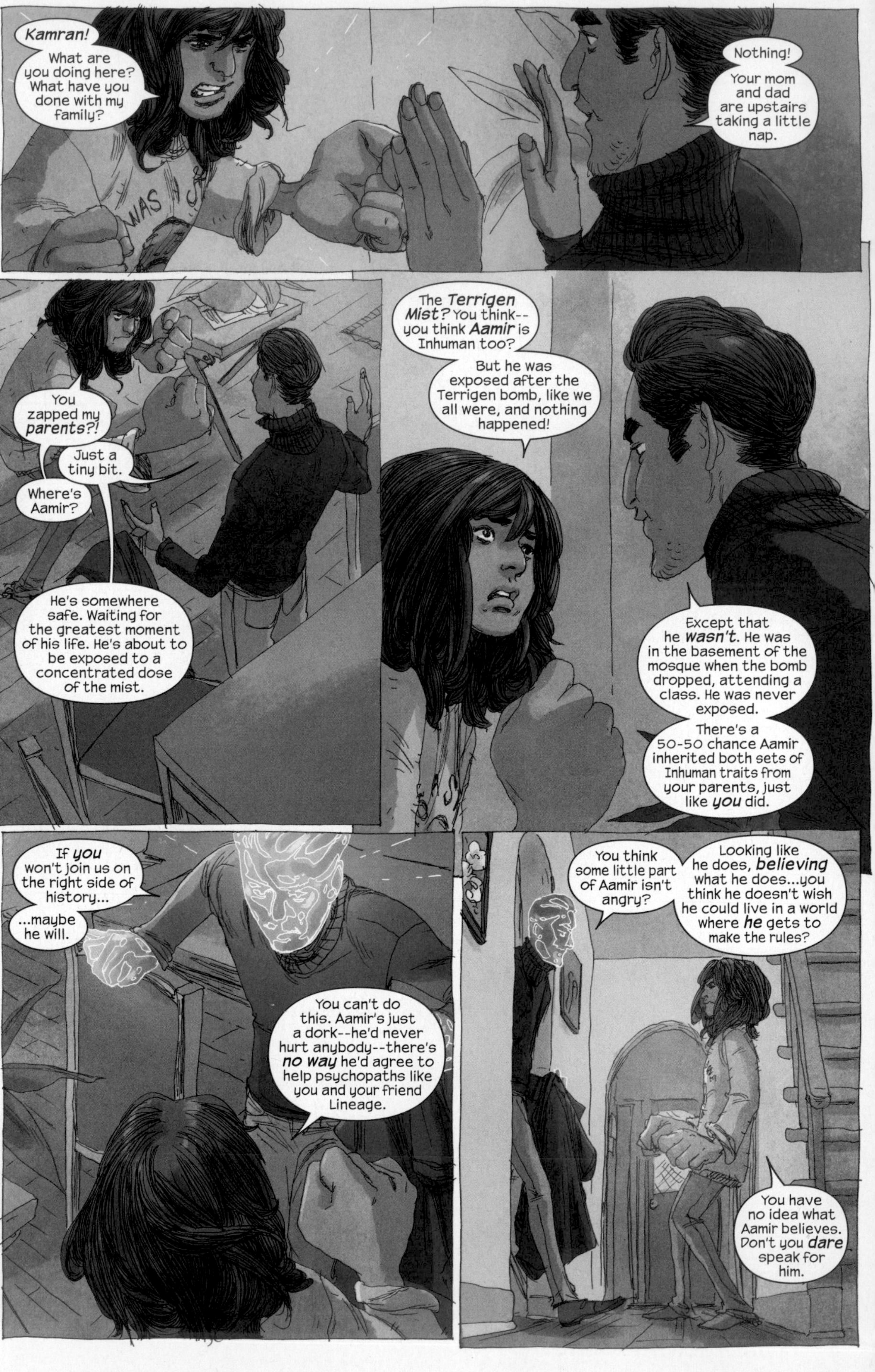
Kamran!
What are you doing here? What have you done with my family?
Nothing!
Your mom and dad are upstairs taking a little nap.
You zapped my parents?!
Just a tiny bit.
Where's Aamir?
He's somewhere safe. Waiting for the greatest moment of his life. He's about to be exposed to a concentrated dose of the mist.
The Terrigen Mist? You think--you think Aamir is Inhuman too?
But he was exposed after the Terrigen bomb, like we all were, and nothing happened!
Except that he wasn't. He was in the basement of the mosque when the bomb dropped, attending a class. He was never exposed.
There's a 50-50 chance Aamir inherited both sets of Inhuman traits from your parents, just like you did.
If you won't join us on the right side of history...
...maybe he will.
You can't do this. Aamir's just a dork--he'd never hurt anybody--there's no way he'd agree to help psychopaths like you and your friend Lineage.
You think some little part of Aamir isn't angry?
Looking like he does, believing what he does...you think he doesn't wish he could live in a world where he gets to make the rules?
You have no idea what Aamir believes. Don't you dare speak for him.

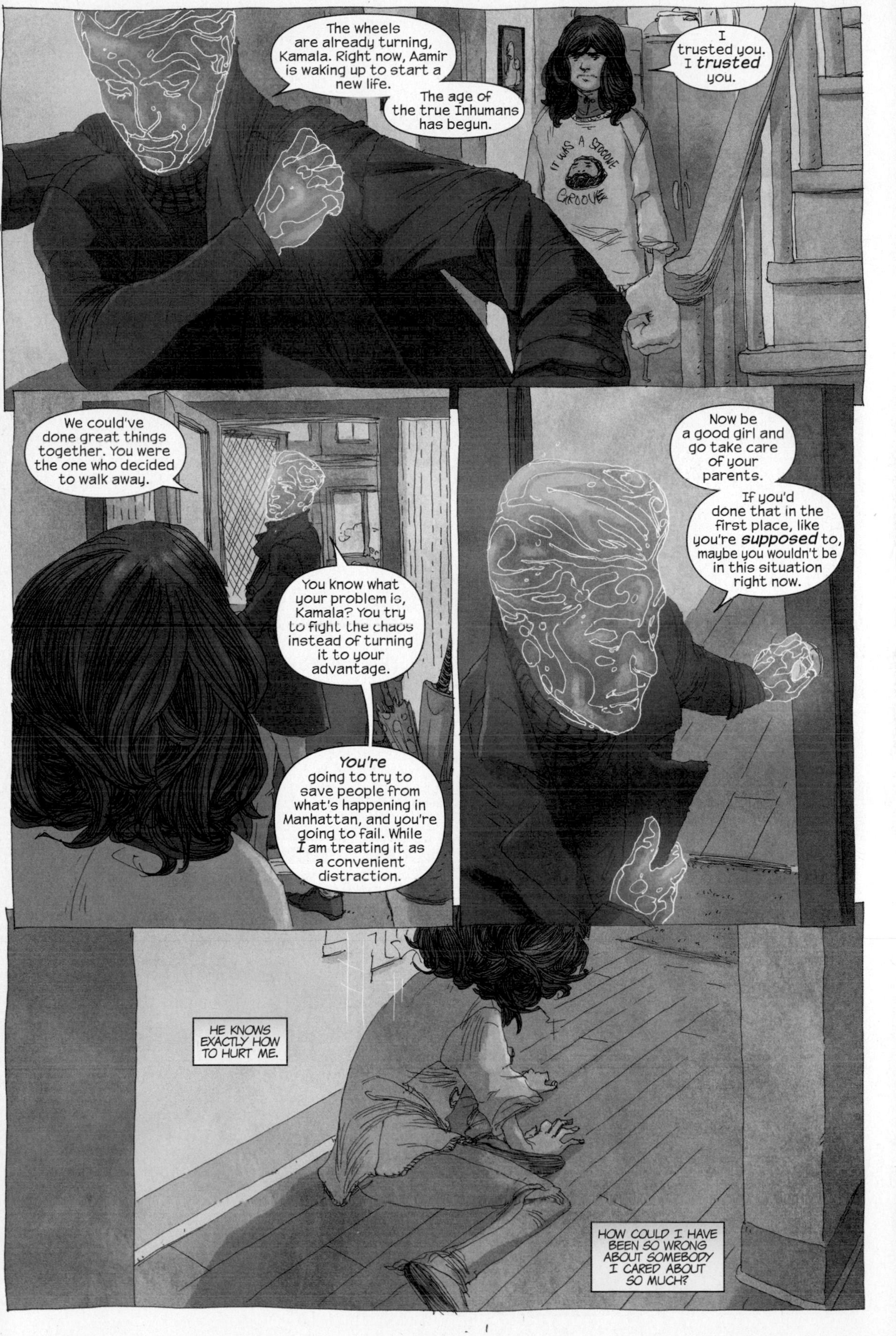
The wheels are already turning, Kamala. Right now, Aamir is waking up to start a new life.
The age of the true Inhumans has begun.
I trusted you. I *trusted* you.
IT WAS A STOOONE GROOVE
We could've done great things together. You were the one who decided to walk away.
You know what your problem is, Kamala? You try to fight the chaos instead of turning it to your advantage.
You're going to try to save people from what's happening in Manhattan, and you're going to fail. While *I* am treating it as a convenient distraction.
Now be a good girl and go take care of your parents.
If you'd done that in the first place, like you're *supposed* to, maybe you wouldn't be in this situation right now.
HE KNOWS EXACTLY HOW TO HURT ME.
HOW COULD I HAVE BEEN SO WRONG ABOUT SOMEBODY I CARED ABOUT SO MUCH?

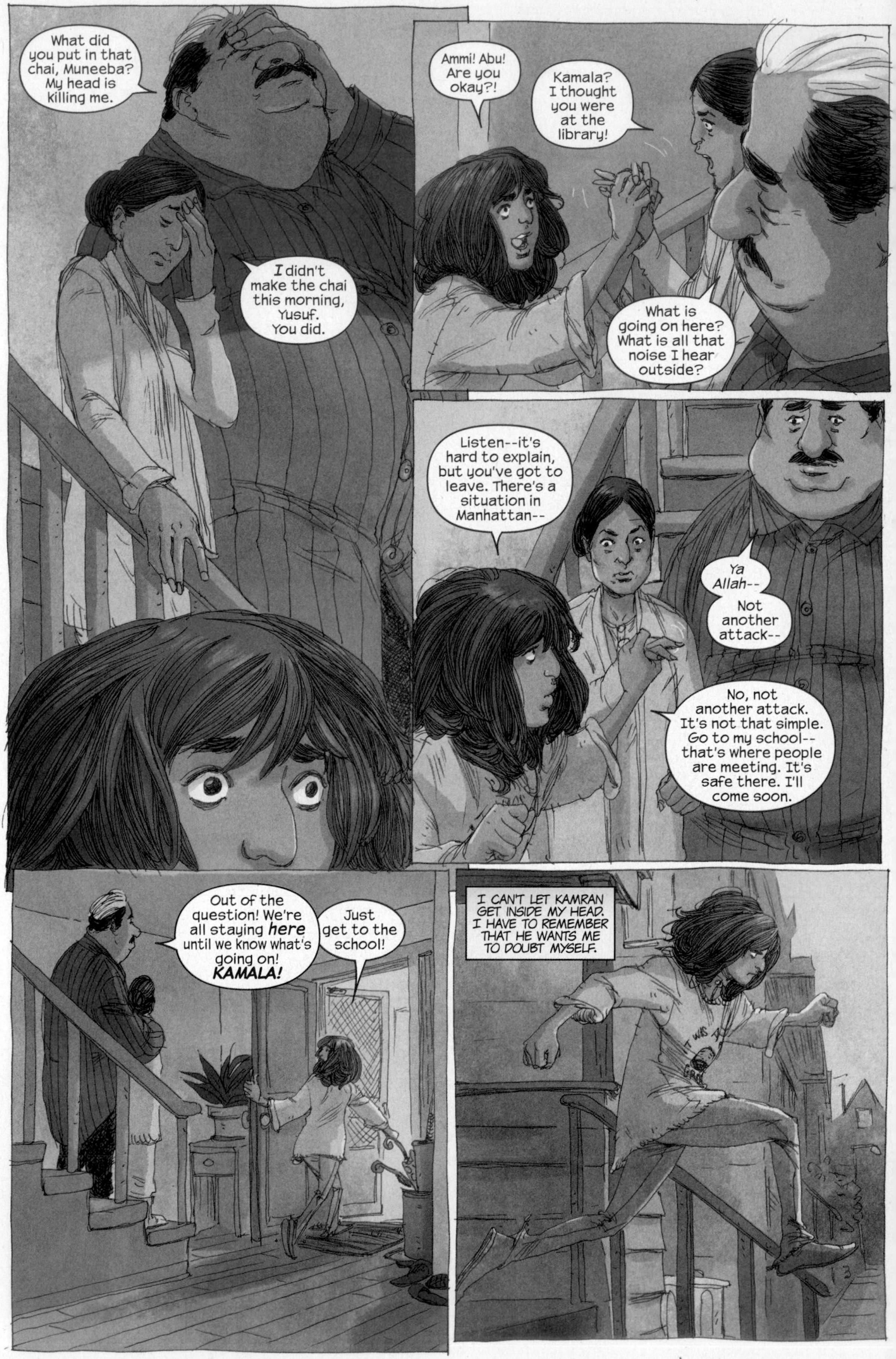
What did you put in that chai, Muneeba? My head is killing me.
I didn't make the chai this morning, Yusuf. You did.
Ammi! Abu! Are you okay?!
Kamala? I thought you were at the library!
What is going on here? What is all that noise I hear outside?
Listen--it's hard to explain, but you've got to leave. There's a situation in Manhattan--
Ya Allah--
Not another attack--
No, not another attack. It's not that simple. Go to my school--that's where people are meeting. It's safe there. I'll come soon.
Out of the question! We're all staying here until we know what's going on! KAMALA!
Just get to the school!
I CAN'T LET KAMRAN GET INSIDE MY HEAD. I HAVE TO REMEMBER THAT HE WANTS ME TO DOUBT MYSELF.

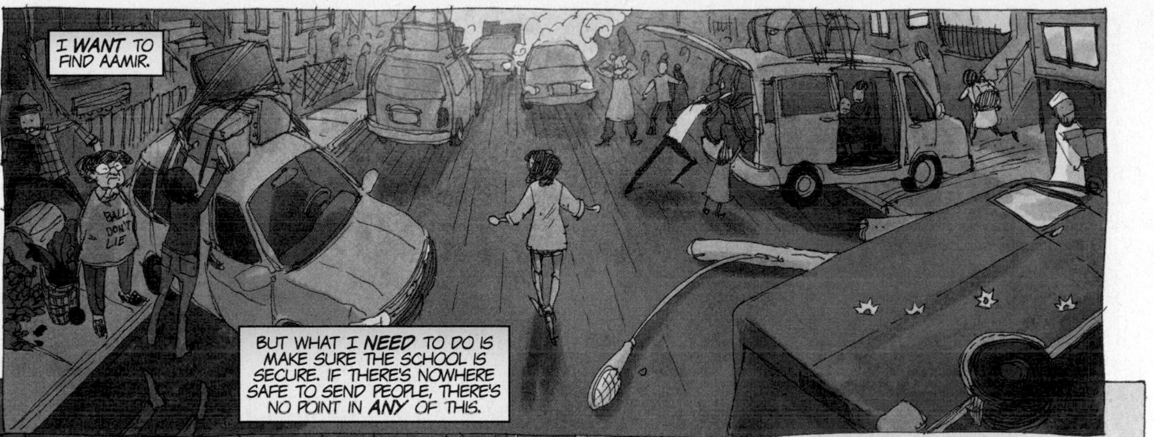
I WANT TO FIND AAMIR.
BALL DON'T LIE
BUT WHAT I NEED TO DO IS MAKE SURE THE SCHOOL IS SECURE. IF THERE'S NOWHERE SAFE TO SEND PEOPLE, THERE'S NO POINT IN ANY OF THIS.
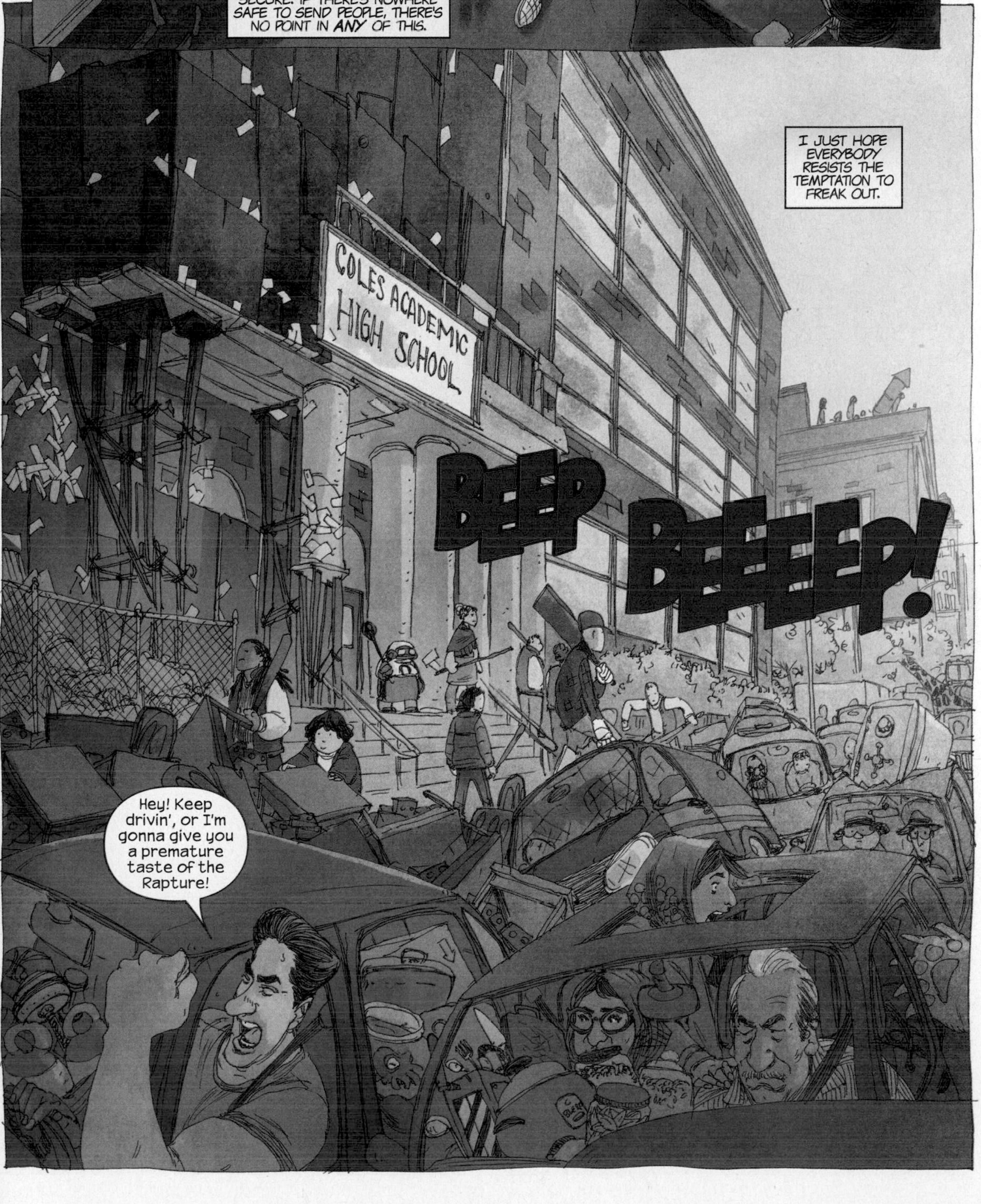
I JUST HOPE EVERYBODY RESISTS THE TEMPTATION TO FREAK OUT.
COLES ACADEMIC HIGH SCHOOL
BEEP
BEEEEP!
Hey! Keep drivin', or I'm gonna give you a premature taste of the Rapture!

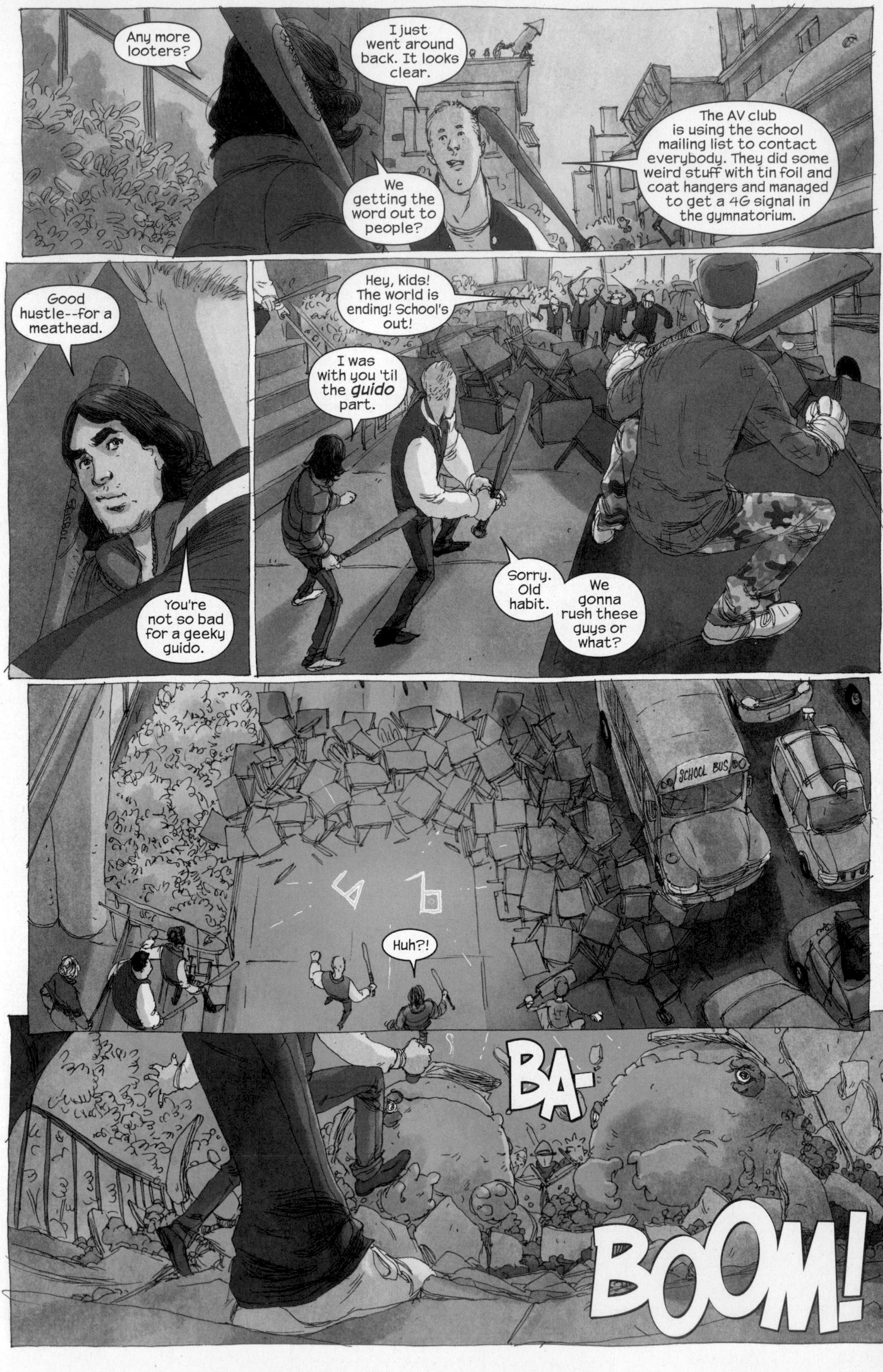
Any more looters?
I just went around back. It looks clear.
We getting the word out to people?
The AV club is using the school mailing list to contact everybody. They did some weird stuff with tin foil and coat hangers and managed to get a 4G signal in the gymnatorium.
Good hustle--for a meathead.
You're not so bad for a geeky guido.
Hey, kids! The world is ending! School's out!
I was with you 'til the *guido* part.
Sorry. Old habit.
We gonna rush these guys or what?
SCHOOL BUS
Huh?!
BA-BOOM!

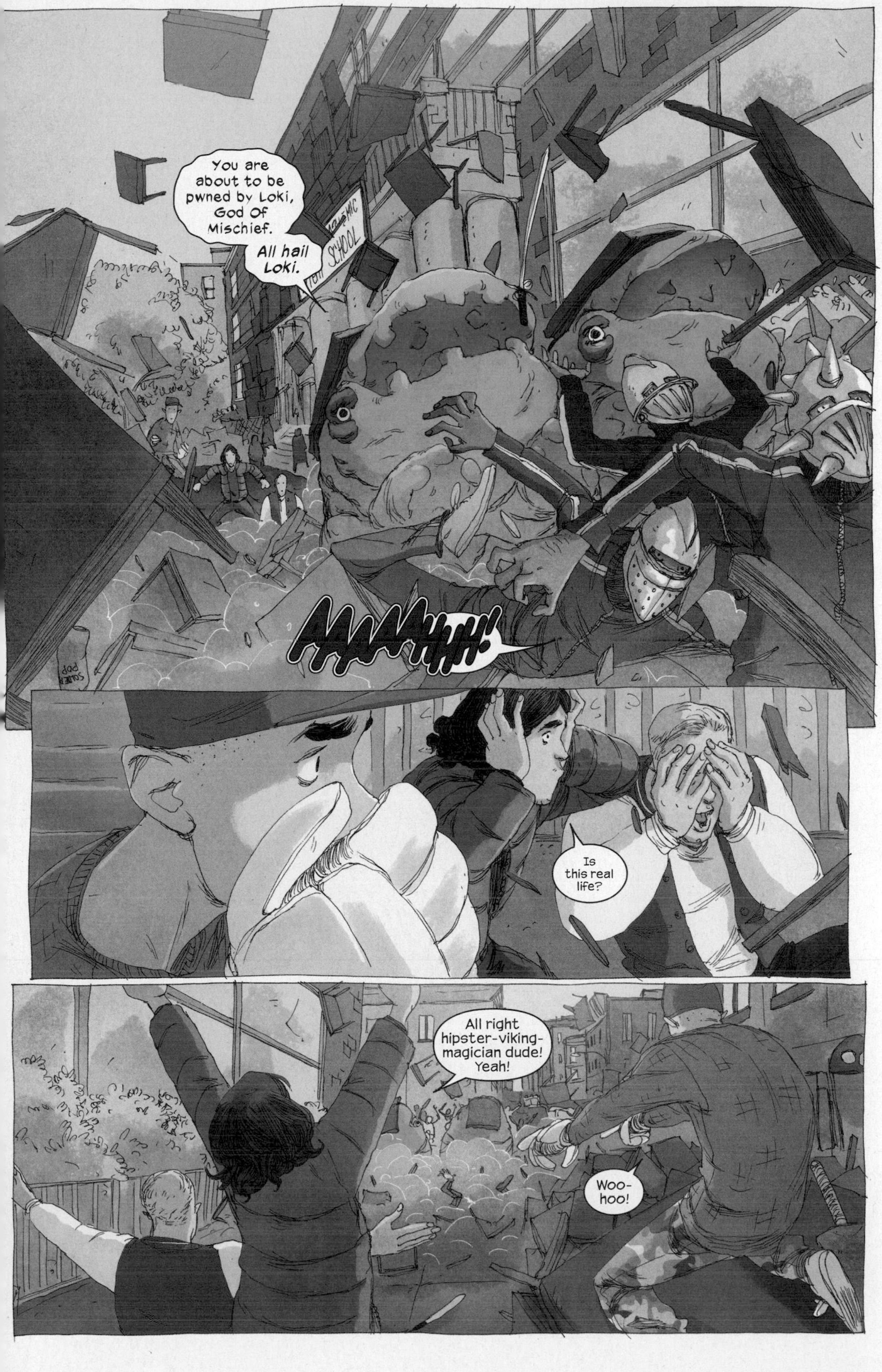
You are about to be pwned by Loki, God Of Mischief.
All hail Loki.
SCHOOL
AAAAHHH!
Is this real life?
All right hipster-viking-magician dude! Yeah!
Woo-hoo!

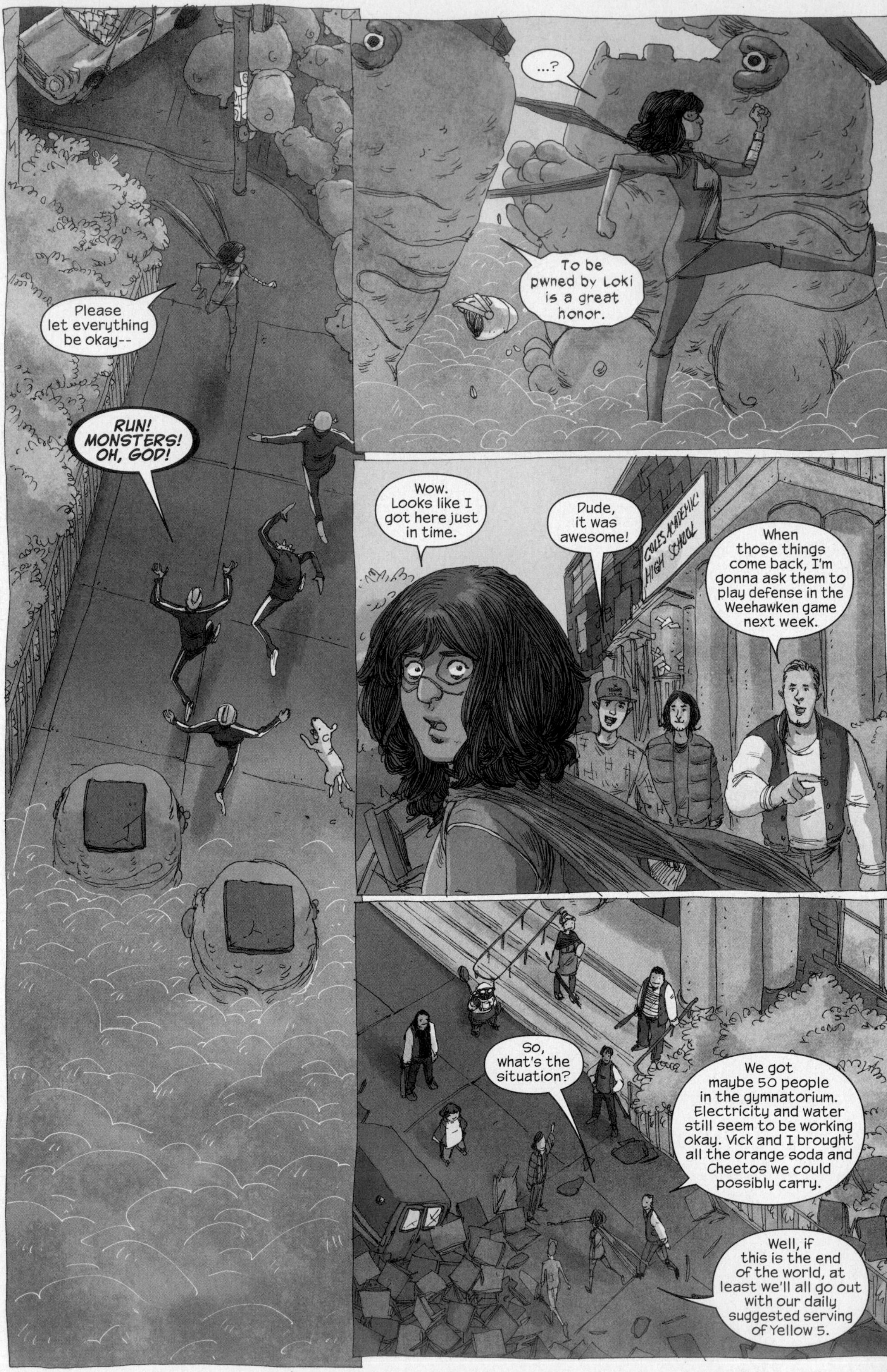
Please let everything be okay--
RUN! MONSTERS! OH, GOD!
...?
To be pwned by Loki is a great honor.
Wow. Looks like I got here just in time.
Dude, it was awesome!
COLES ACADEMIC HIGH SCHOOL
When those things come back, I'm gonna ask them to play defense in the Weehawken game next week.
So, what's the situation?
We got maybe 50 people in the gymnatorium. Electricity and water still seem to be working okay. Vick and I brought all the orange soda and Cheetos we could possibly carry.
Well, if this is the end of the world, at least we'll all go out with our daily suggested serving of Yellow 5.

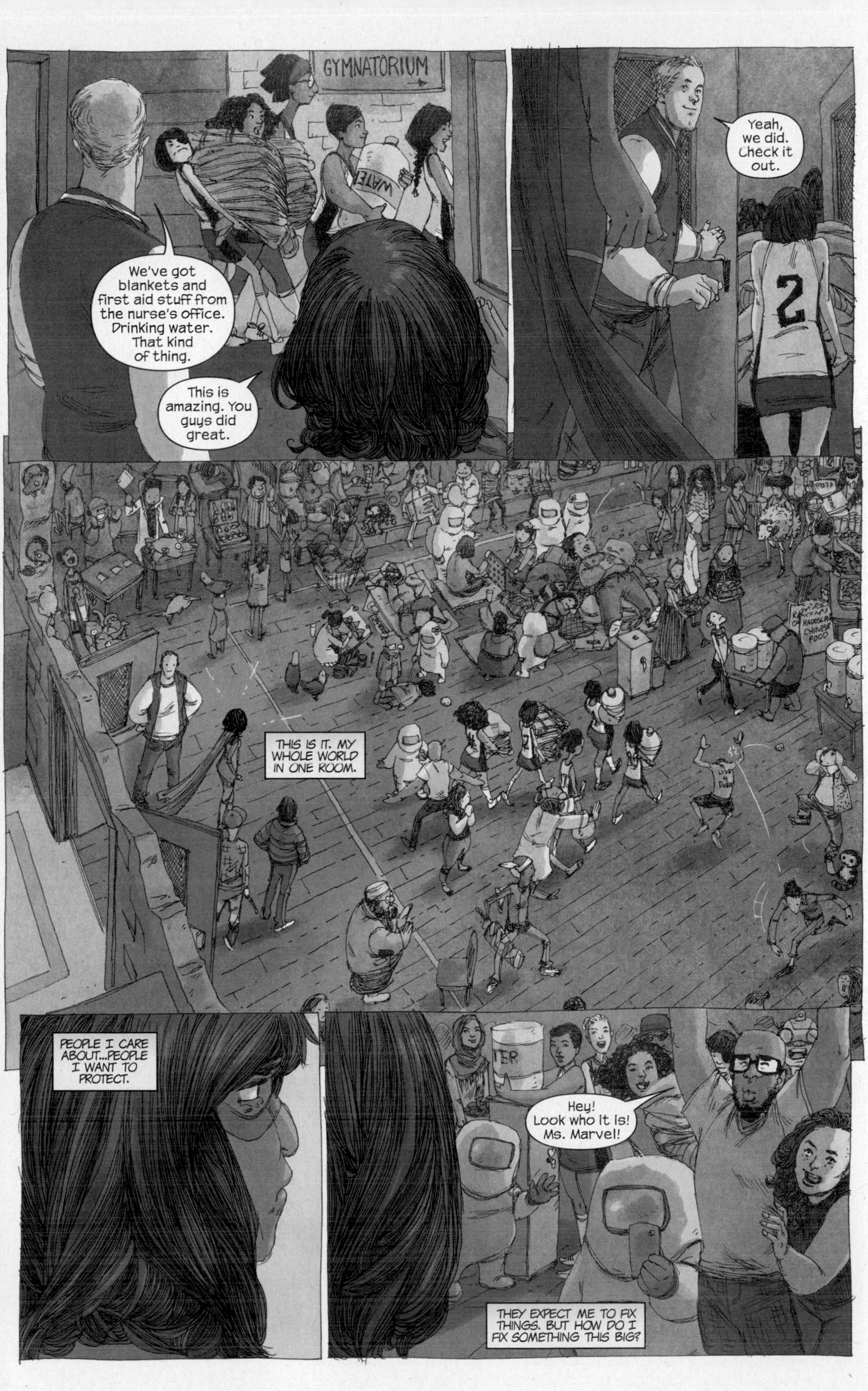
GYMNATORIUM
WATER
We've got blankets and first aid stuff from the nurse's office. Drinking water. That kind of thing.
This is amazing. You guys did great.
Yeah, we did. Check it out.
2
THIS IS IT. MY WHOLE WORLD IN ONE ROOM.
CHINESE FOOD
PEOPLE I CARE ABOUT...PEOPLE I WANT TO PROTECT.
Hey! Look who it is! Ms. Marvel!
THEY EXPECT ME TO FIX THINGS. BUT HOW DO I FIX SOMETHING THIS BIG?

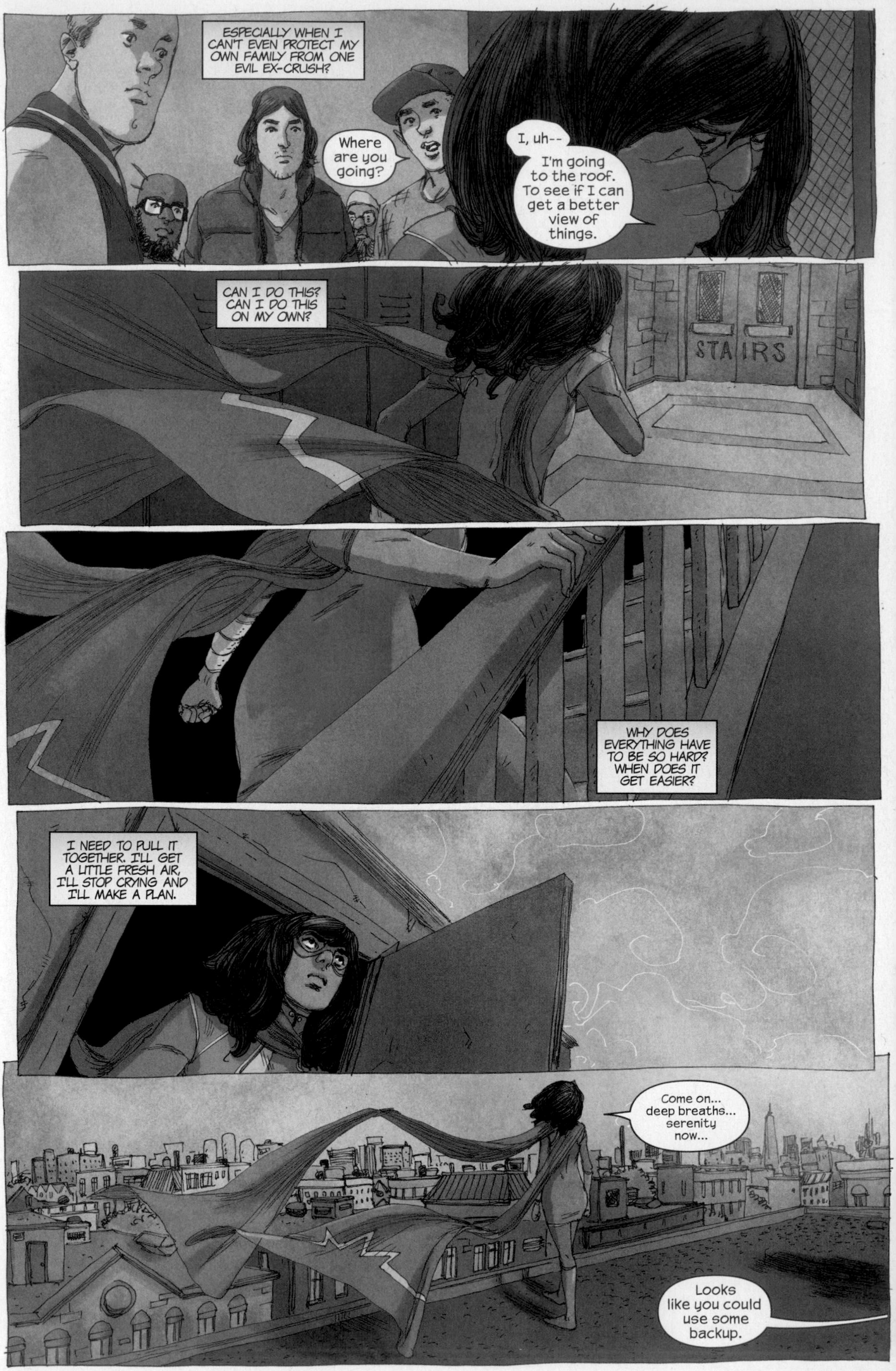
ESPECIALLY WHEN I CAN'T EVEN PROTECT MY OWN FAMILY FROM ONE EVIL EX-CRUSH?
Where are you going?
I, uh--
I'm going to the roof. To see if I can get a better view of things.
CAN I DO THIS? CAN I DO THIS ON MY OWN?
STAIRS
WHY DOES EVERYTHING HAVE TO BE SO HARD? WHEN DOES IT GET EASIER?
I NEED TO PULL IT TOGETHER. I'LL GET A LITTLE FRESH AIR, I'LL STOP CRYING AND I'LL MAKE A PLAN.
Come on... deep breaths... serenity now...
Looks like you could use some backup.

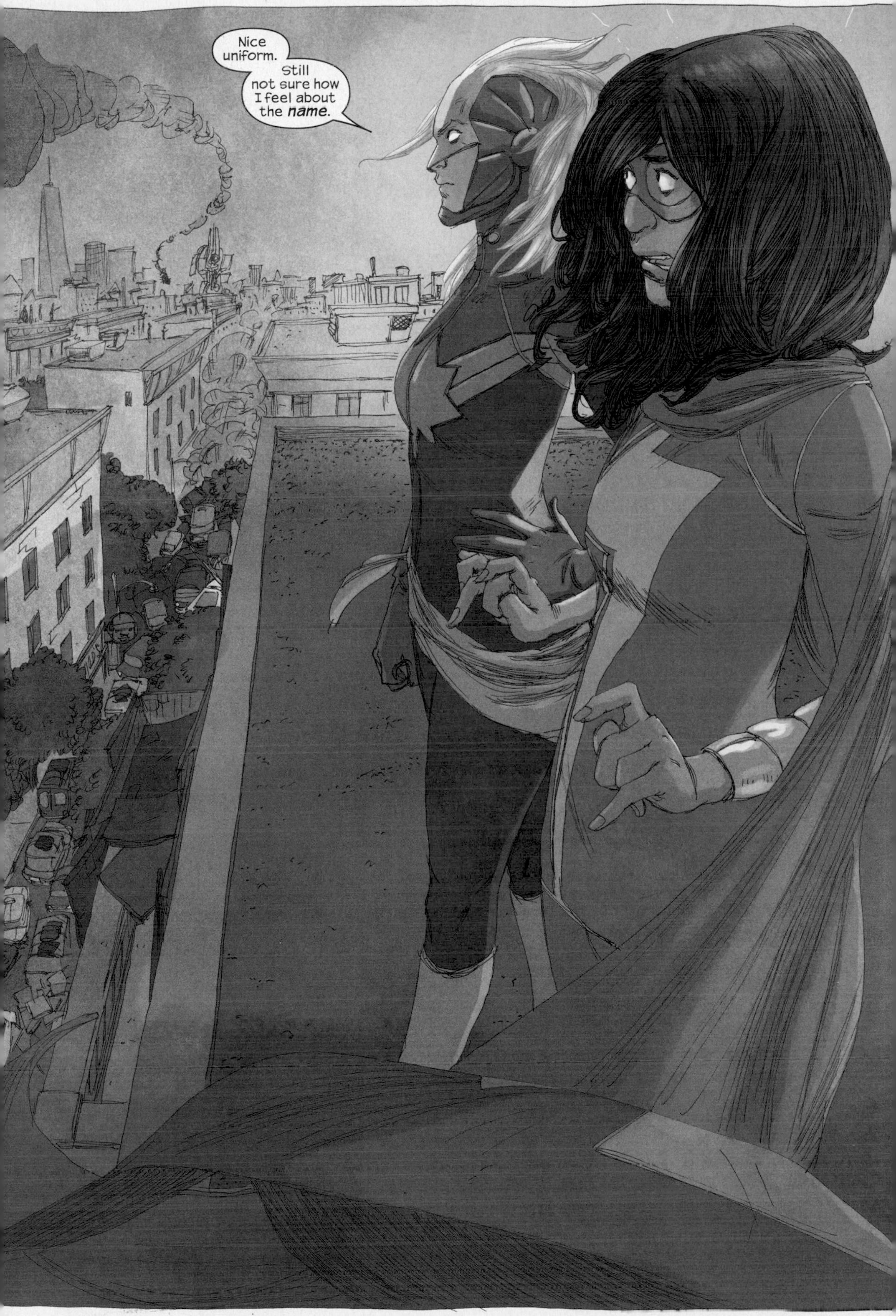
Nice uniform.
Still not sure how I feel about the *name*.

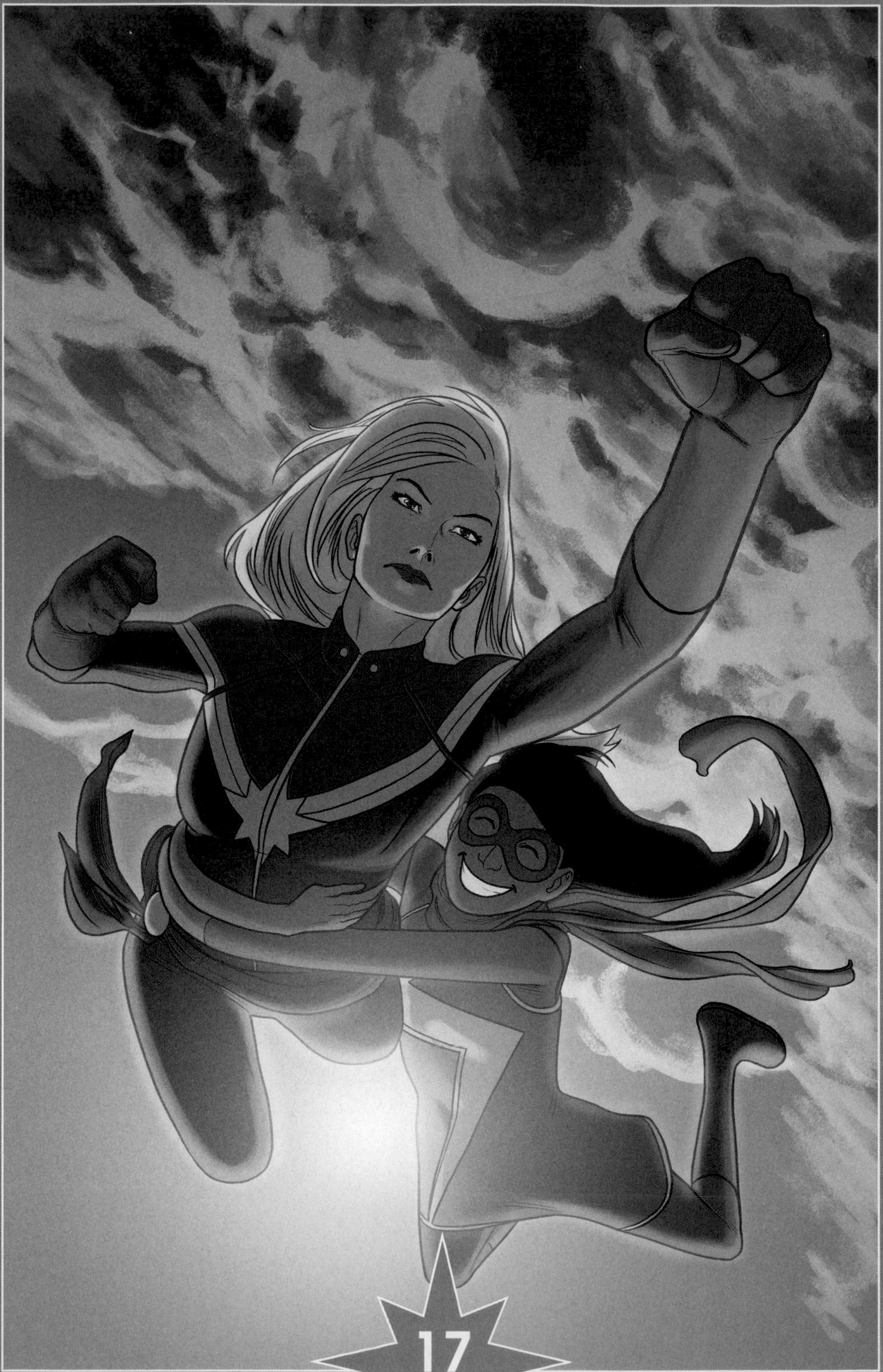

17

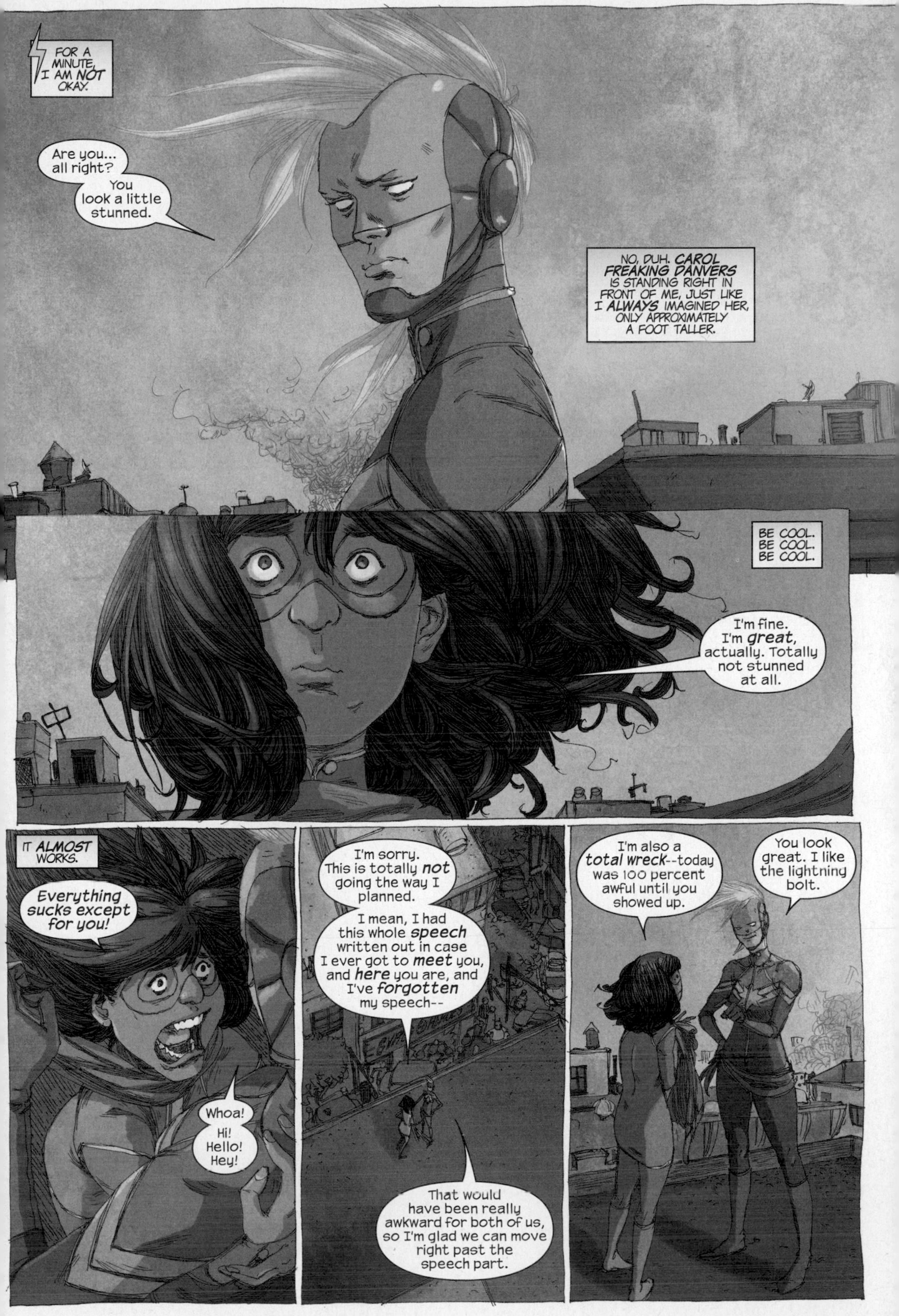
FOR A MINUTE, I AM NOT OKAY.
Are you... all right? You look a little stunned.
NO, DUH. CAROL FREAKING DANVERS IS STANDING RIGHT IN FRONT OF ME, JUST LIKE I ALWAYS IMAGINED HER, ONLY APPROXIMATELY A FOOT TALLER.
BE COOL. BE COOL. BE COOL.
I'm fine. I'm great, actually. Totally not stunned at all.
IT ALMOST WORKS.
Everything sucks except for you!
Whoa! Hi! Hello! Hey!
I'm sorry. This is totally not going the way I planned.
I mean, I had this whole speech written out in case I ever got to meet you, and here you are, and I've forgotten my speech--
That would have been really awkward for both of us, so I'm glad we can move right past the speech part.
I'm also a total wreck--today was 100 percent awful until you showed up.
You look great. I like the lightning bolt.

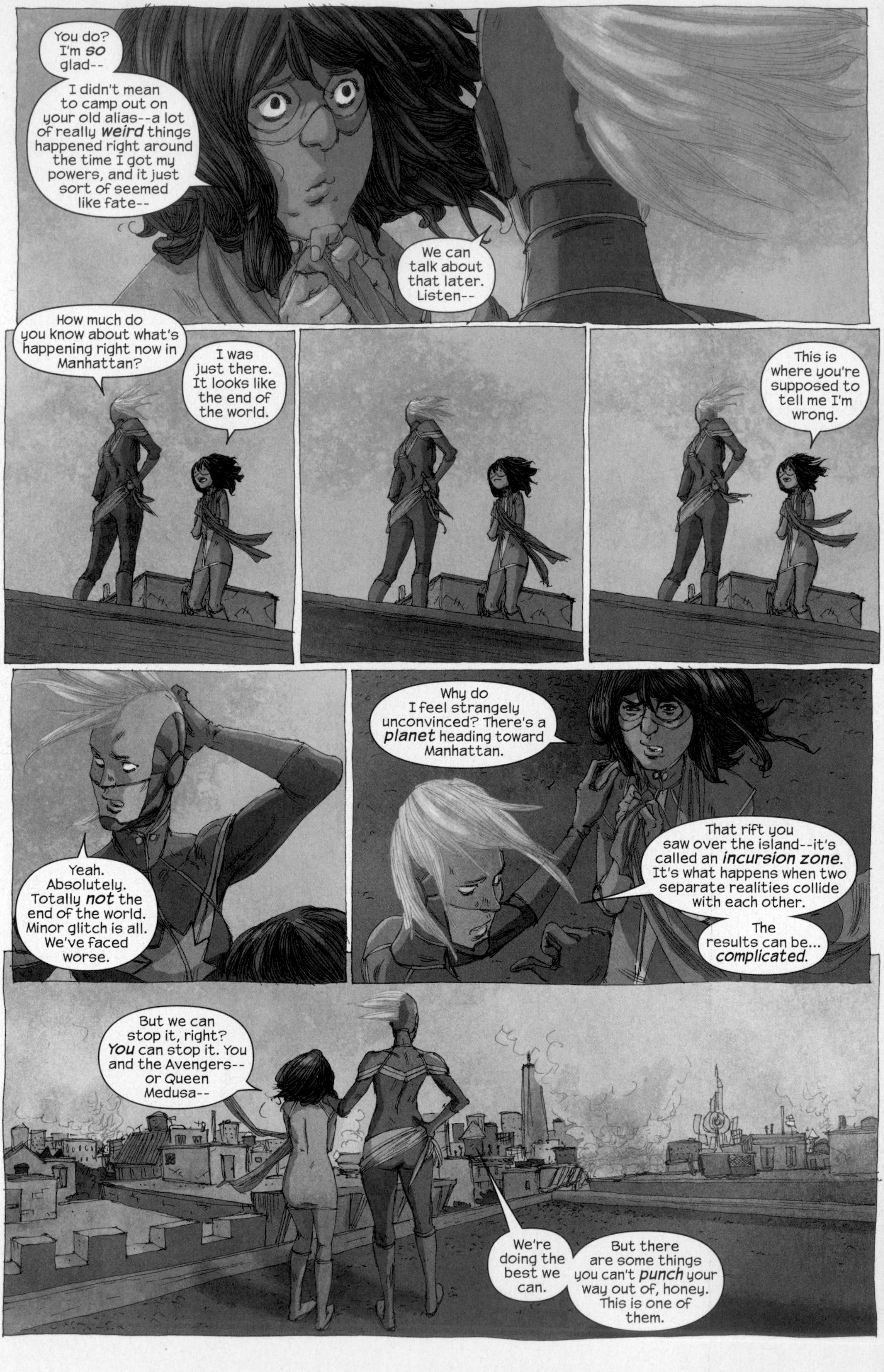
You do? I'm SO glad--
I didn't mean to camp out on your old alias--a lot of really weird things happened right around the time I got my powers, and it just sort of seemed like fate--
We can talk about that later. Listen--
How much do you know about what's happening right now in Manhattan?
I was just there. It looks like the end of the world.
This is where you're supposed to tell me I'm wrong.
Yeah. Absolutely. Totally not the end of the world. Minor glitch is all. We've faced worse.
Why do I feel strangely unconvinced? There's a planet heading toward Manhattan.
That rift you saw over the island--it's called an incursion zone. It's what happens when two separate realities collide with each other.
The results can be... complicated.
But we can stop it, right? You can stop it. You and the Avengers--or Queen Medusa--
We're doing the best we can.
But there are some things you can't punch your way out of, honey. This is one of them.

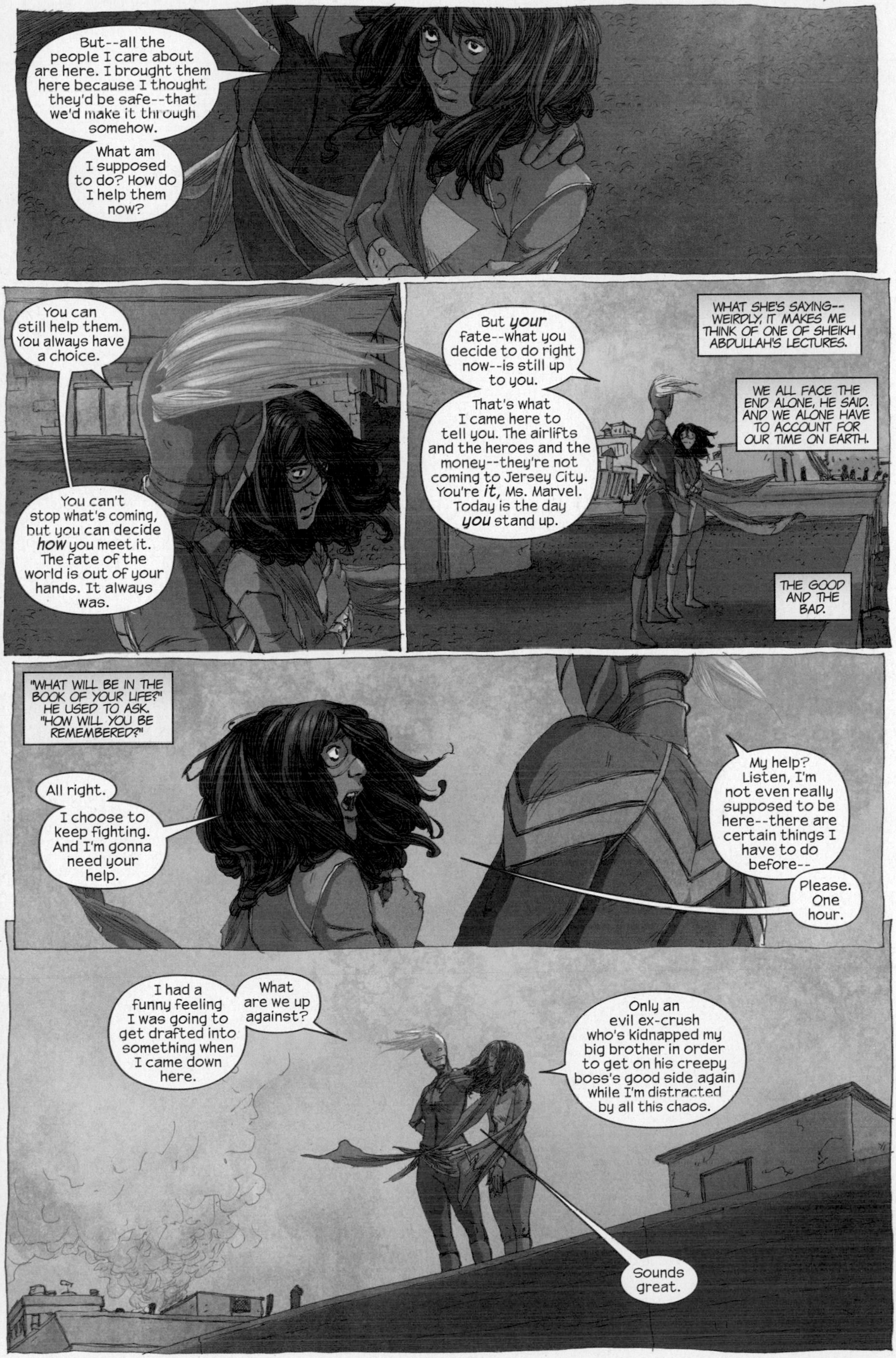

But--all the people I care about are here. I brought them here because I thought they'd be safe--that we'd make it through somehow.
What am I supposed to do? How do I help them now?
You can still help them. You always have a choice.
You can't stop what's coming, but you can decide *how* you meet it. The fate of the world is out of your hands. It always was.
But *your* fate--what you decide to do right now--is still up to you.
That's what I came here to tell you. The airlifts and the heroes and the money--they're not coming to Jersey City. You're *it*, Ms. Marvel. Today is the day *you* stand up.
WHAT SHE'S SAYING-- WEIRDLY, IT MAKES ME THINK OF ONE OF SHEIKH ABDULLAH'S LECTURES.
WE ALL FACE THE END ALONE, HE SAID. AND WE ALONE HAVE TO ACCOUNT FOR OUR TIME ON EARTH.
THE GOOD AND THE BAD.
"WHAT WILL BE IN THE BOOK OF YOUR LIFE?" HE USED TO ASK. "HOW WILL YOU BE REMEMBERED?"
All right.
I choose to keep fighting. And I'm gonna need your help.
My help? Listen, I'm not even really supposed to be here--there are certain things I have to do before--
Please. One hour.
I had a funny feeling I was going to get drafted into something when I came down here.
What are we up against?
Only an evil ex-crush who's kidnapped my big brother in order to get on his creepy boss's good side again while I'm distracted by all this chaos.
Sounds great.

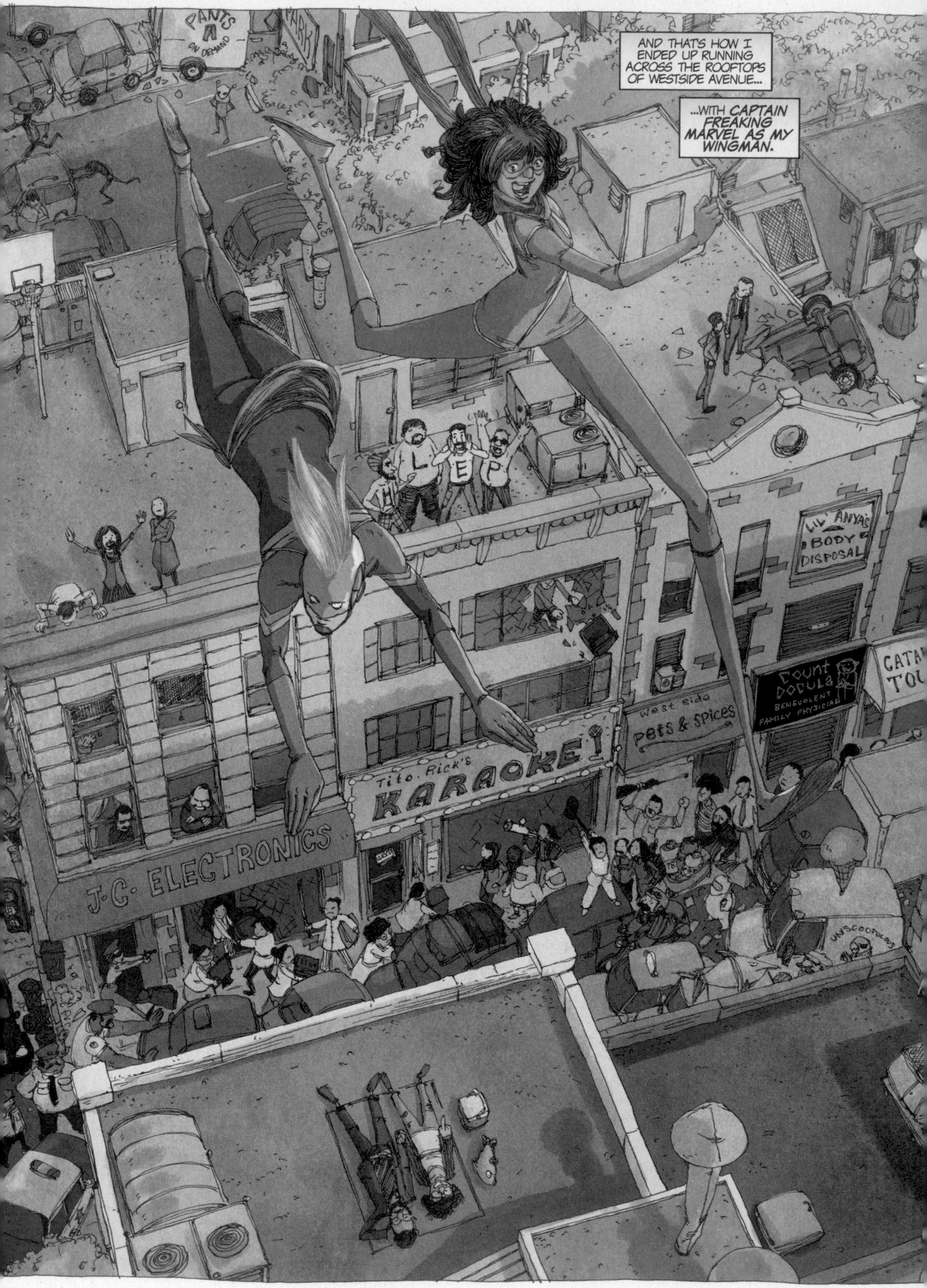
AND THAT'S HOW I ENDED UP RUNNING ACROSS THE ROOFTOPS OF WESTSIDE AVENUE...
...WITH CAPTAIN FREAKING MARVEL AS MY WINGMAN.
PANTS ON DEMAND
PARK
H L E P
LIL' ANYA'S BODY DISPOSAL
Count Docula BENEVOLENT FAMILY PHYSICIAN
West side pets & spices
Tito Rick's KARAOKE!
J·C· ELECTRONICS
UNSCOOPULOUS

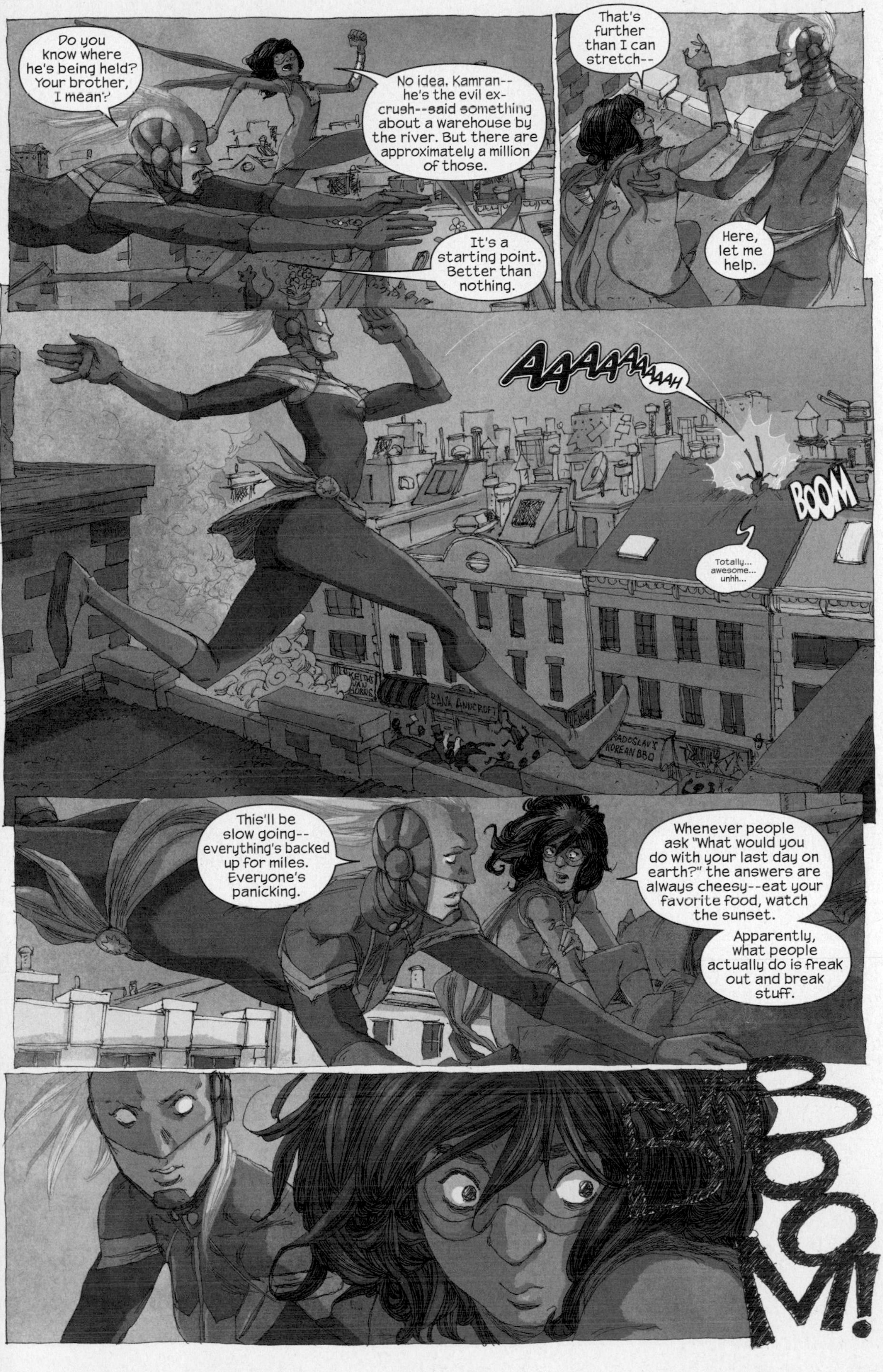
Do you know where he's being held? Your brother, I mean?
No idea. Kamran--he's the evil ex-crush--said something about a warehouse by the river. But there are approximately a million of those.
It's a starting point. Better than nothing.
That's further than I can stretch--
Here, let me help.
AAAAAAAAAH
BOOM
Totally... awesome... unhh...
KORIEAN BBQ
This'll be slow going--everything's backed up for miles. Everyone's panicking.
Whenever people ask "What would you do with your last day on earth?" the answers are always cheesy--eat your favorite food, watch the sunset.
Apparently, what people actually do is freak out and break stuff.
BOOOM!

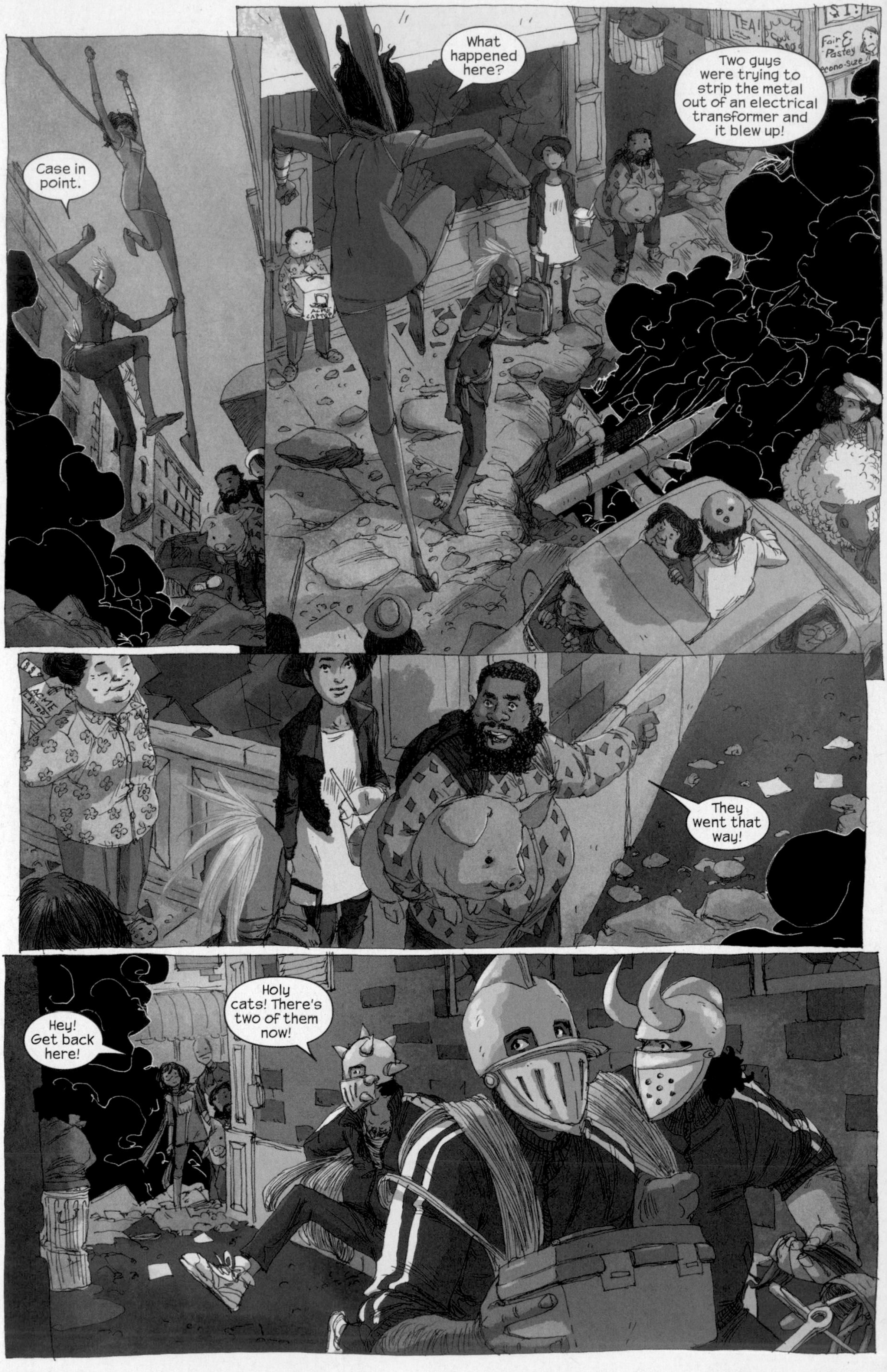
Case in point.
What happened here?
Two guys were trying to strip the metal out of an electrical transformer and it blew up!
TEA!
Fair & Pastey
econo-size
ACME
They went that way!
Hey! Get back here!
Holy cats! There's two of them now!

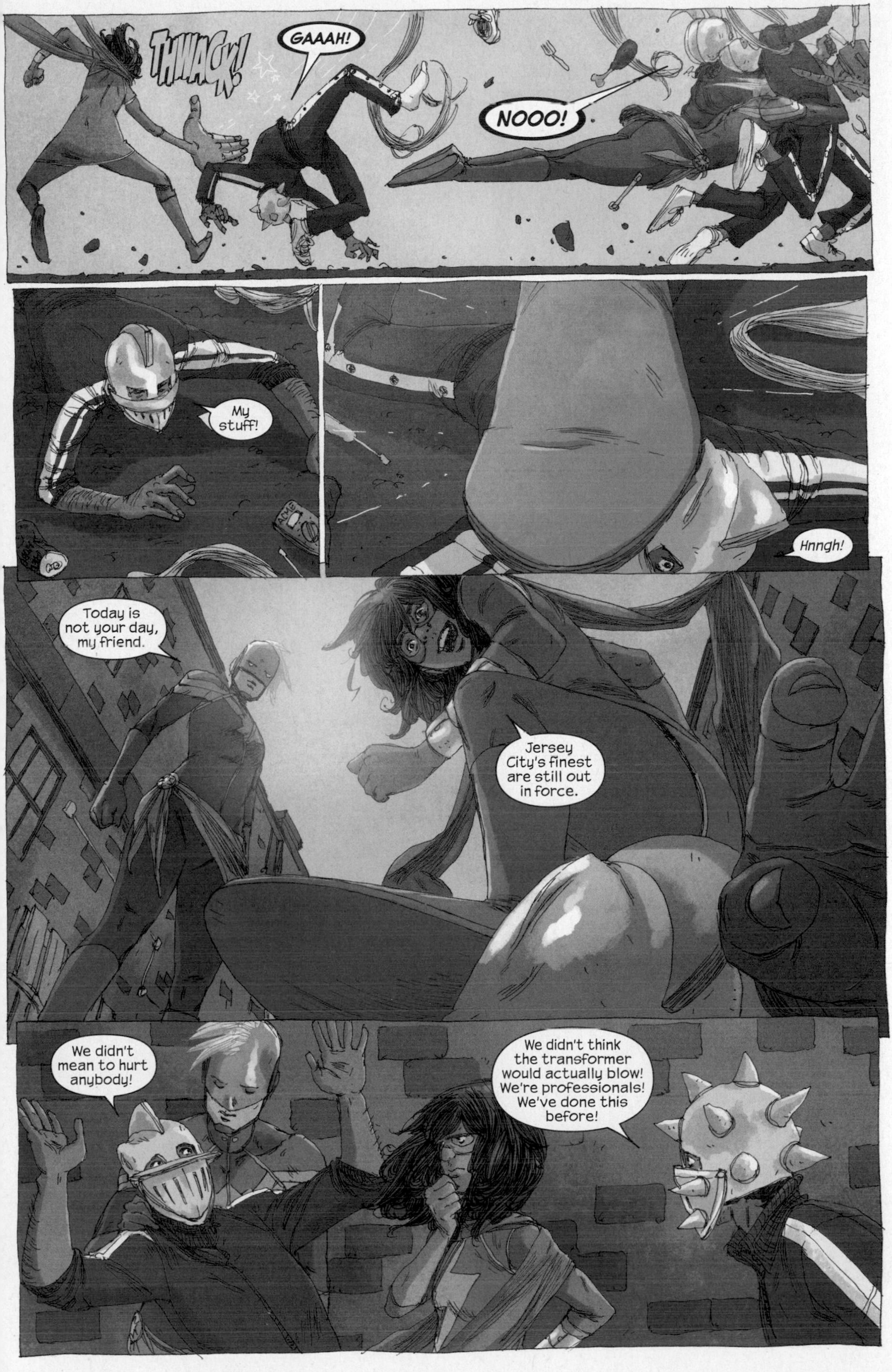
THWACK!
GAAAH!
NOOO!
My stuff!
Hnngh!
Today is not your day, my friend.
Jersey City's finest are still out in force.
We didn't mean to hurt anybody!
We didn't think the transformer would actually blow! We're professionals! We've done this before!

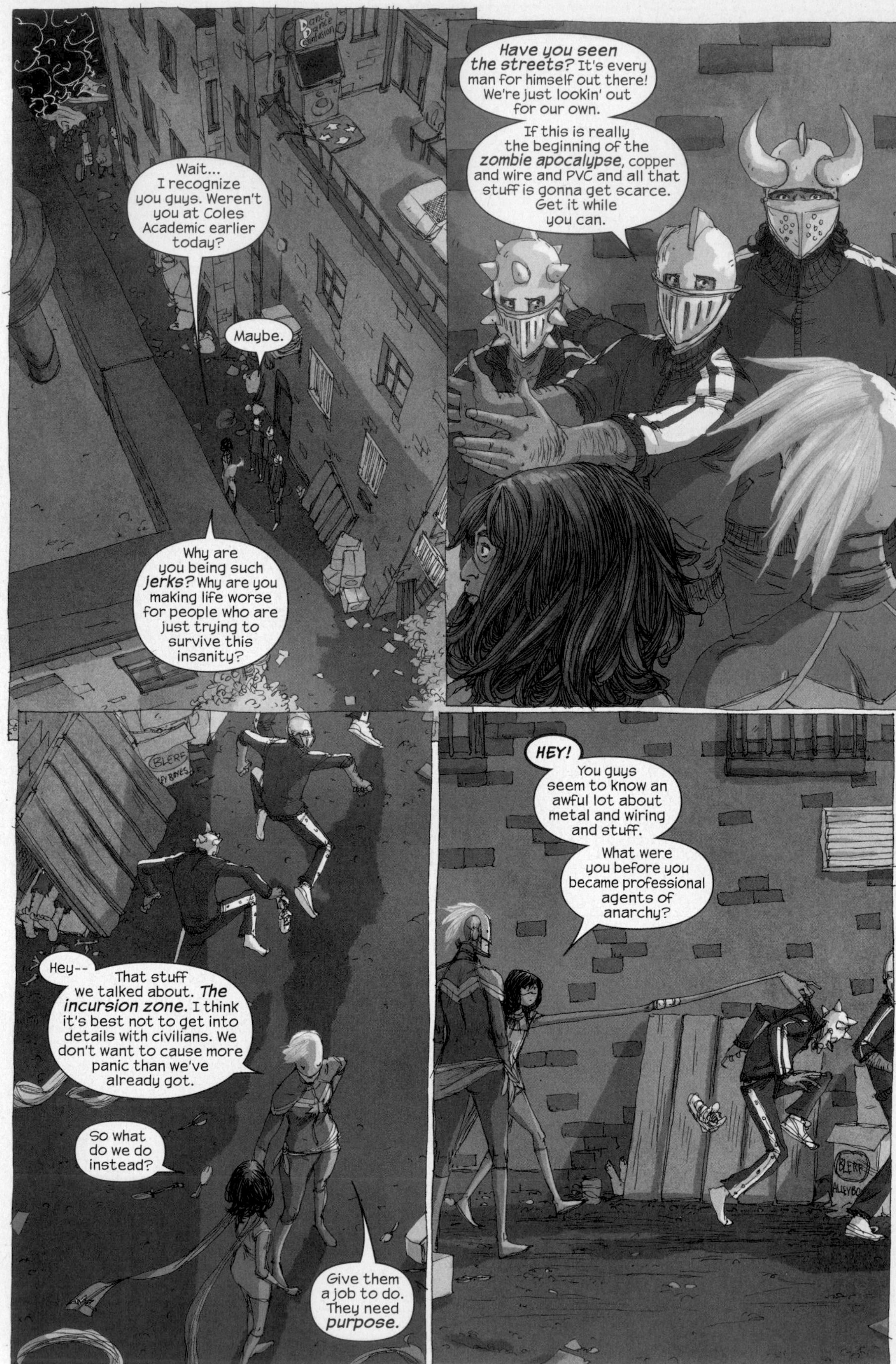

Wait... I recognize you guys. Weren't you at Coles Academic earlier today?
Maybe.
Why are you being such *jerks?* Why are you making life worse for people who are just trying to survive this insanity?
Have you seen the streets? It's every man for himself out there! We're just lookin' out for our own.
If this is really the beginning of the ***zombie apocalypse***, copper and wire and PVC and all that stuff is gonna get scarce. Get it while you can.
Hey--
That stuff we talked about. ***The incursion zone.*** I think it's best not to get into details with civilians. We don't want to cause more panic than we've already got.
So what do we do instead?
Give them a job to do. They need ***purpose.***
HEY!
You guys seem to know an awful lot about metal and wiring and stuff.
What were you before you became professional agents of anarchy?

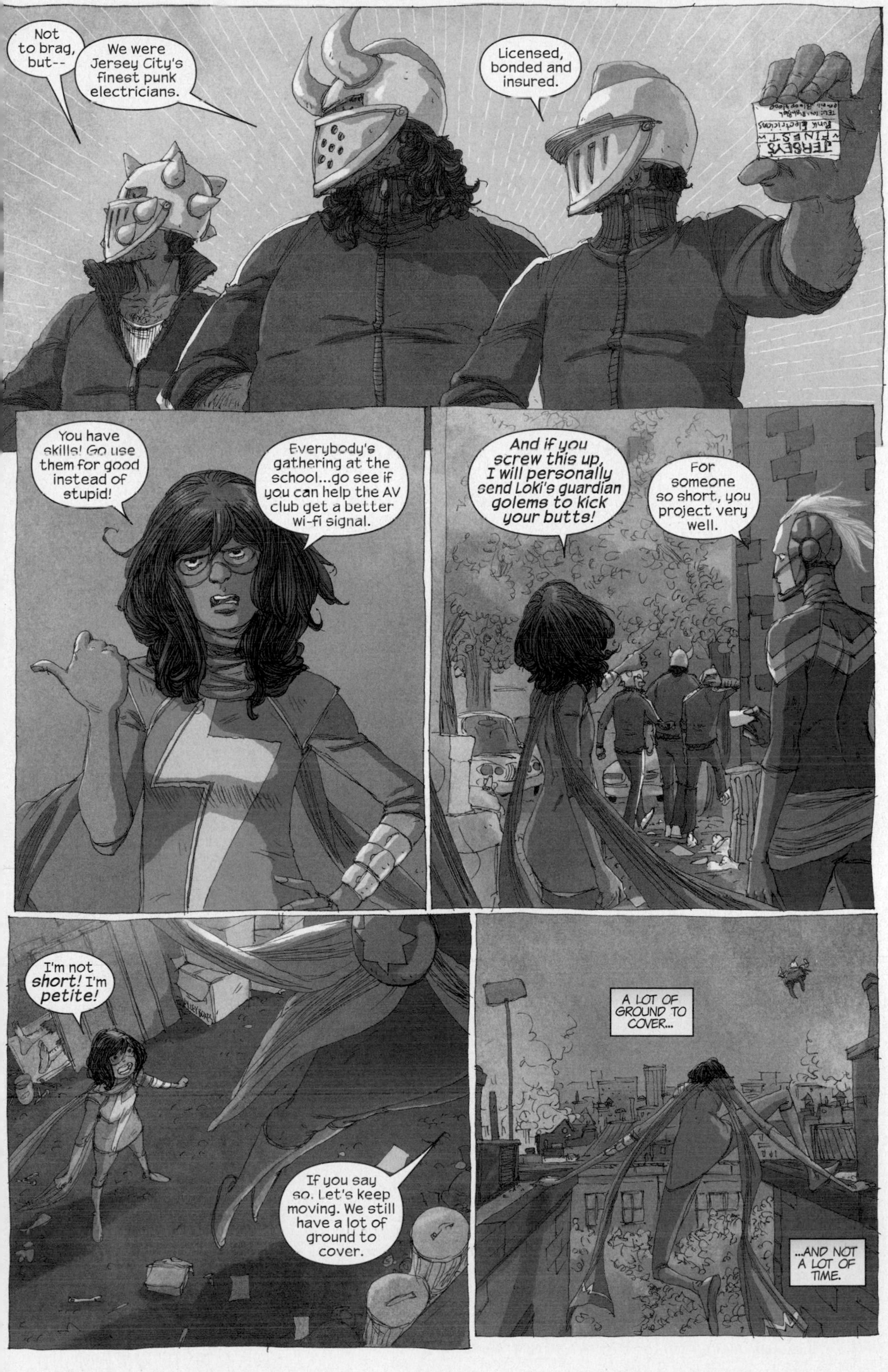

Not to brag, but--
We were Jersey City's finest punk electricians.
Licensed, bonded and insured.
You have skills! Go use them for good instead of stupid!
Everybody's gathering at the school...go see if you can help the AV club get a better wi-fi signal.
And if you screw this up, I will personally send Loki's guardian golems to kick your butts!
For someone so short, you project very well.
I'm not short! I'm petite!
If you say so. Let's keep moving. We still have a lot of ground to cover.
A LOT OF GROUND TO COVER...
...AND NOT A LOT OF TIME.

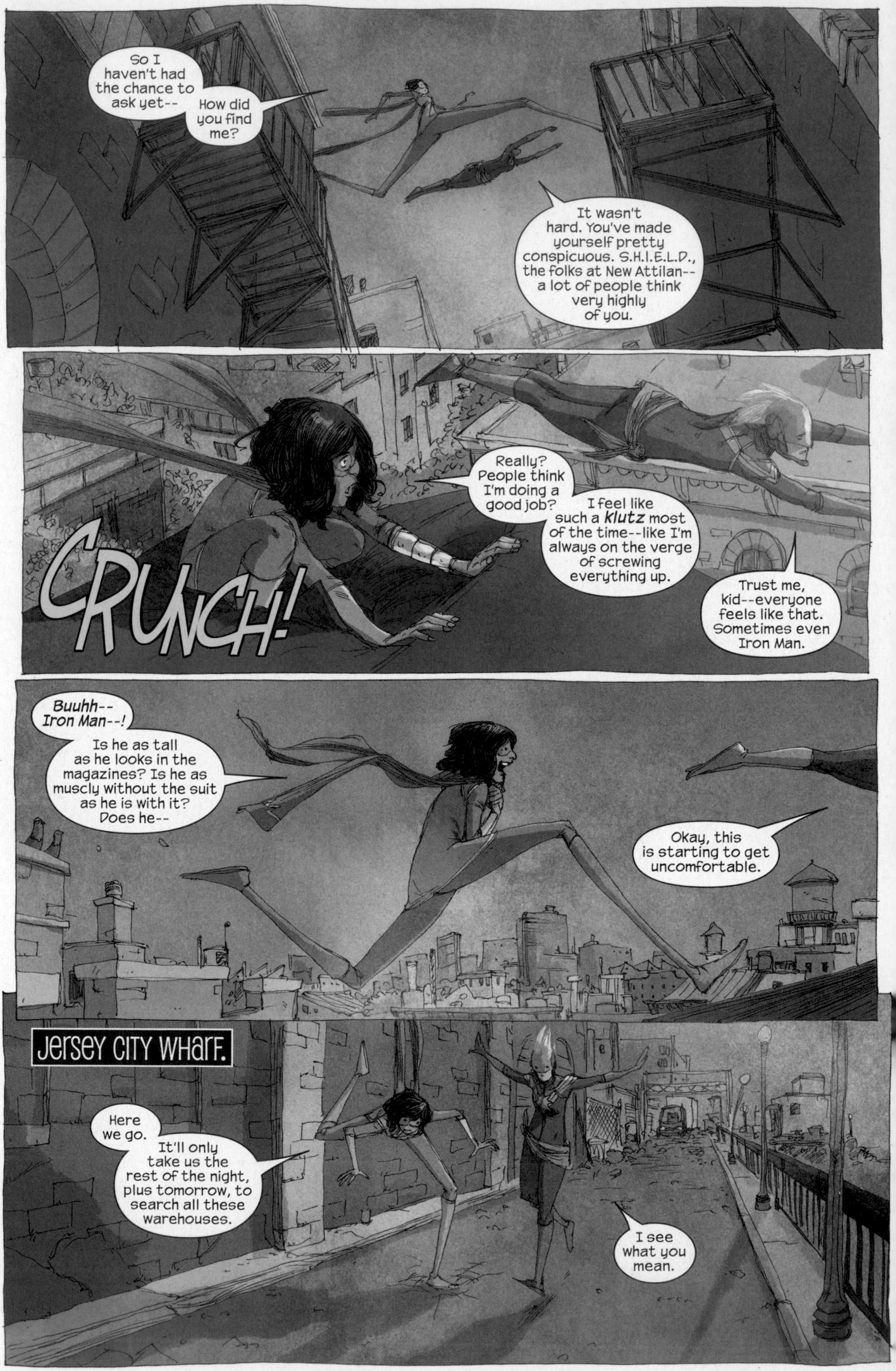

So I haven't had the chance to ask yet--
How did you find me?
It wasn't hard. You've made yourself pretty conspicuous. S.H.I.E.L.D., the folks at New Attilan--a lot of people think very highly of you.
Really? People think I'm doing a good job?
I feel like such a klutz most of the time--like I'm always on the verge of screwing everything up.
CRUNCH!
Trust me, kid--everyone feels like that. Sometimes even Iron Man.
Buuhh-- Iron Man--!
Is he as tall as he looks in the magazines? Is he as muscly without the suit as he is with it? Does he--
Okay, this is starting to get uncomfortable.
Jersey City Wharf.
Here we go.
It'll only take us the rest of the night, plus tomorrow, to search all these warehouses.
I see what you mean.

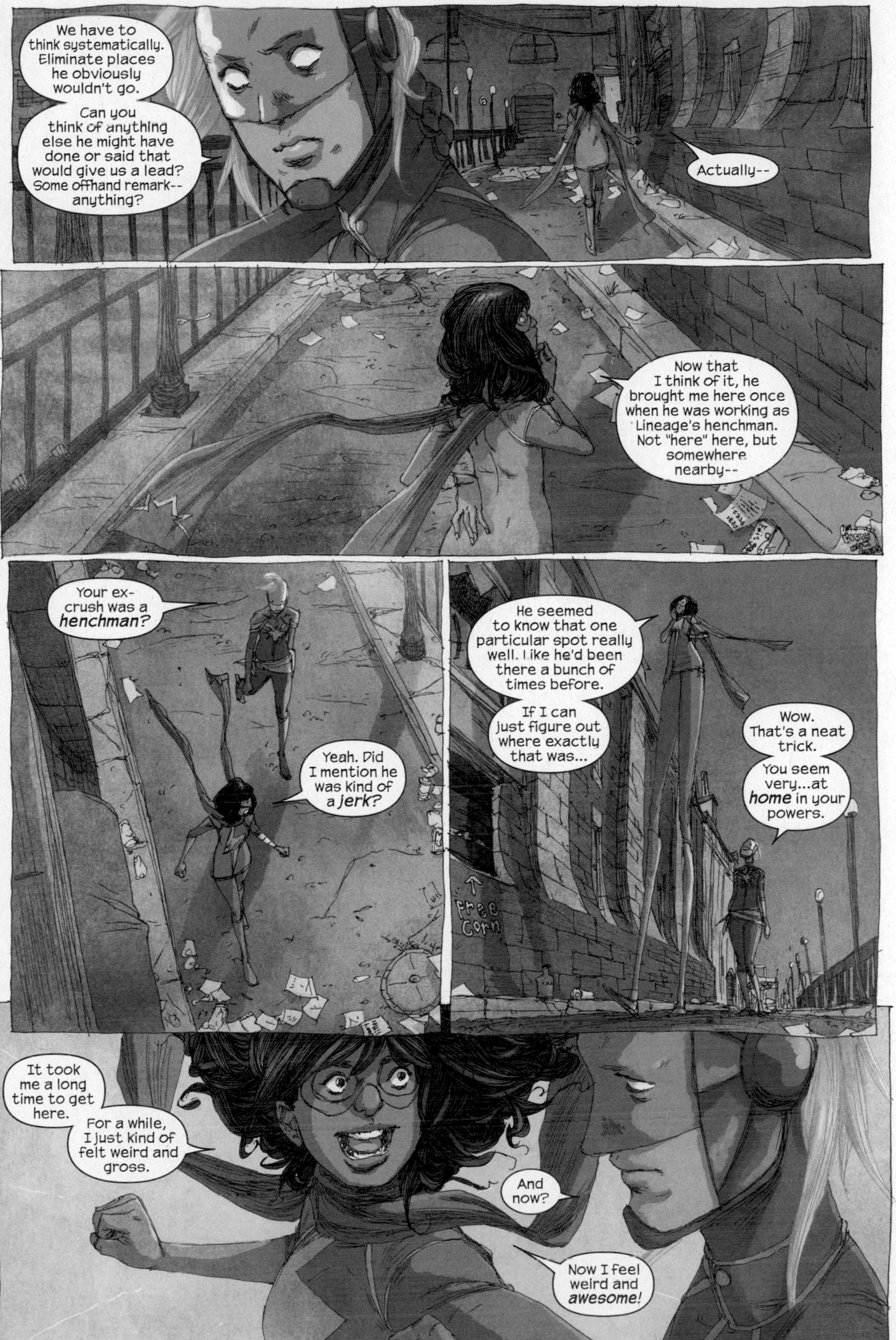
We have to think systematically. Eliminate places he obviously wouldn't go.
Can you think of anything else he might have done or said that would give us a lead? Some offhand remark--anything?
Actually--
Now that I think of it, he brought me here once when he was working as Lineage's henchman. Not "here" here, but somewhere nearby--
Your ex-crush was a *henchman*?
Yeah. Did I mention he was kind of a *jerk*?
He seemed to know that one particular spot really well. Like he'd been there a bunch of times before.
If I can just figure out where exactly that was...
Wow. That's a neat trick.
You seem very...at *home* in your powers.
Free Corn
It took me a long time to get here.
For a while, I just kind of felt weird and gross.
And now?
Now I feel weird and *awesome!*

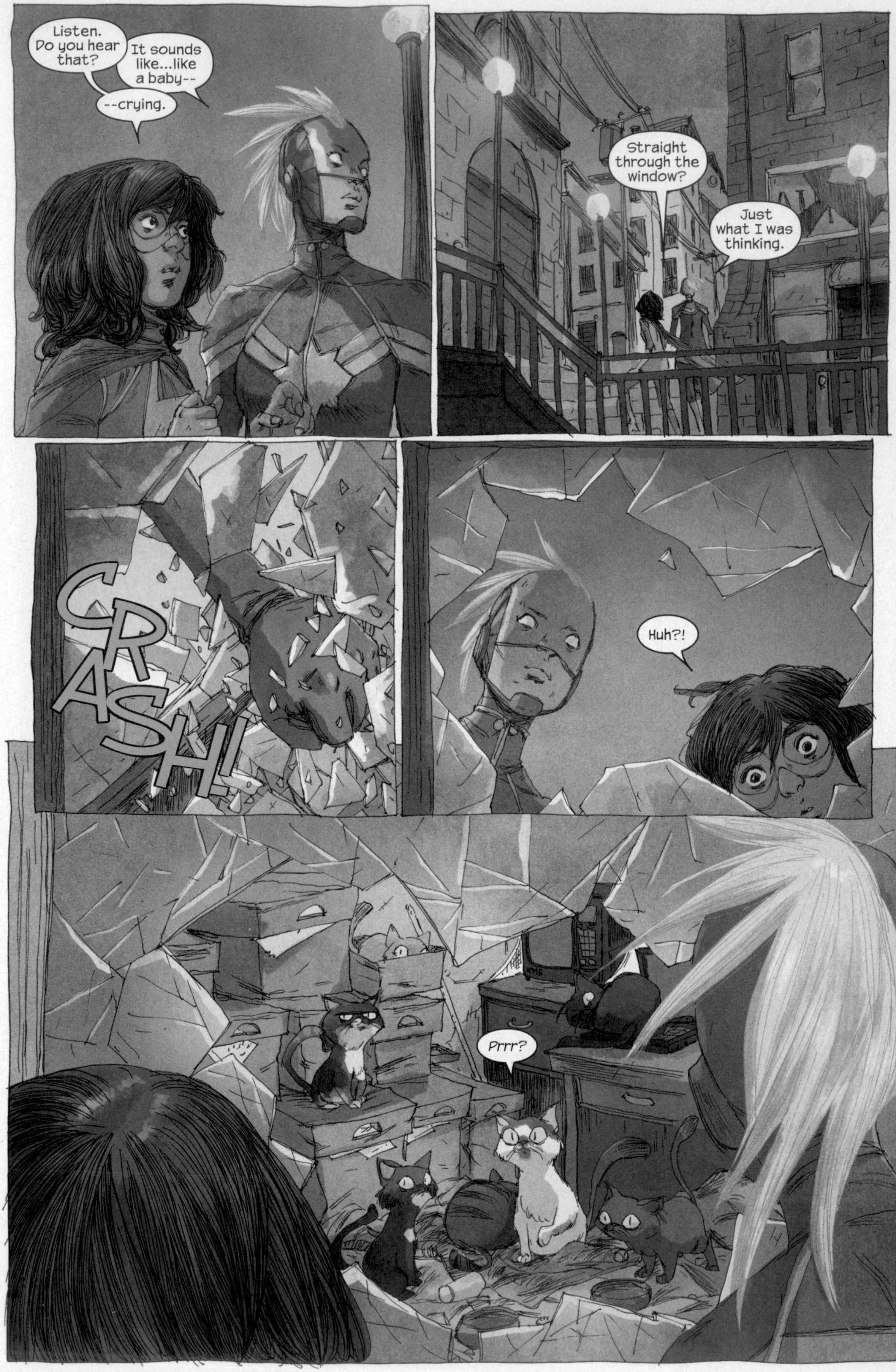
Listen. Do you hear that?
It sounds like...like a baby--
--crying.
Straight through the window?
Just what I was thinking.
CRASH!
Huh?!
Prrr?

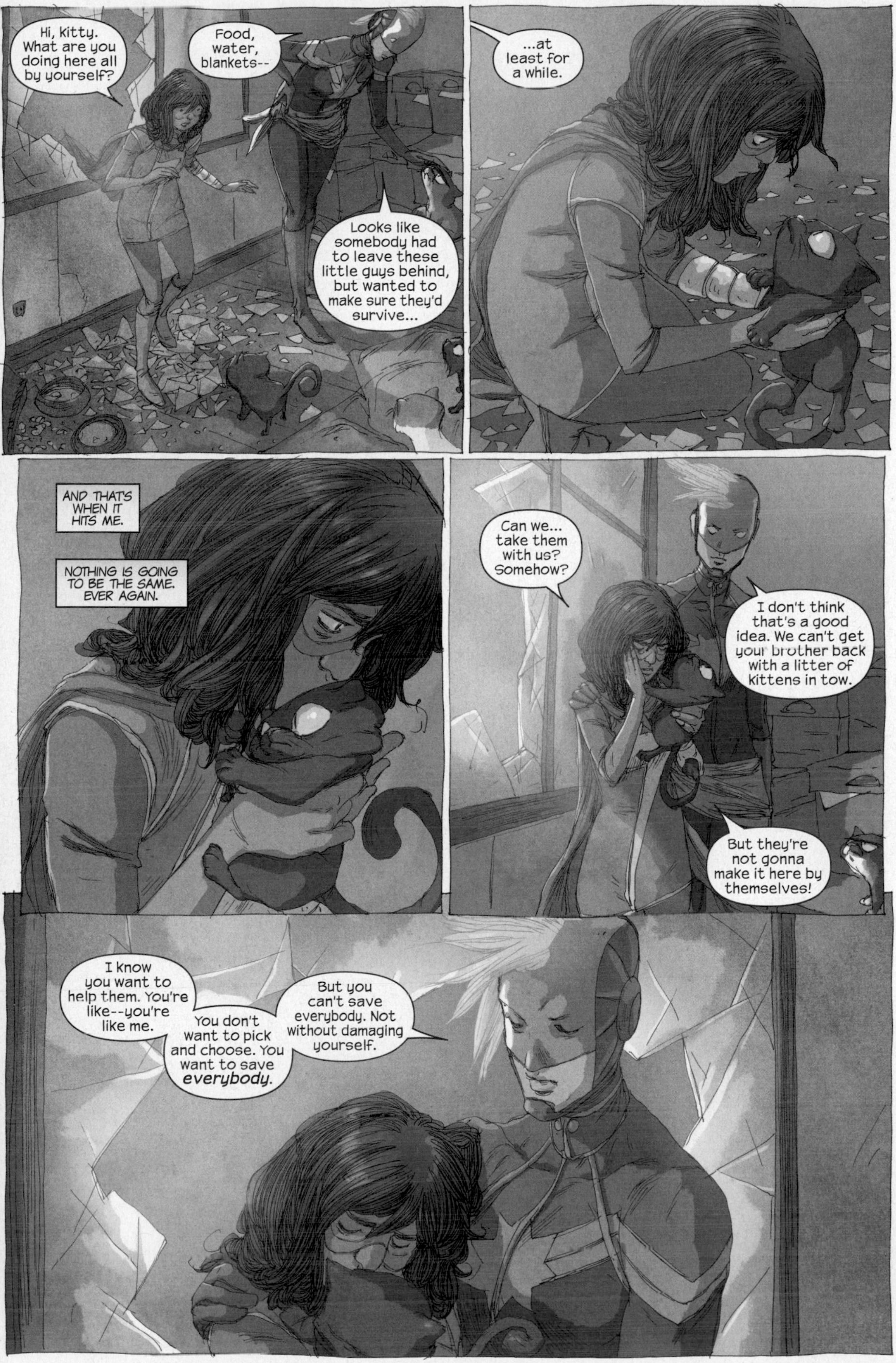
Hi, kitty. What are you doing here all by yourself?
Food, water, blankets--
Looks like somebody had to leave these little guys behind, but wanted to make sure they'd survive...
...at least for a while.
AND THAT'S WHEN IT HITS ME.
NOTHING IS GOING TO BE THE SAME. EVER AGAIN.
Can we... take them with us? Somehow?
I don't think that's a good idea. We can't get your brother back with a litter of kittens in tow.
But they're not gonna make it here by themselves!
I know you want to help them. You're like--you're like me.
You don't want to pick and choose. You want to save *everybody*.
But you can't save everybody. Not without damaging yourself.

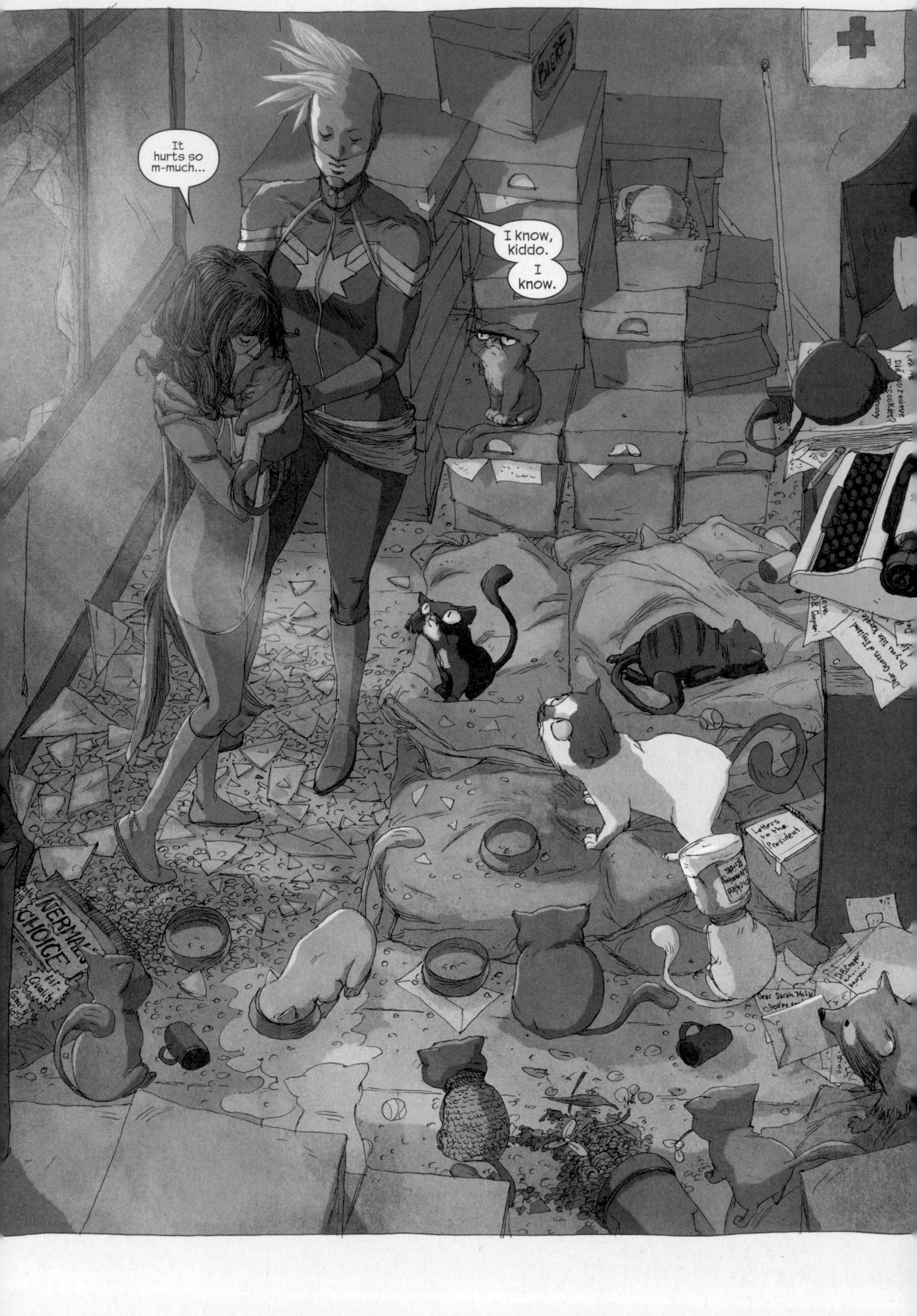
It hurts so m-much...
I know, kiddo.
I know.
Letters to the President.

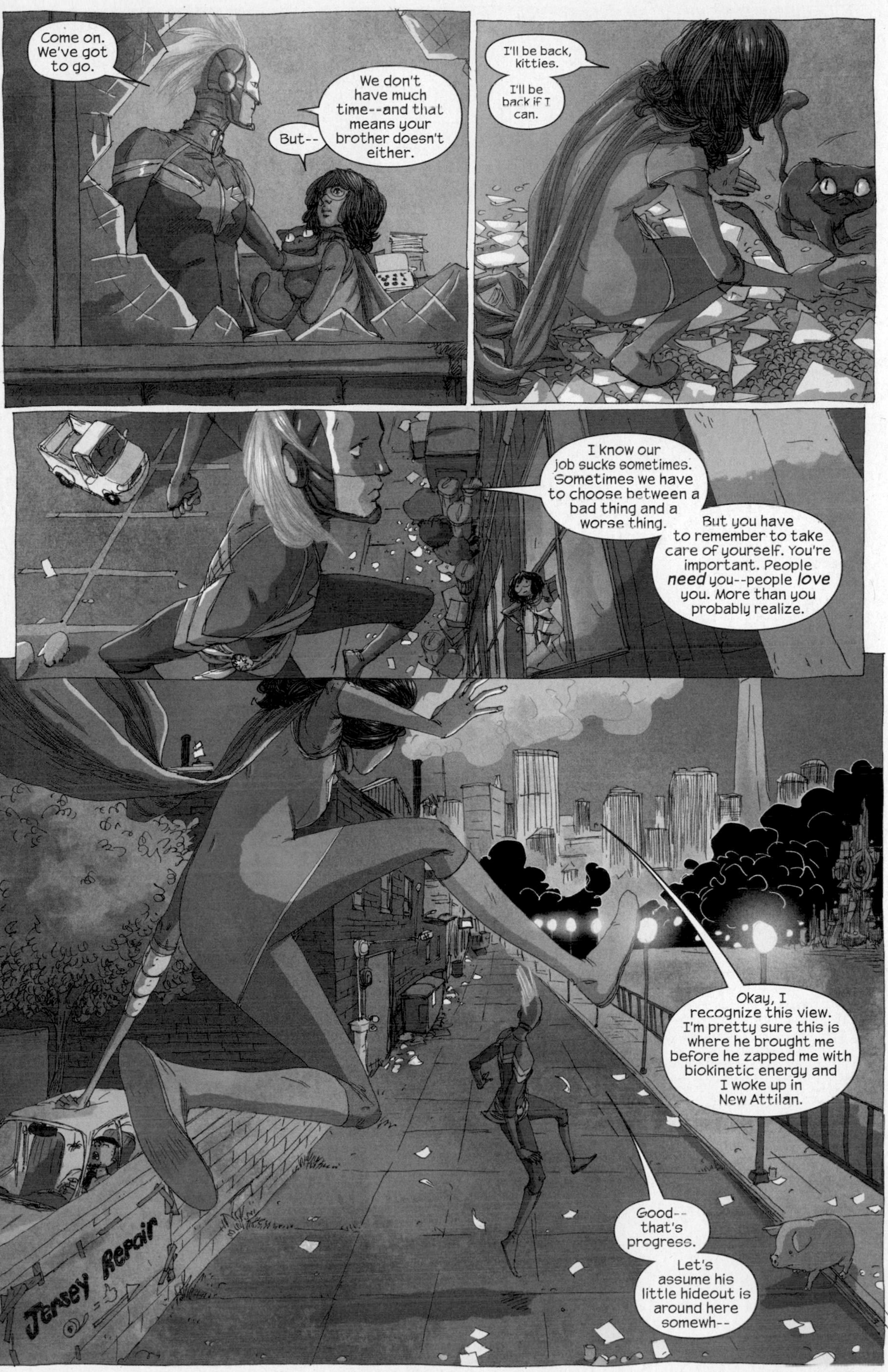
Come on. We've got to go.
But--
We don't have much time--and that means your brother doesn't either.
I'll be back, kitties.
I'll be back if I can.
I know our job sucks sometimes. Sometimes we have to choose between a bad thing and a worse thing.
But you have to remember to take care of yourself. You're important. People **need** you--people **love** you. More than you probably realize.
Okay, I recognize this view. I'm pretty sure this is where he brought me before he zapped me with biokinetic energy and I woke up in New Attilan.
Good--that's progress.
Let's assume his little hideout is around here somewh--
Jersey Repair

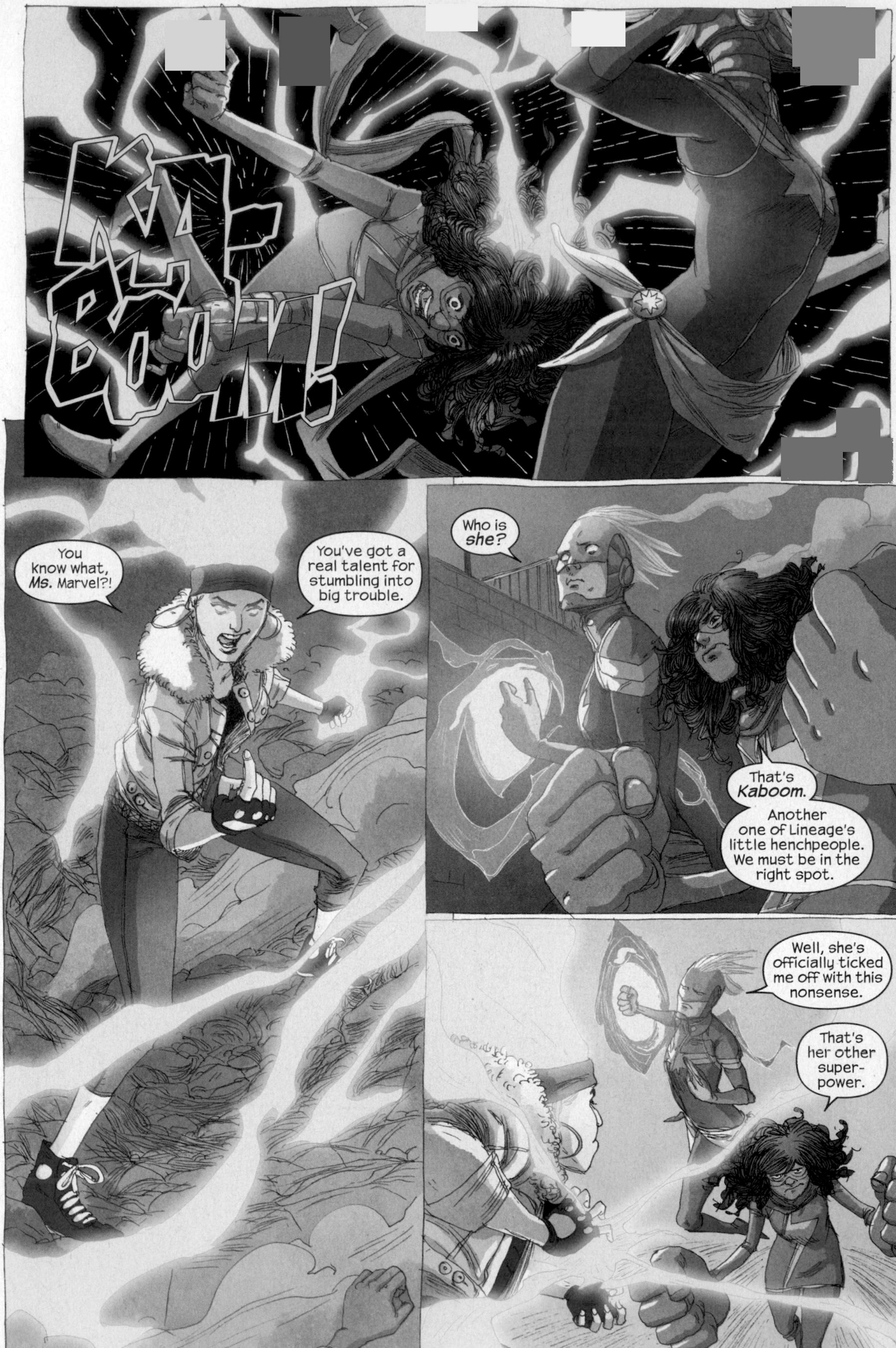

You know what, Ms. Marvel?!
You've got a real talent for stumbling into big trouble.
Who is she?
That's Kaboom.
Another one of Lineage's little henchpeople. We must be in the right spot.
Well, she's officially ticked me off with this nonsense.
That's her other super-power.

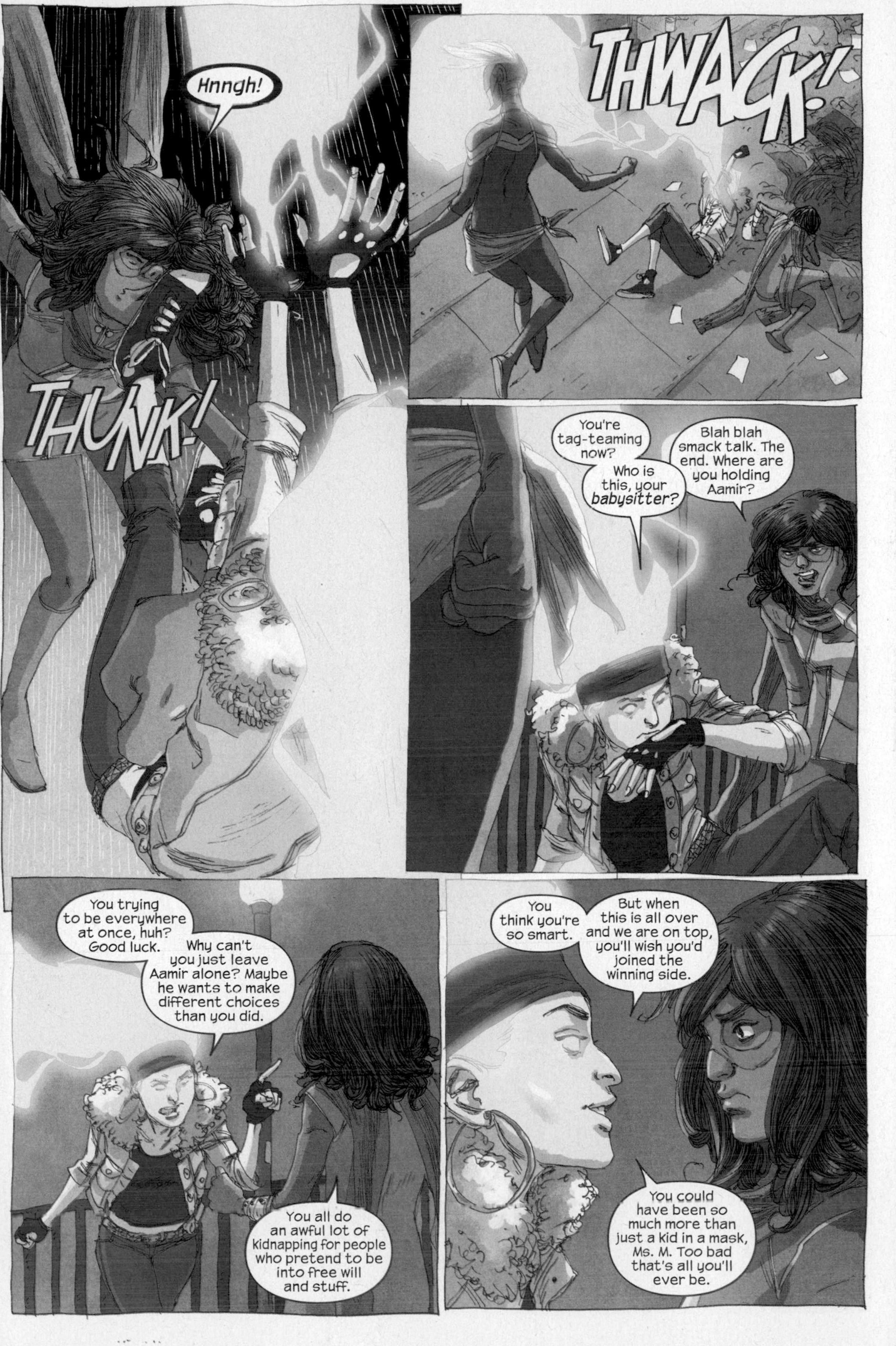
Hnngh!
THUNK!
THWACK!
You're tag-teaming now?
Who is this, your *babysitter?*
Blah blah smack talk. The end. Where are you holding Aamir?
You trying to be everywhere at once, huh? Good luck.
Why can't you just leave Aamir alone? Maybe he wants to make different choices than you did.
You all do an awful lot of kidnapping for people who pretend to be into free will and stuff.
You think you're so smart.
But when this is all over and we are on top, you'll wish you'd joined the winning side.
You could have been so much more than just a kid in a mask, Ms. M. Too bad that's all you'll ever be.

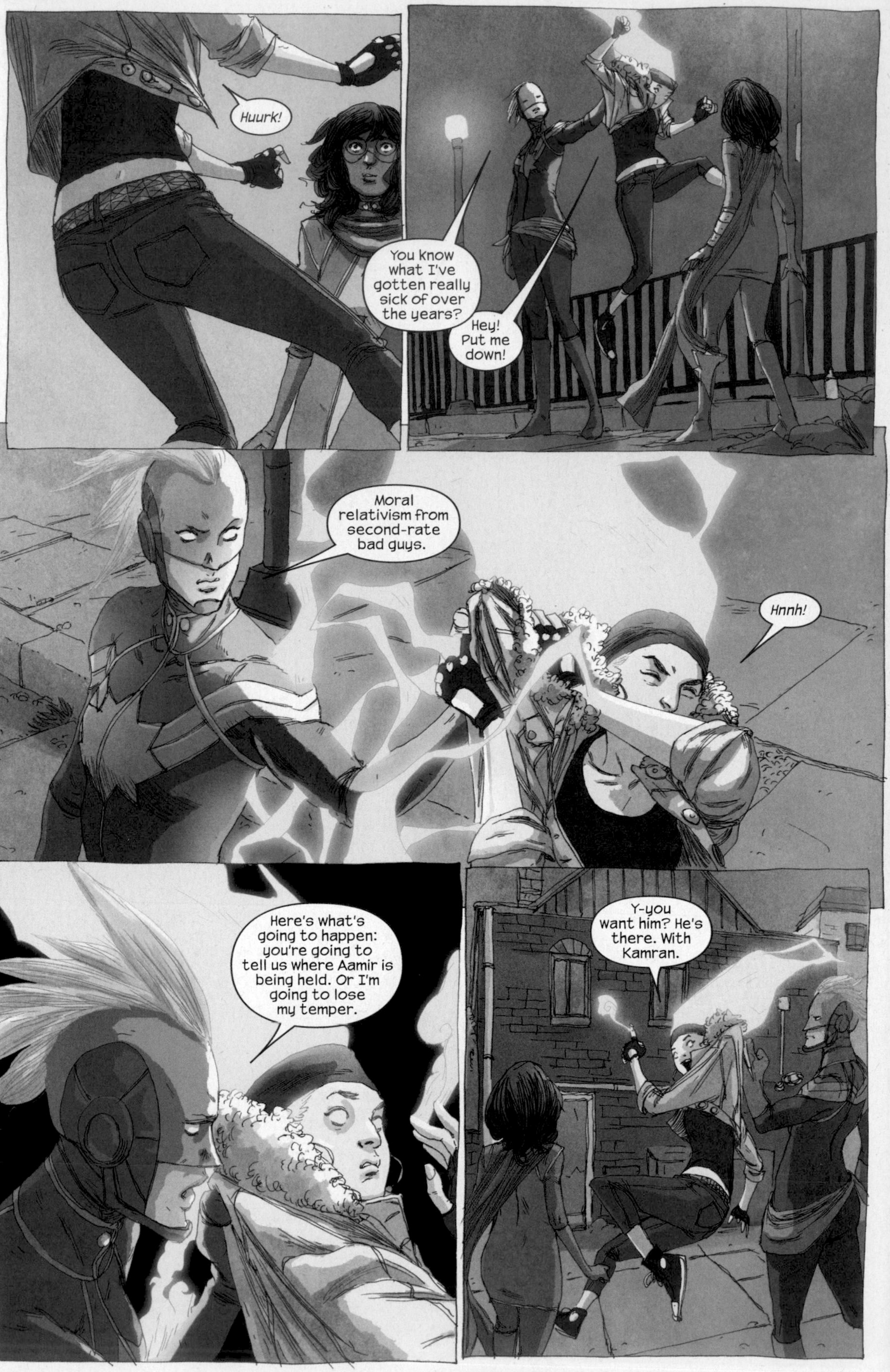
Huurk!
You know what I've gotten really sick of over the years?
Hey! Put me down!
Moral relativism from second-rate bad guys.
Hnnh!
Here's what's going to happen: you're going to tell us where Aamir is being held. Or I'm going to lose my temper.
Y-you want him? He's there. With Kamran.

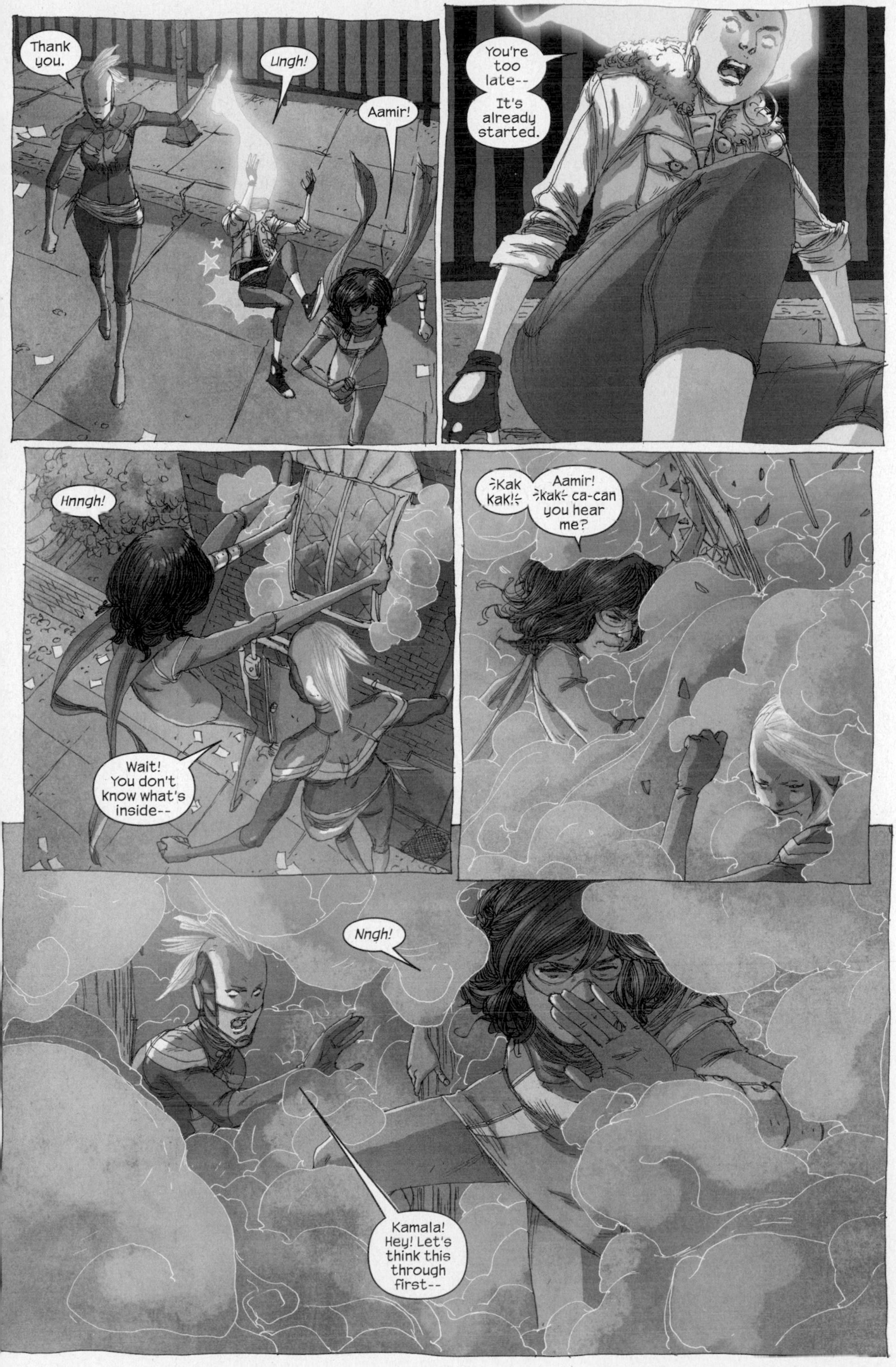
Thank you.
Ungh!
Aamir!
You're too late--
It's already started.
Hnngh!
Wait! You don't know what's inside--
Kak kak!
Aamir! kak ca-can you hear me?
Nngh!
Kamala! Hey! Let's think this through first--

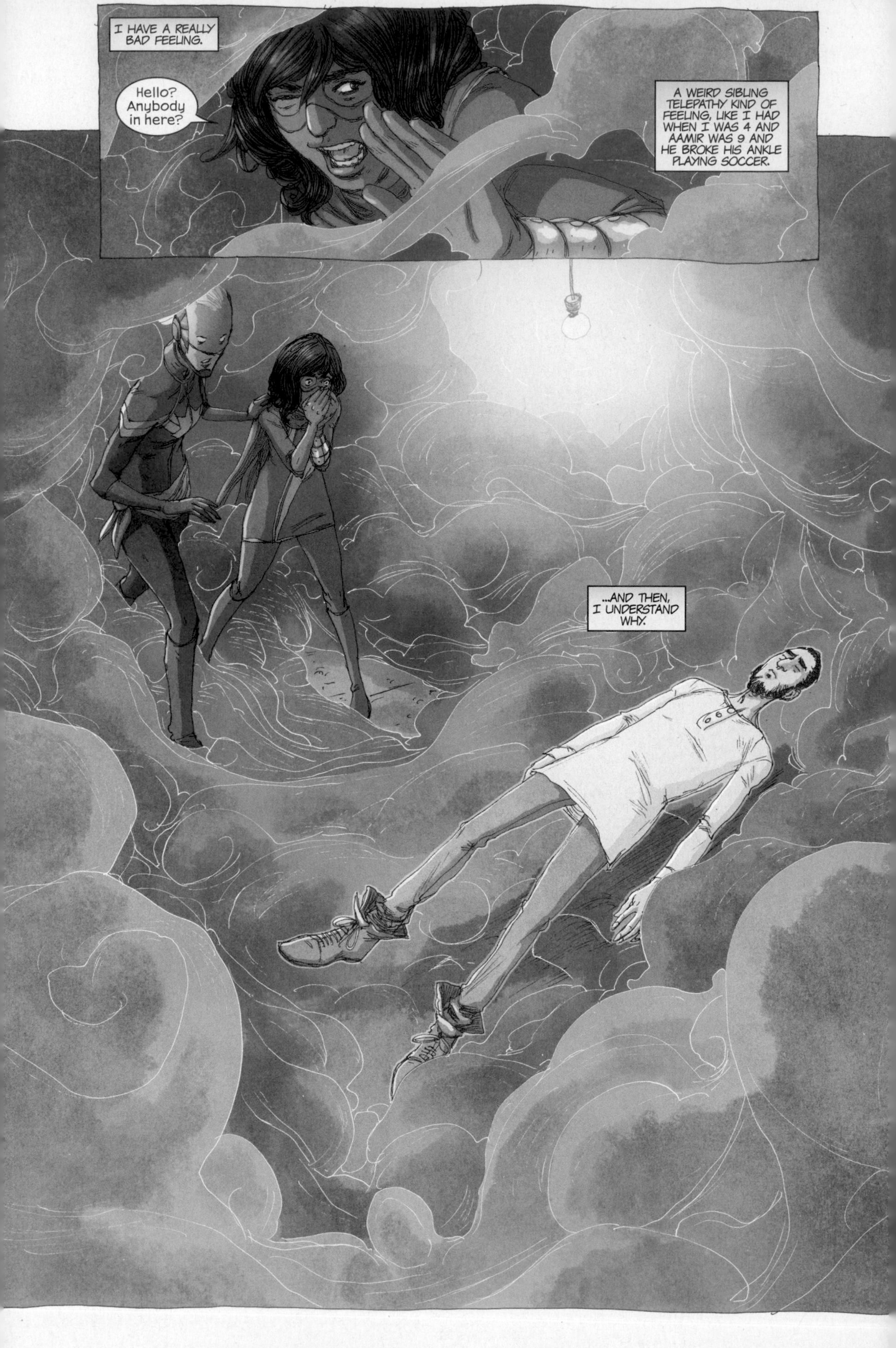
I HAVE A REALLY BAD FEELING.
Hello? Anybody in here?
A WEIRD SIBLING TELEPATHY KIND OF FEELING, LIKE I HAD WHEN I WAS 4 AND AAMIR WAS 9 AND HE BROKE HIS ANKLE PLAYING SOCCER.
...AND THEN, I UNDERSTAND WHY.

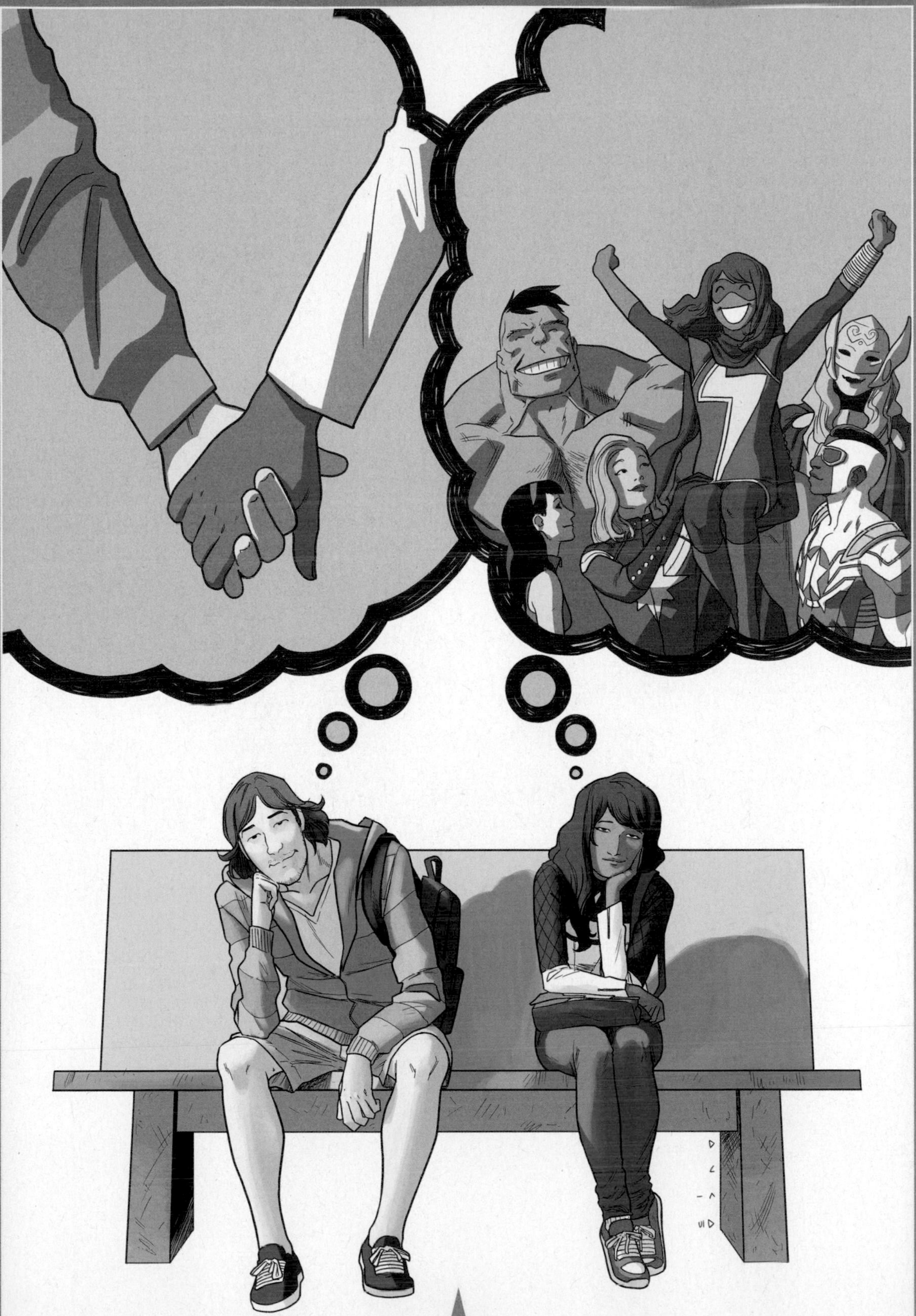

18

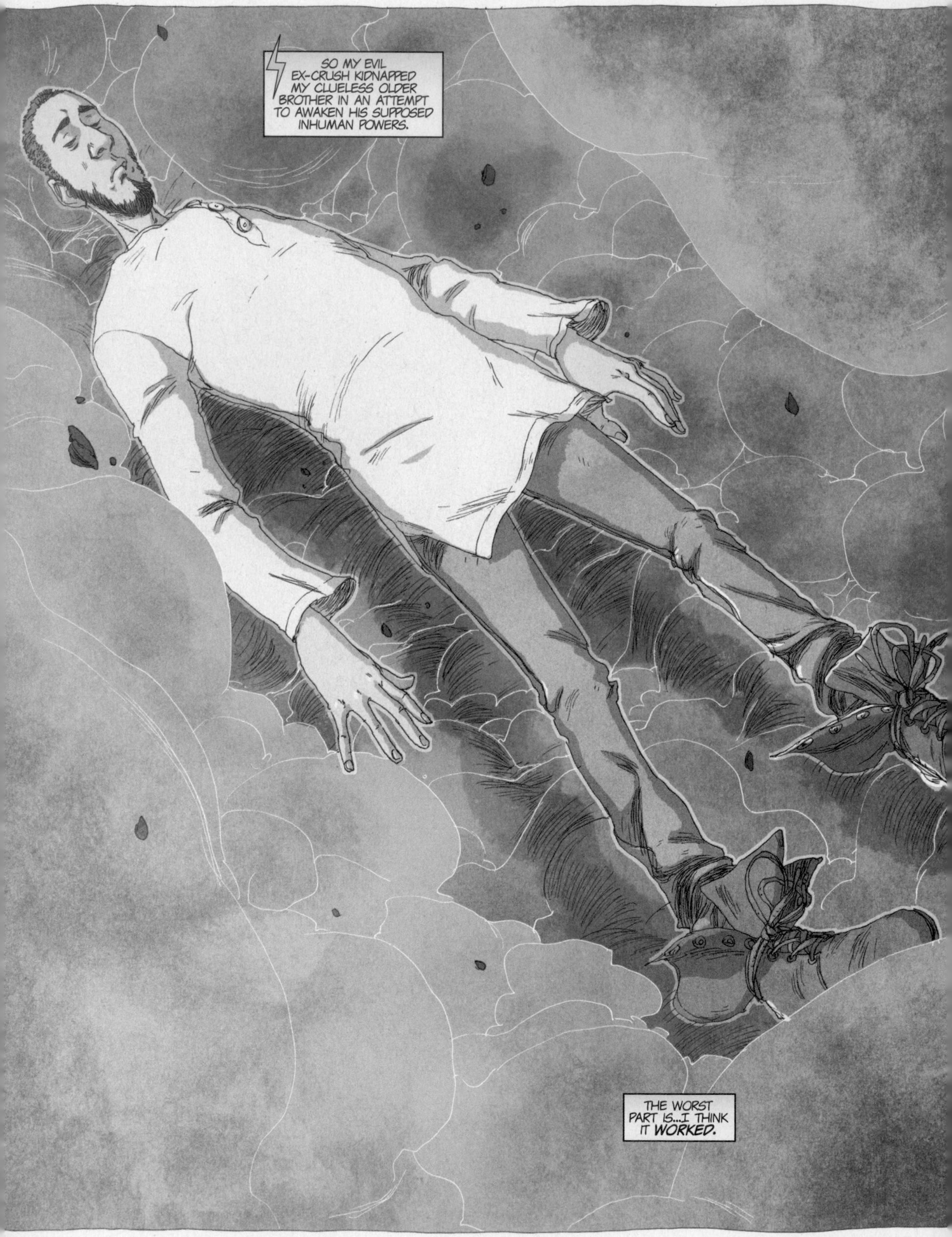
SO MY EVIL EX-CRUSH KIDNAPPED MY CLUELESS OLDER BROTHER IN AN ATTEMPT TO AWAKEN HIS SUPPOSED INHUMAN POWERS.
THE WORST PART IS...I THINK IT *WORKED.*

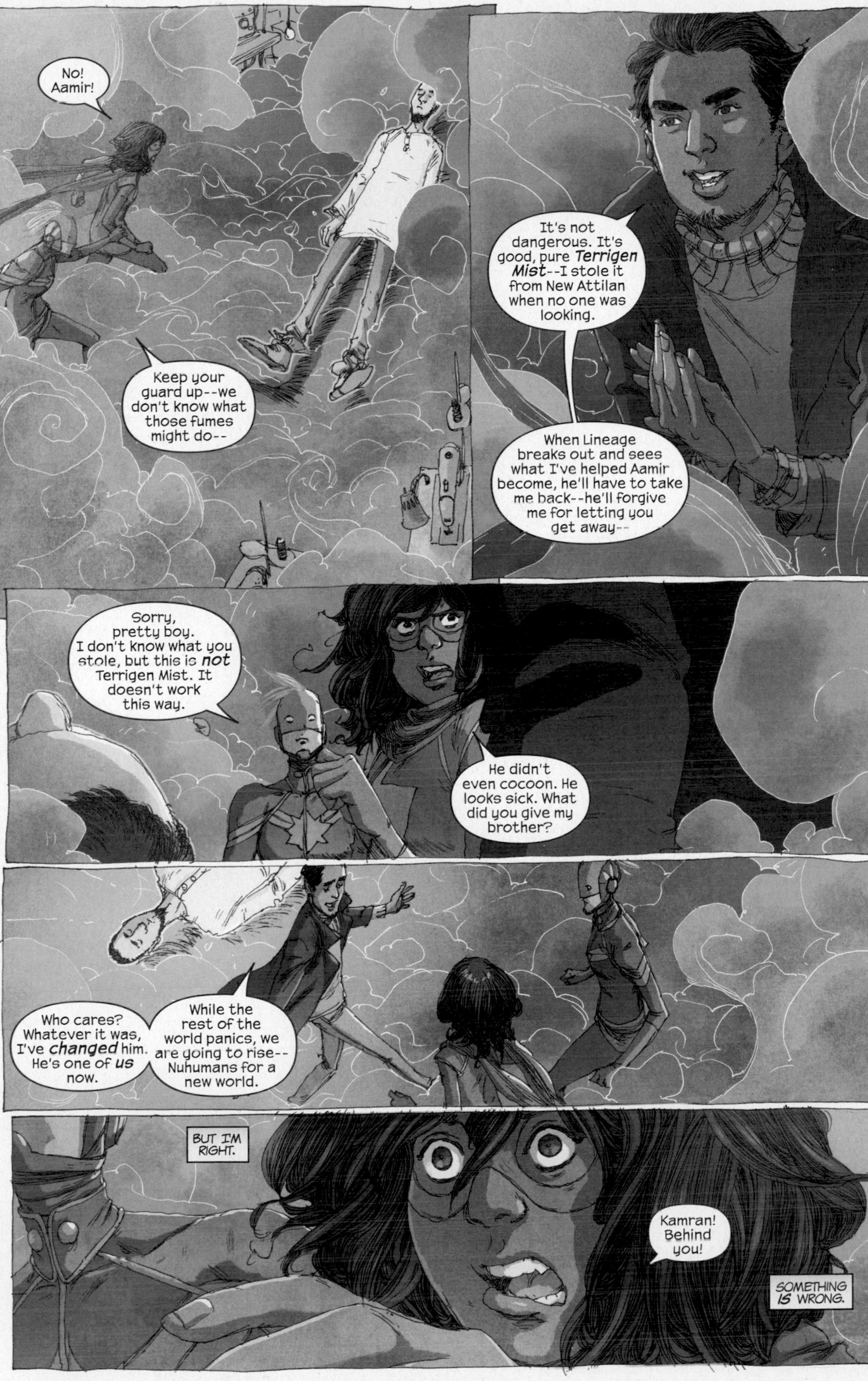

No! Aamir!
Keep your guard up--we don't know what those fumes might do--
It's not dangerous. It's good, pure Terrigen Mist--I stole it from New Attilan when no one was looking.
When Lineage breaks out and sees what I've helped Aamir become, he'll have to take me back--he'll forgive me for letting you get away--
Sorry, pretty boy. I don't know what you stole, but this is not Terrigen Mist. It doesn't work this way.
He didn't even cocoon. He looks sick. What did you give my brother?
Who cares? Whatever it was, I've changed him. He's one of us now.
While the rest of the world panics, we are going to rise--Nuhumans for a new world.
BUT I'M RIGHT.
Kamran! Behind you!
SOMETHING IS WRONG.

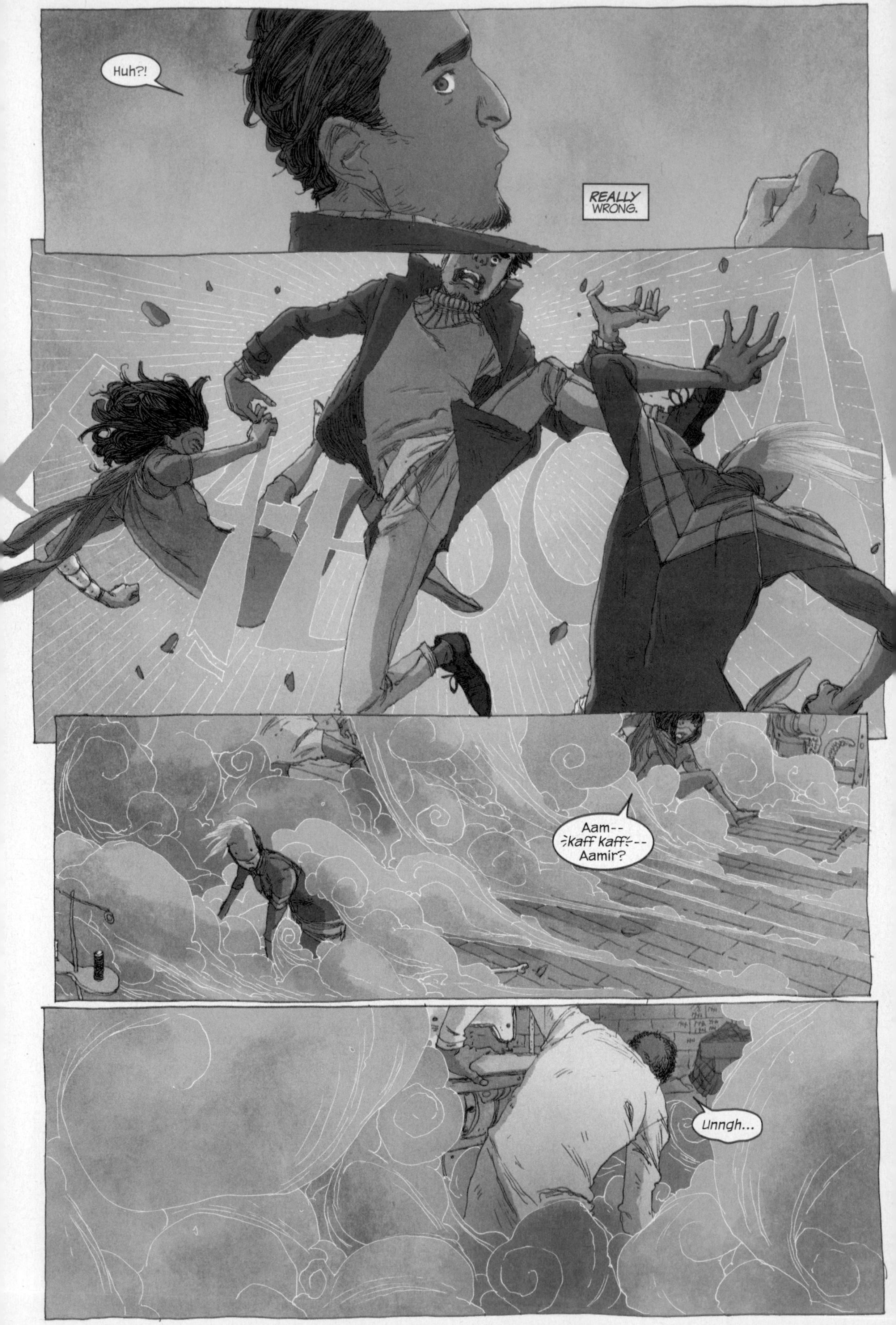
Huh?!
REALLY WRONG.
Aam-- -kaff kaff- -- Aamir?
Unngh...

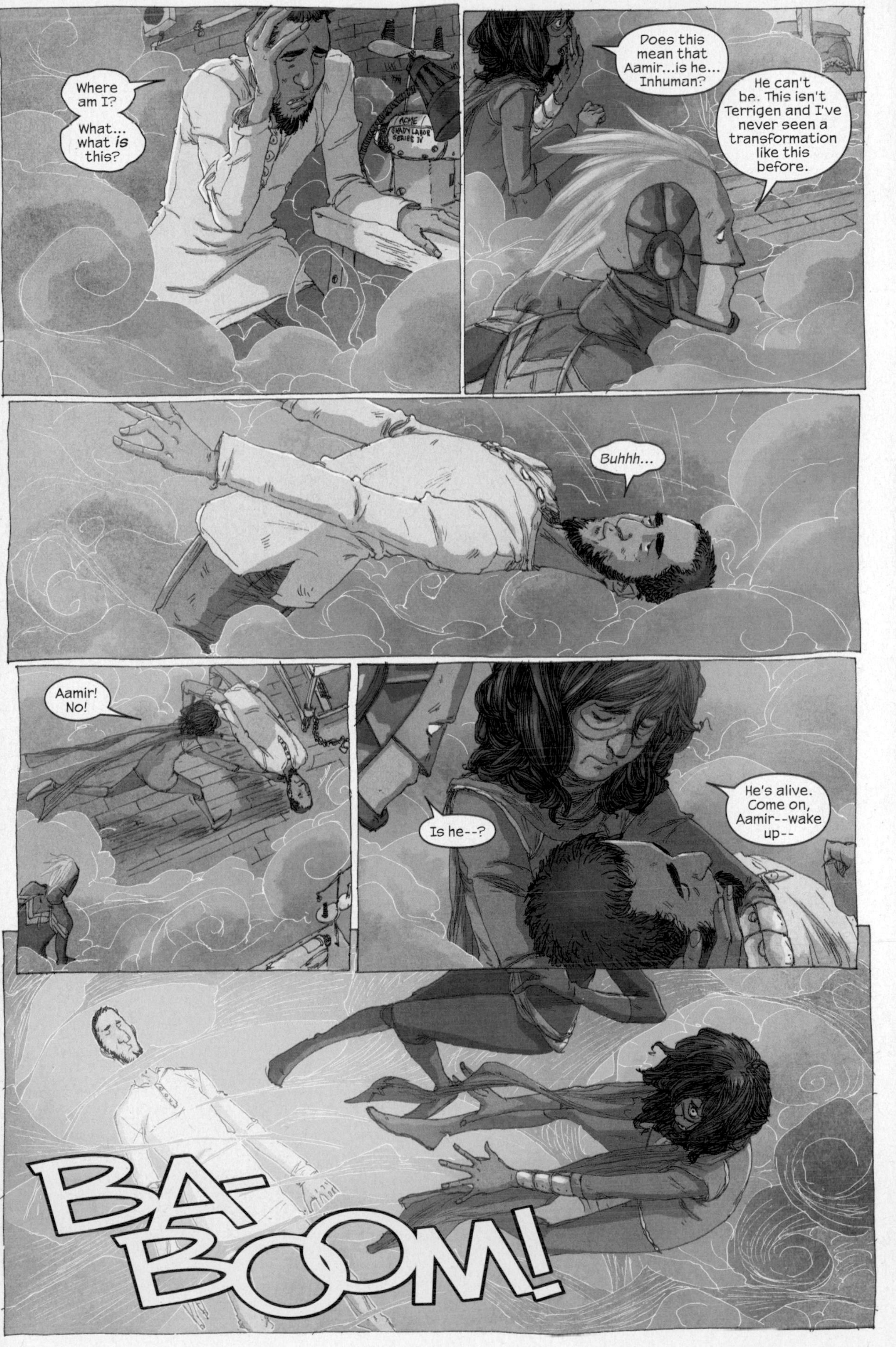
Where am I?
What... what *is* this?
ACME SHADY LABOR SERIES IV
Does this mean that Aamir...is he... Inhuman?
He can't be. This isn't Terrigen and I've never seen a transformation like this before.
Buhhh...
Aamir! No!
Is he--?
He's alive. Come on, Aamir--wake up--
BA-BOOM!

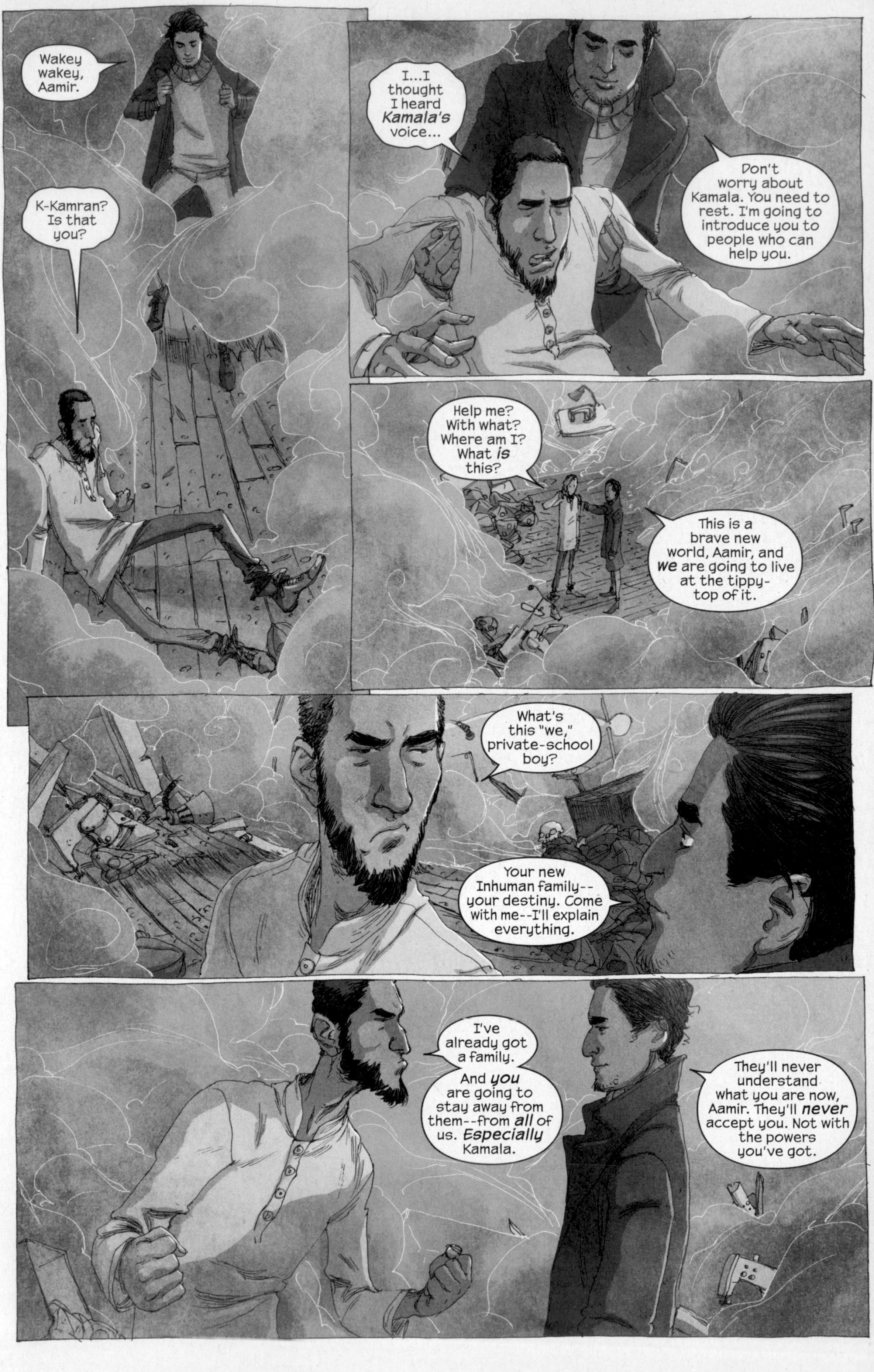
Wakey wakey, Aamir.
K-Kamran? Is that you?
I...I thought I heard Kamala's voice...
Don't worry about Kamala. You need to rest. I'm going to introduce you to people who can help you.
Help me? With what? Where am I? What is this?
This is a brave new world, Aamir, and we are going to live at the tippy-top of it.
What's this "we," private-school boy?
Your new Inhuman family--your destiny. Come with me--I'll explain everything.
I've already got a family.
And you are going to stay away from them--from all of us. Especially Kamala.
They'll never understand what you are now, Aamir. They'll never accept you. Not with the powers you've got.

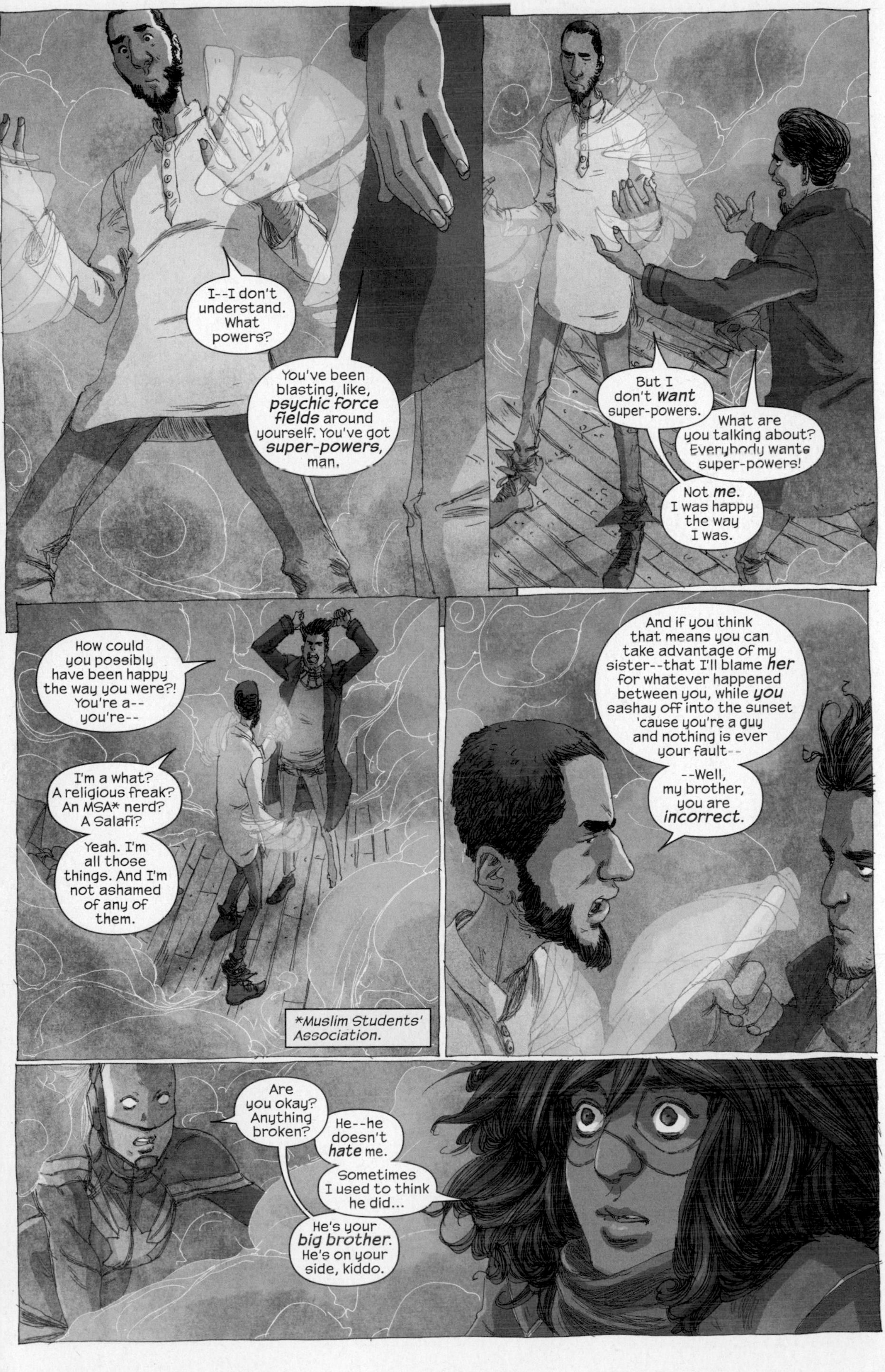
I--I don't understand. What powers?
You've been blasting, like, psychic force fields around yourself. You've got super-powers, man.
But I don't want super-powers.
What are you talking about? Everybody wants super-powers!
Not me. I was happy the way I was.
How could you possibly have been happy the way you were?! You're a-- you're--
I'm a what? A religious freak? An MSA* nerd? A Salafi?
Yeah. I'm all those things. And I'm not ashamed of any of them.
*Muslim Students' Association.
And if you think that means you can take advantage of my sister--that I'll blame her for whatever happened between you, while you sashay off into the sunset 'cause you're a guy and nothing is ever your fault--
--Well, my brother, you are incorrect.
Are you okay? Anything broken?
He--he doesn't hate me.
Sometimes I used to think he did...
He's your big brother. He's on your side, kiddo.

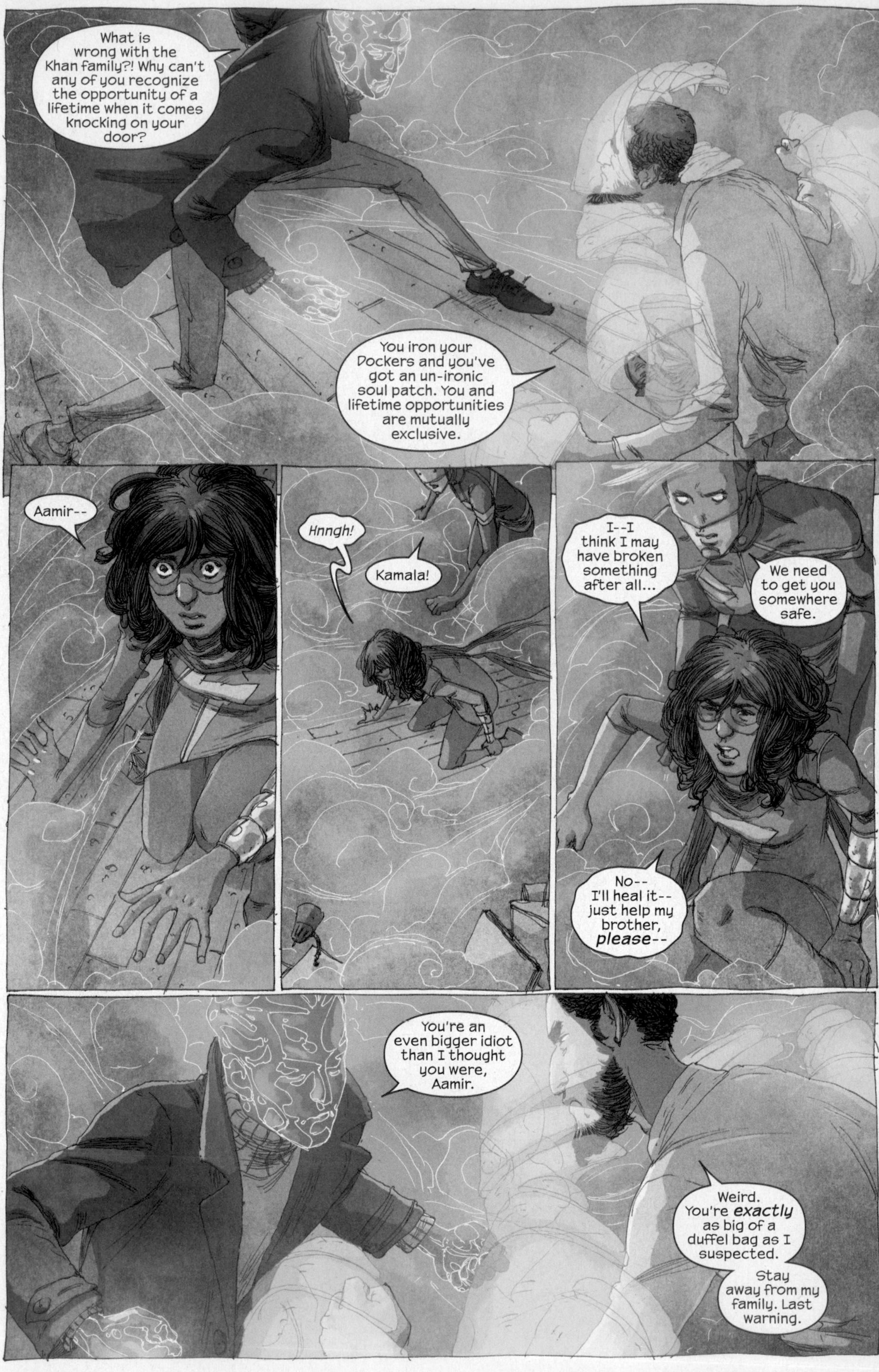
What is wrong with the Khan family?! Why can't any of you recognize the opportunity of a lifetime when it comes knocking on your door?
You iron your Dockers and you've got an un-ironic soul patch. You and lifetime opportunities are mutually exclusive.
Aamir--
Hnngh!
Kamala!
I--I think I may have broken something after all...
We need to get you somewhere safe.
No-- I'll heal it-- just help my brother, *please*--
You're an even bigger idiot than I thought you were, Aamir.
Weird. You're *exactly* as big of a duffel bag as I suspected.
Stay away from my family. Last warning.

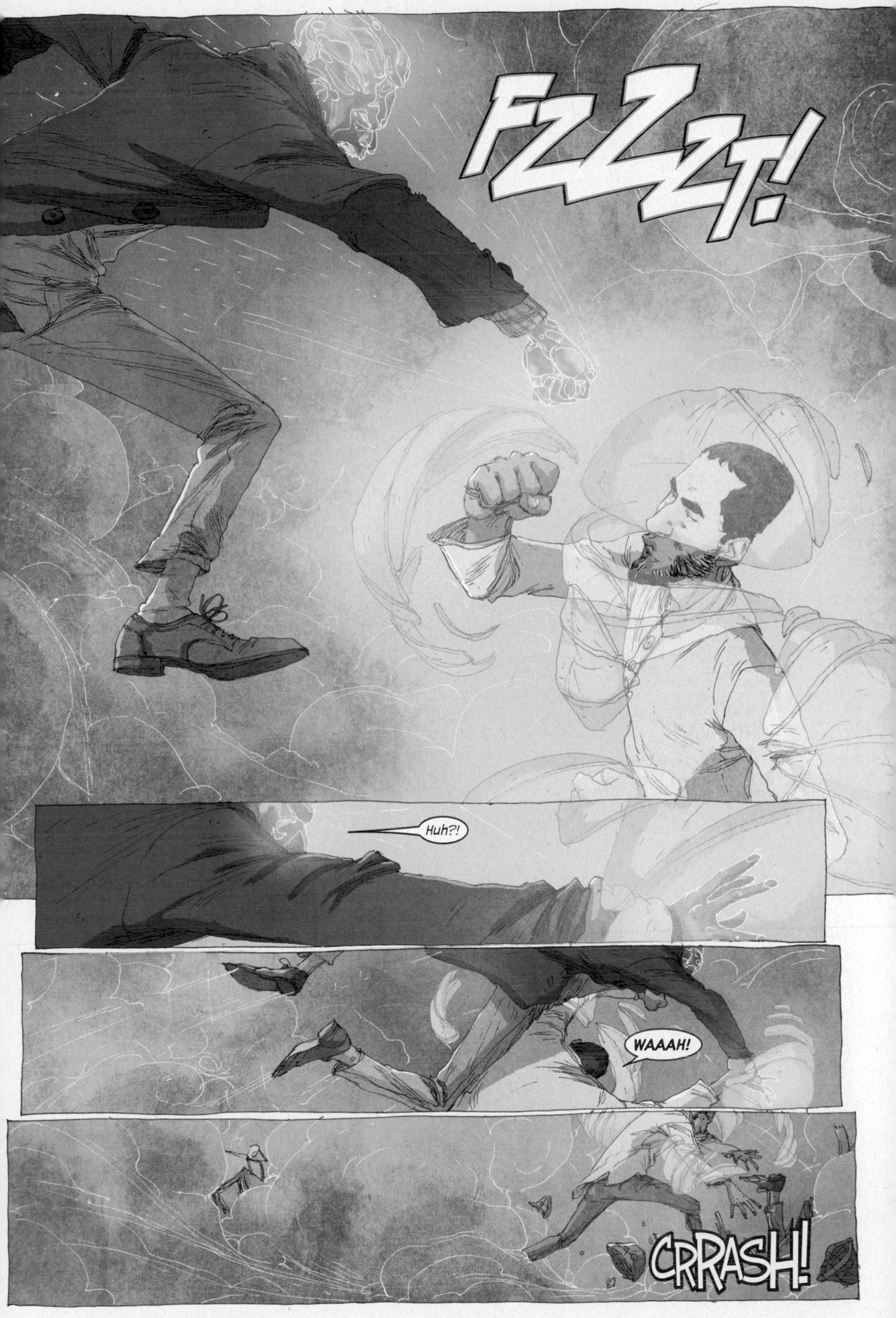

FZZZZT!
Huh?!
WAAAH!
CRRASH!

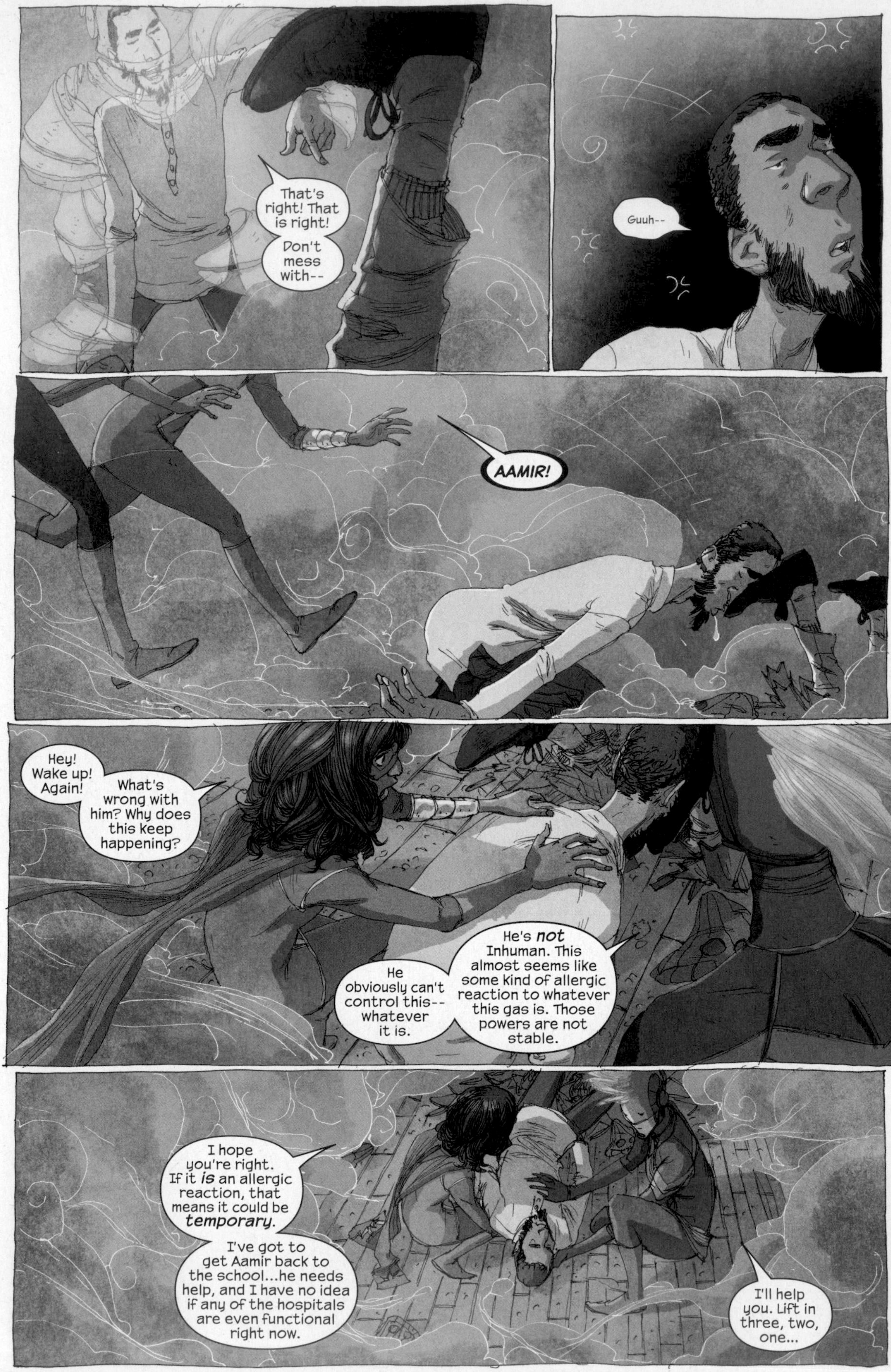
That's right! That is right!
Don't mess with--
Guuh--
AAMIR!
Hey! Wake up! Again!
What's wrong with him? Why does this keep happening?
He obviously can't control this--whatever it is.
He's not Inhuman. This almost seems like some kind of allergic reaction to whatever this gas is. Those powers are not stable.
I hope you're right. If it is an allergic reaction, that means it could be temporary.
I've got to get Aamir back to the school...he needs help, and I have no idea if any of the hospitals are even functional right now.
I'll help you. Lift in three, two, one...

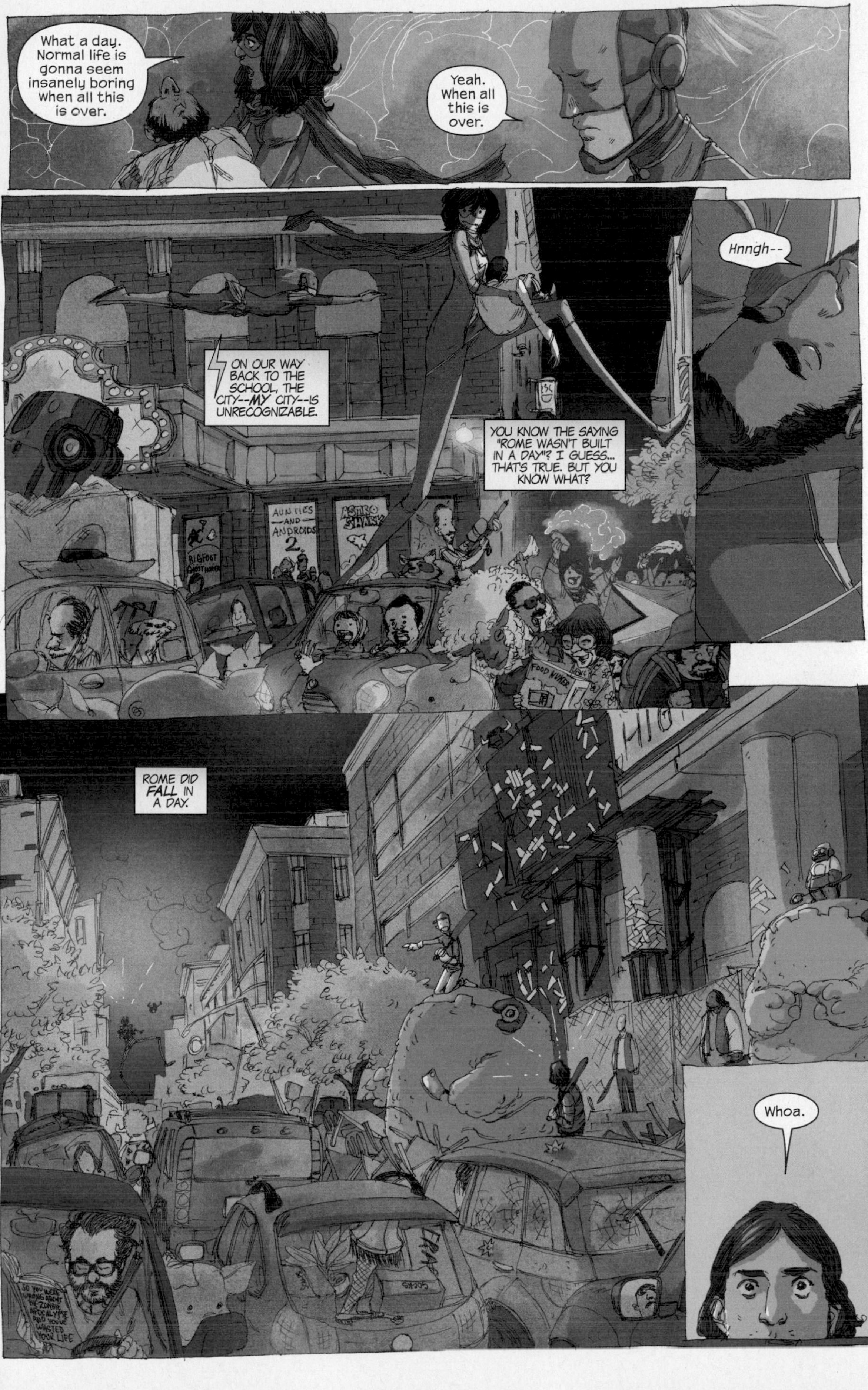

What a day. Normal life is gonna seem insanely boring when all this is over.
Yeah. When all this is over.
ON OUR WAY BACK TO THE SCHOOL, THE CITY--MY CITY--IS UNRECOGNIZABLE.
YOU KNOW THE SAYING "ROME WASN'T BUILT IN A DAY"? I GUESS... THAT'S TRUE. BUT YOU KNOW WHAT?
Hnngh--
AUNTIES AND ANDROIDS 2
ASTRO SHARK
BIGFOOT
ROME DID FALL IN A DAY.
Whoa.

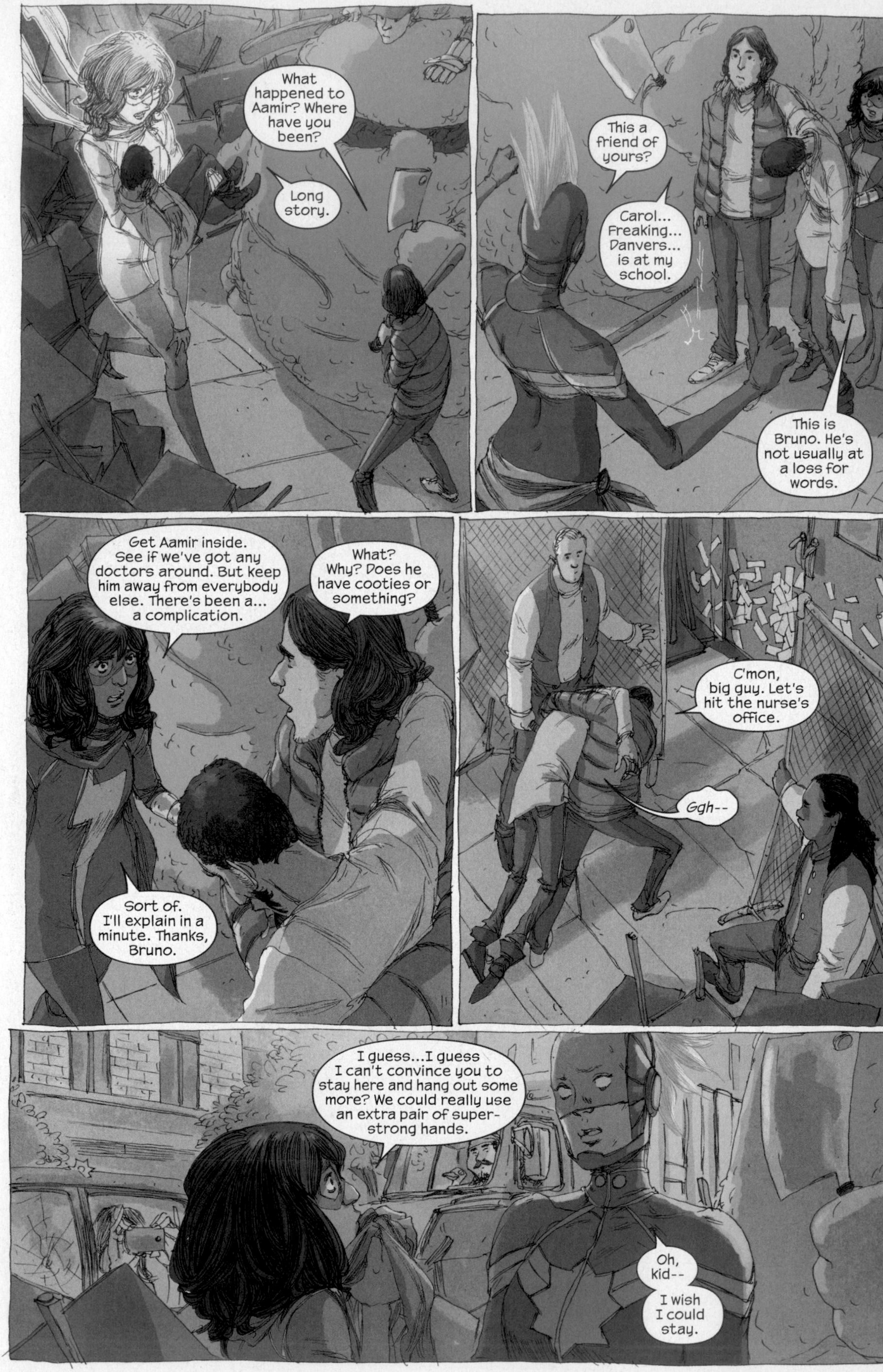
What happened to Aamir? Where have you been?
Long story.
This a friend of yours?
Carol... Freaking... Danvers... is at my school.
This is Bruno. He's not usually at a loss for words.
Get Aamir inside. See if we've got any doctors around. But keep him away from everybody else. There's been a... a complication.
What? Why? Does he have cooties or something?
Sort of. I'll explain in a minute. Thanks, Bruno.
C'mon, big guy. Let's hit the nurse's office.
Ggh--
I guess...I guess I can't convince you to stay here and hang out some more? We could really use an extra pair of super-strong hands.
Oh, kid--
I wish I could stay.

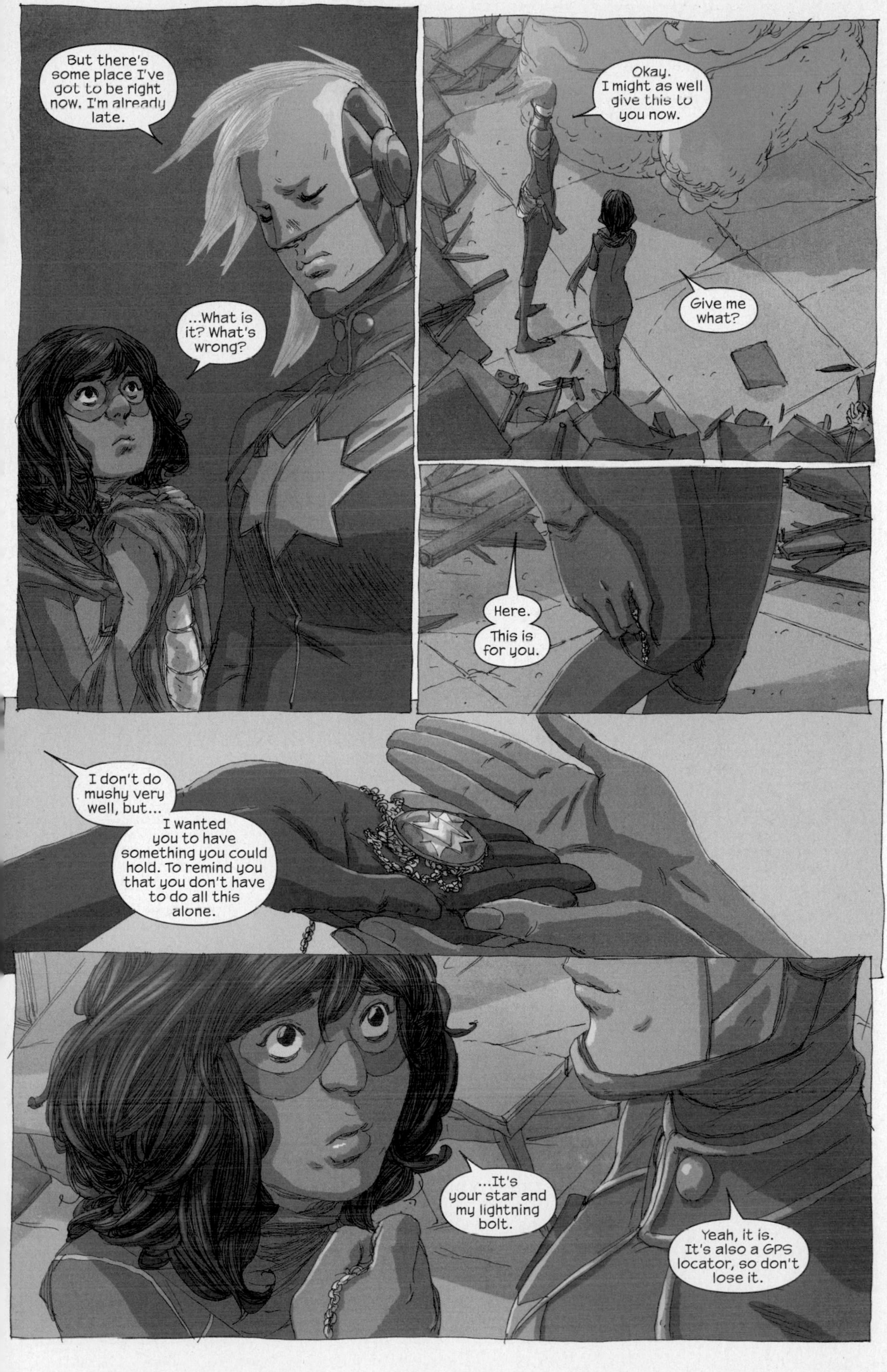
But there's some place I've got to be right now. I'm already late.
...What is it? What's wrong?
Okay. I might as well give this to you now.
Give me what?
Here. This is for you.
I don't do mushy very well, but...
I wanted you to have something you could hold. To remind you that you don't have to do all this alone.
...It's your star and my lightning bolt.
Yeah, it is. It's also a GPS locator, so don't lose it.

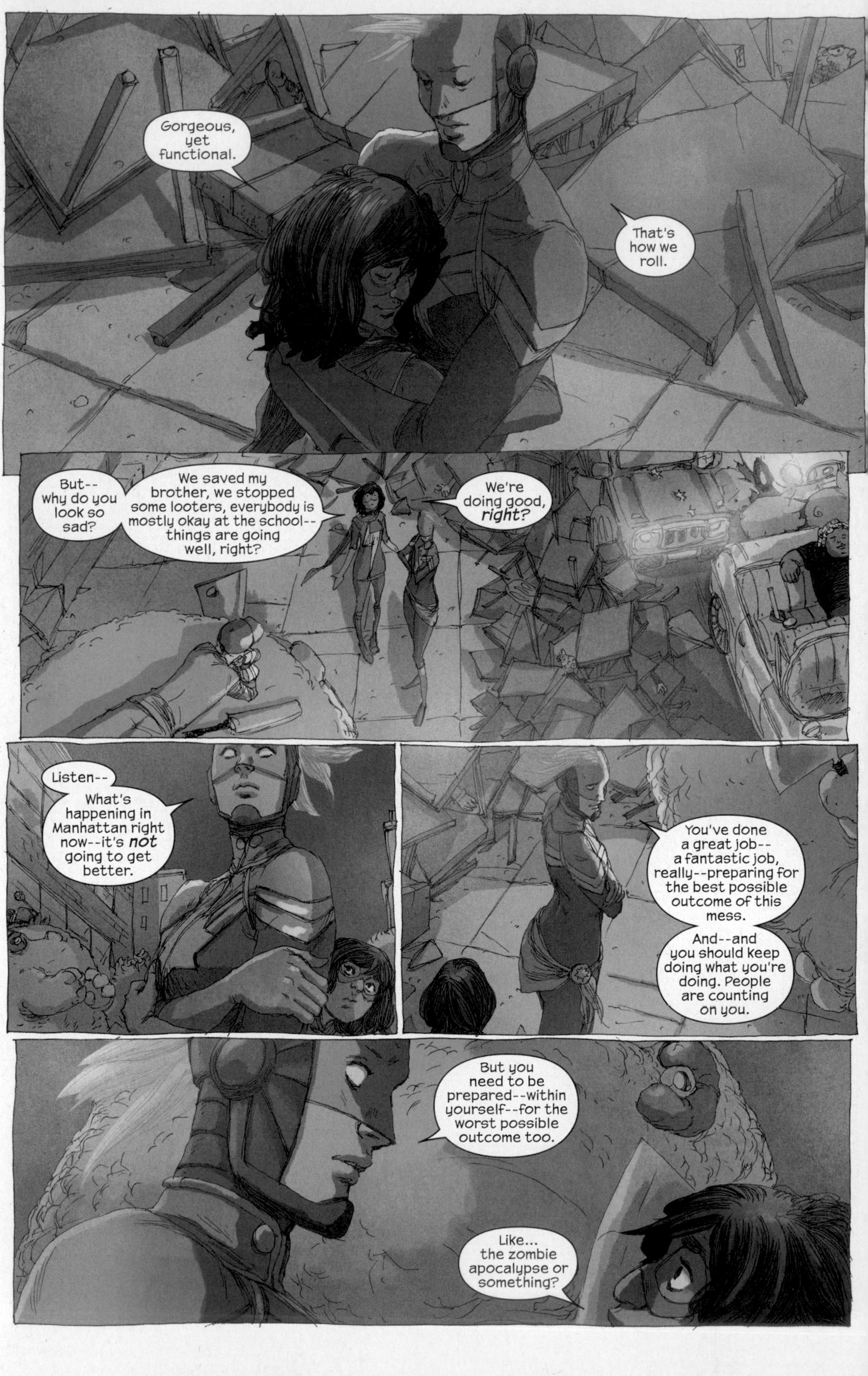
Gorgeous, yet functional.
That's how we roll.
But-- why do you look so sad?
We saved my brother, we stopped some looters, everybody is mostly okay at the school-- things are going well, right?
We're doing good, *right?*
Listen--
What's happening in Manhattan right now--it's *not* going to get better.
You've done a great job-- a fantastic job, really--preparing for the best possible outcome of this mess.
And--and you should keep doing what you're doing. People are counting on you.
But you need to be prepared--within yourself--for the worst possible outcome too.
Like... the zombie apocalypse or something?

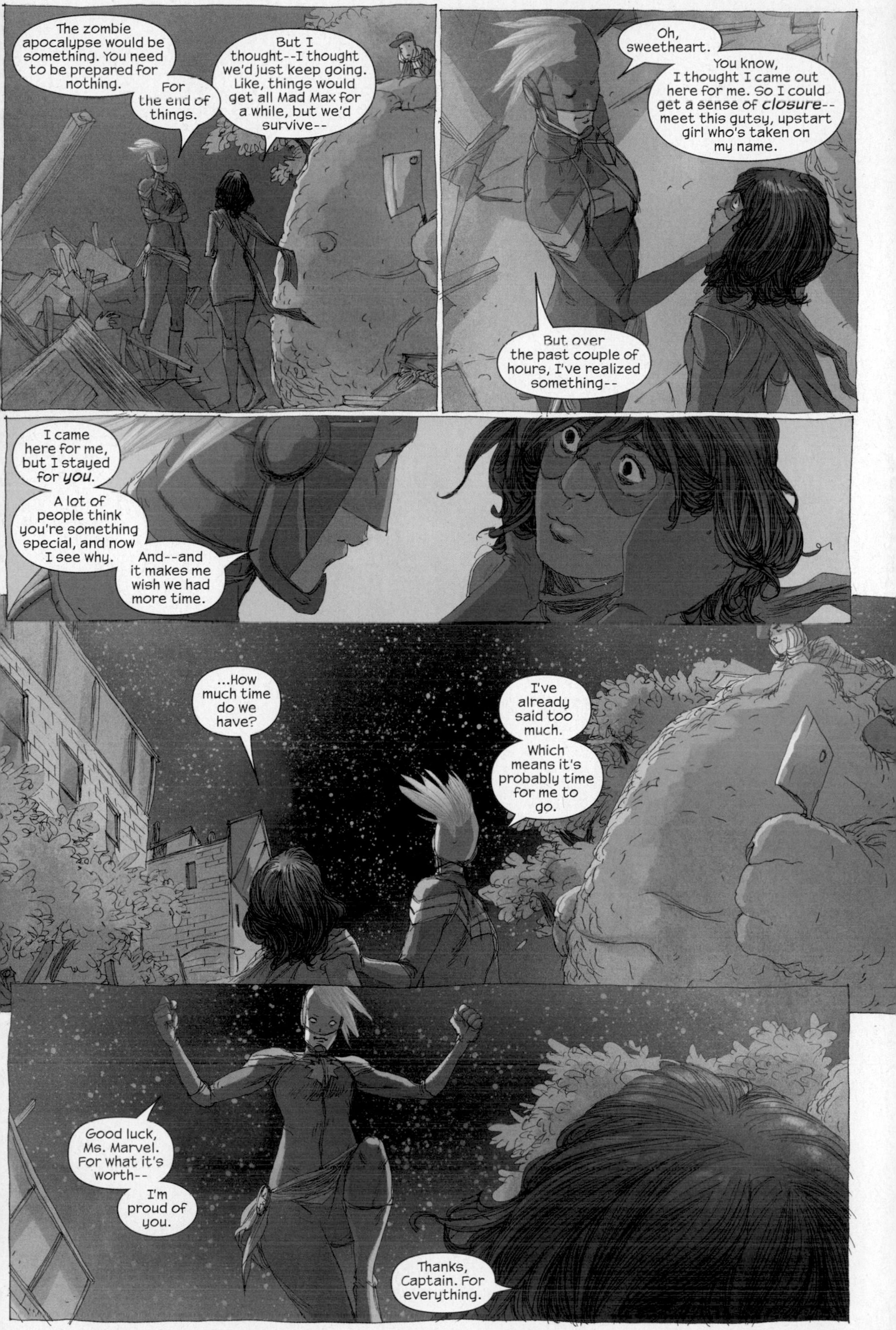
The zombie apocalypse would be something. You need to be prepared for nothing.
For the end of things.
But I thought--I thought we'd just keep going. Like, things would get all Mad Max for a while, but we'd survive--
Oh, sweetheart.
You know, I thought I came out here for me. So I could get a sense of *closure*-- meet this gutsy, upstart girl who's taken on my name.
But over the past couple of hours, I've realized something--
I came here for me, but I stayed for *you*.
A lot of people think you're something special, and now I see why.
And--and it makes me wish we had more time.
...How much time do we have?
I've already said too much.
Which means it's probably time for me to go.
Good luck, Ms. Marvel. For what it's worth--
I'm proud of you.
Thanks, Captain. For everything.

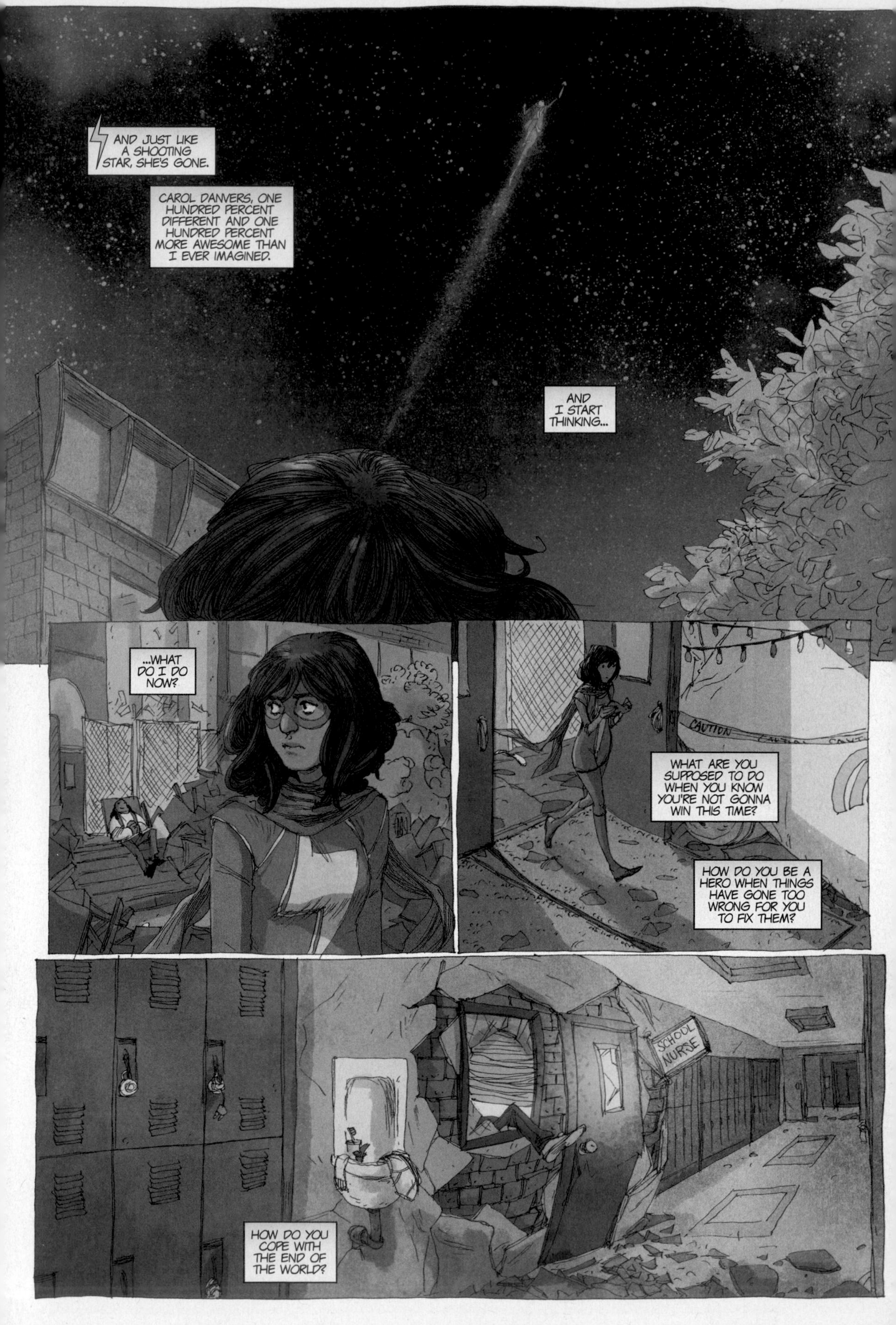
AND JUST LIKE A SHOOTING STAR, SHE'S GONE.
CAROL DANVERS, ONE HUNDRED PERCENT DIFFERENT AND ONE HUNDRED PERCENT MORE AWESOME THAN I EVER IMAGINED.
AND I START THINKING...
...WHAT DO I DO NOW?
CAUTION
WHAT ARE YOU SUPPOSED TO DO WHEN YOU KNOW YOU'RE NOT GONNA WIN THIS TIME?
HOW DO YOU BE A HERO WHEN THINGS HAVE GONE TOO WRONG FOR YOU TO FIX THEM?
SCHOOL NURSE
HOW DO YOU COPE WITH THE END OF THE WORLD?

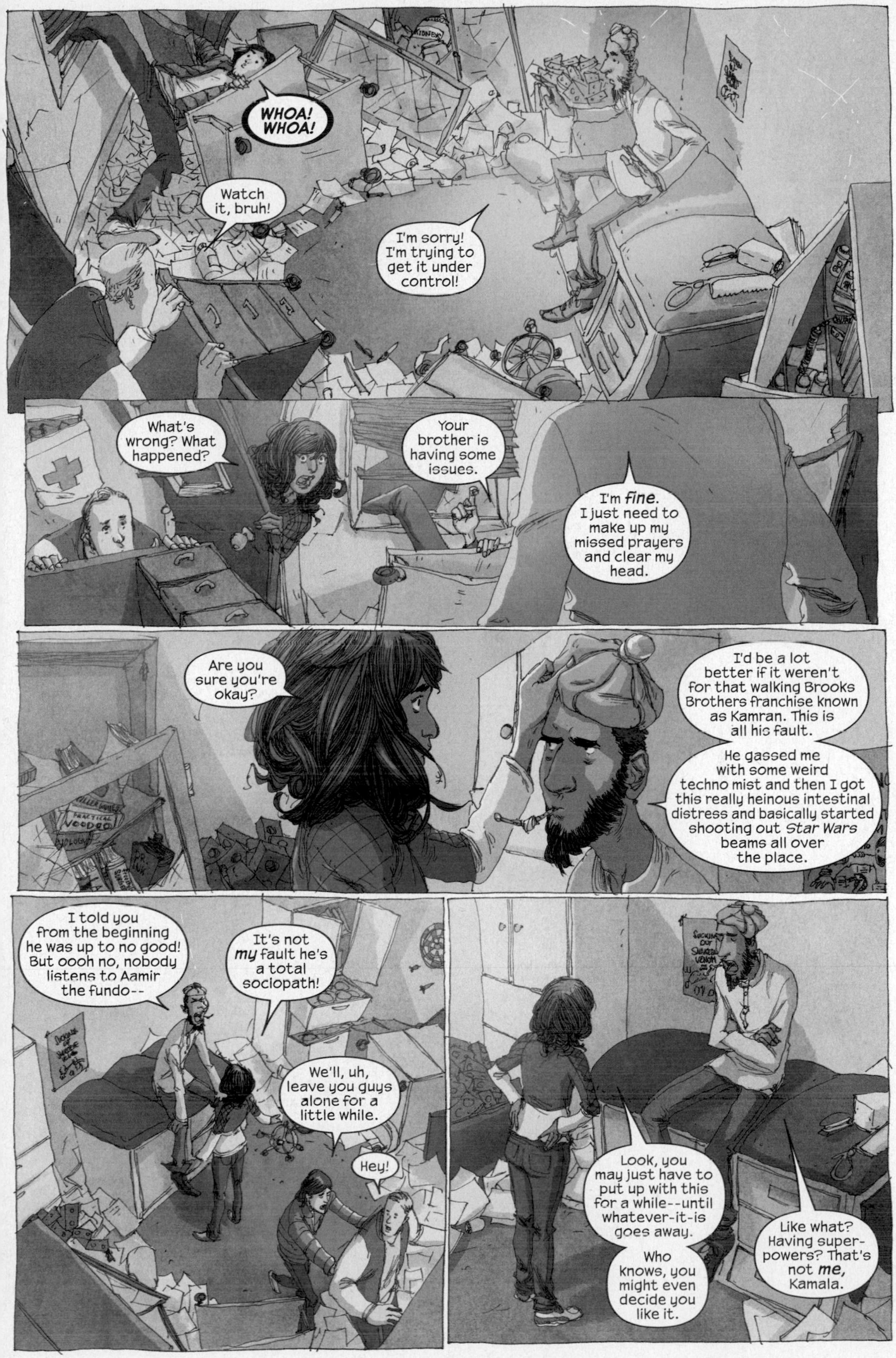
WHOA! WHOA!
Watch it, bruh!
I'm sorry! I'm trying to get it under control!
What's wrong? What happened?
Your brother is having some issues.
I'm *fine*. I just need to make up my missed prayers and clear my head.
Are you sure you're okay?
I'd be a lot better if it weren't for that walking Brooks Brothers franchise known as Kamran. This is all his fault.
He gassed me with some weird techno mist and then I got this really heinous intestinal distress and basically started shooting out *Star Wars* beams all over the place.
I told you from the beginning he was up to no good! But oooh no, nobody listens to Aamir the fundo--
It's not *my* fault he's a total sociopath!
We'll, uh, leave you guys alone for a little while.
Hey!
Look, you may just have to put up with this for a while--until whatever-it-is goes away.
Who knows, you might even decide you like it.
Like what? Having super-powers? That's not *me,* Kamala.

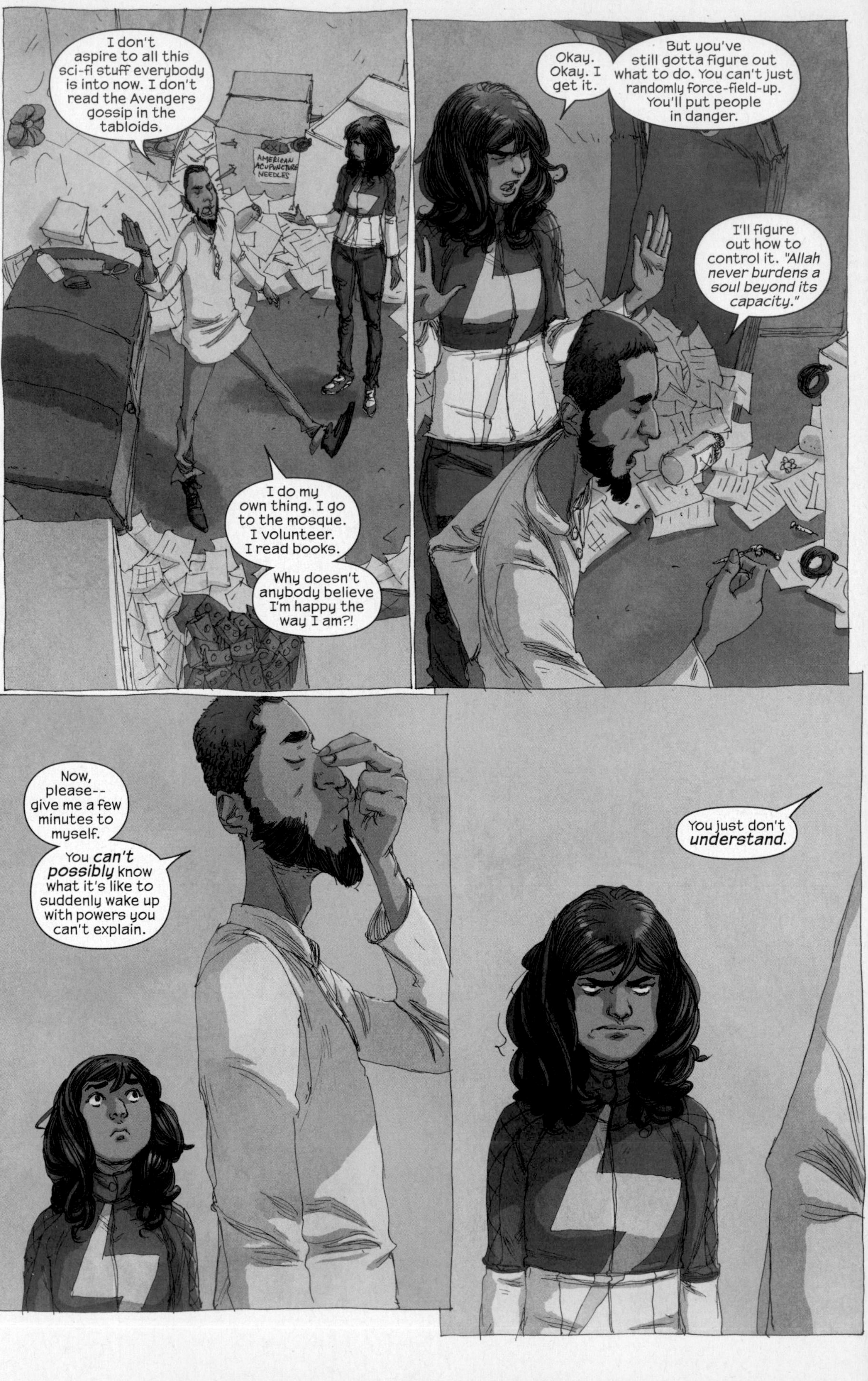

I don't aspire to all this sci-fi stuff everybody is into now. I don't read the Avengers gossip in the tabloids.
XXL
AMERICAN ACUPUNCTURE NEEDLES
I do my own thing. I go to the mosque. I volunteer. I read books.
Why doesn't anybody believe I'm happy the way I am?!
Okay. Okay. I get it.
But you've still gotta figure out what to do. You can't just randomly force-field-up. You'll put people in danger.
I'll figure out how to control it. "Allah never burdens a soul beyond its capacity."
Now, please-- give me a few minutes to myself.
You can't possibly know what it's like to suddenly wake up with powers you can't explain.
You just don't understand.

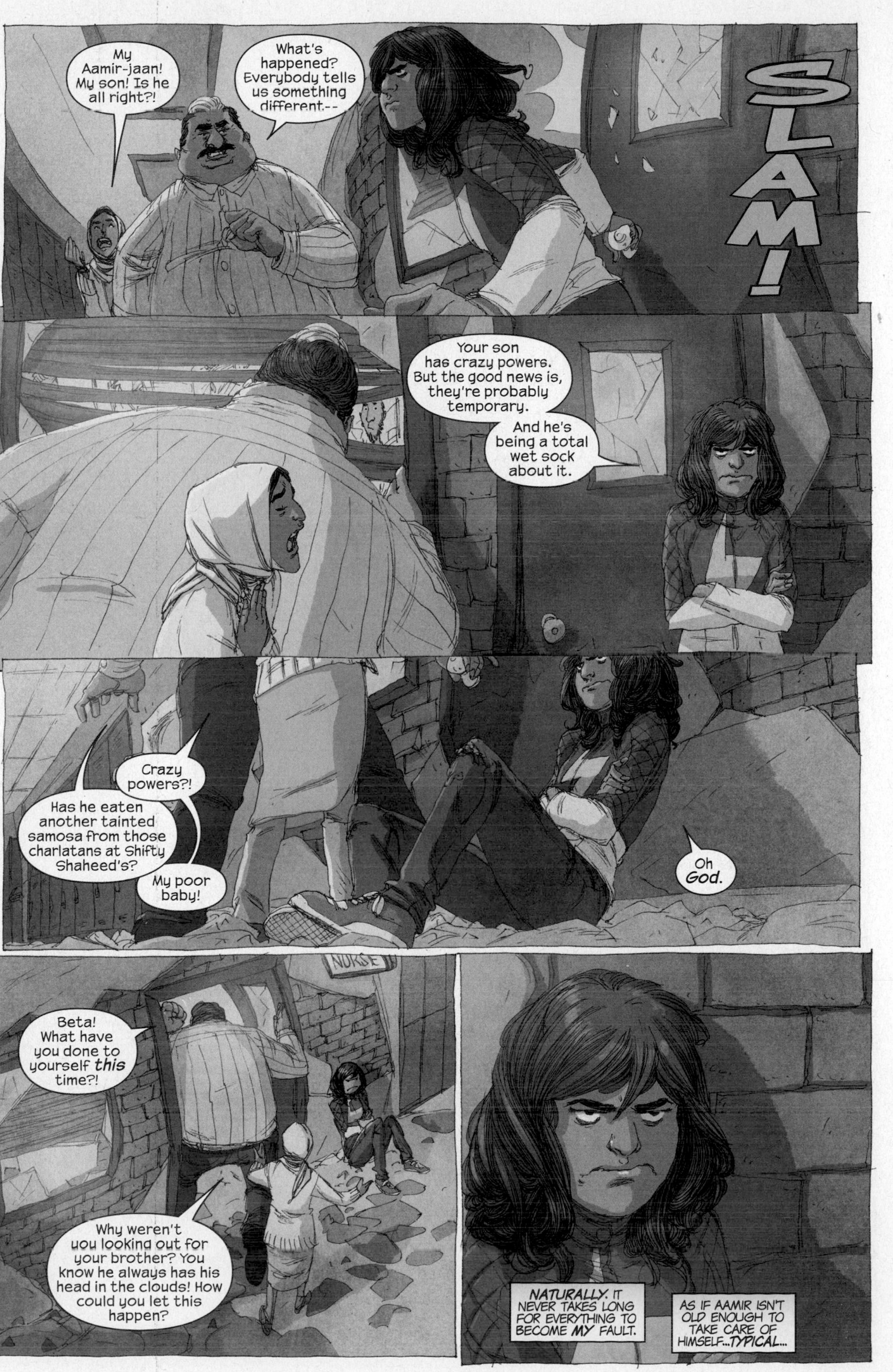
My Aamir-jaan! My son! Is he all right?!
What's happened? Everybody tells us something different.--
SLAM!
Your son has crazy powers. But the good news is, they're probably temporary.
And he's being a total wet sock about it.
Crazy powers?!
Has he eaten another tainted samosa from those charlatans at Shifty Shaheed's?
My poor baby!
Oh God.
NURSE
Beta! What have you done to yourself this time?!
Why weren't you looking out for your brother? You know he always has his head in the clouds! How could you let this happen?
NATURALLY. IT NEVER TAKES LONG FOR EVERYTHING TO BECOME MY FAULT.
AS IF AAMIR ISN'T OLD ENOUGH TO TAKE CARE OF HIMSELF...TYPICAL...

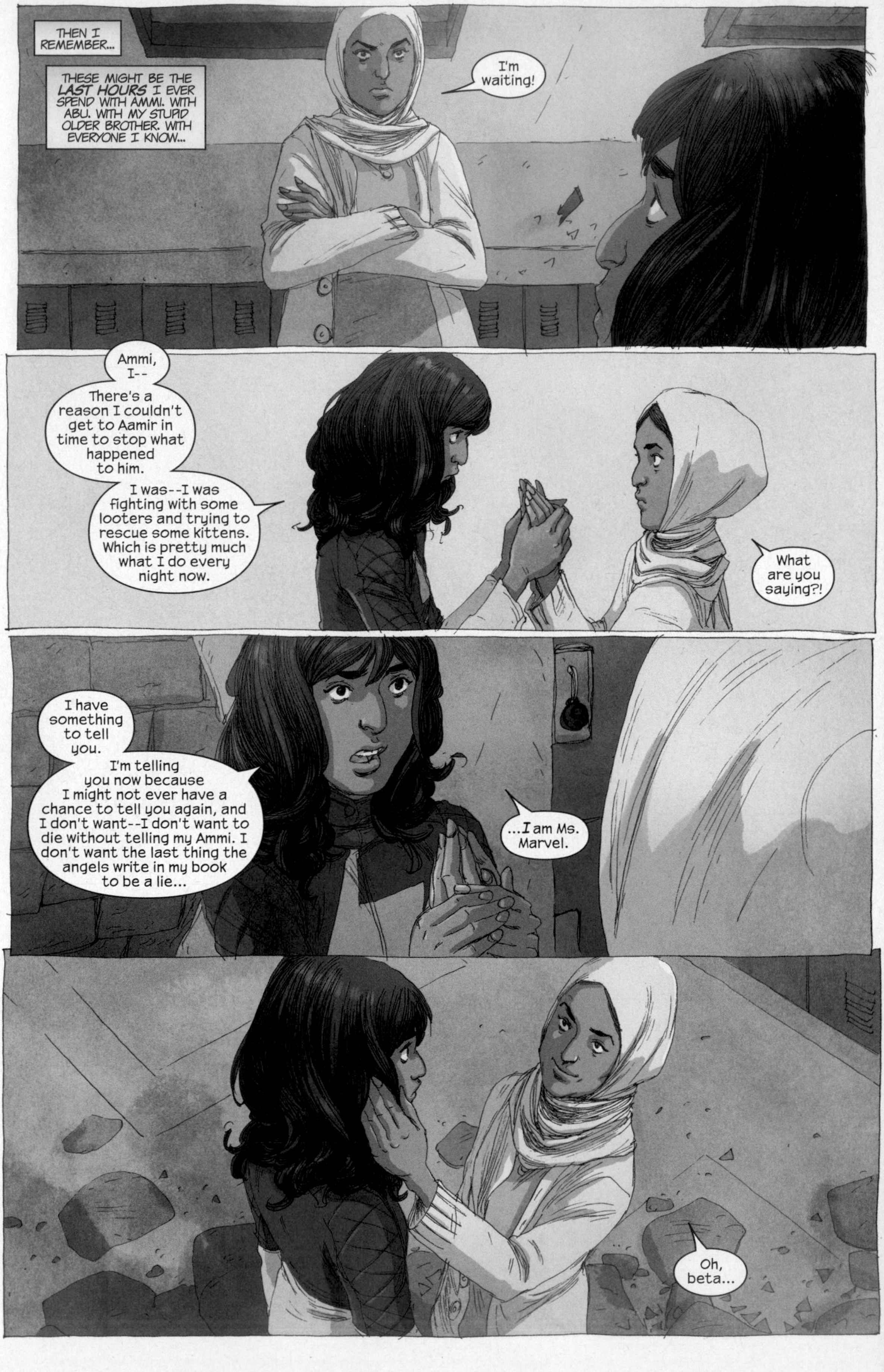

THEN I REMEMBER...
THESE MIGHT BE THE LAST HOURS I EVER SPEND WITH AMMI. WITH ABU. WITH MY STUPID OLDER BROTHER. WITH EVERYONE I KNOW...
I'm waiting!
Ammi, I--
There's a reason I couldn't get to Aamir in time to stop what happened to him.
I was--I was fighting with some looters and trying to rescue some kittens. Which is pretty much what I do every night now.
What are you saying?!
I have something to tell you.
I'm telling you now because I might not ever have a chance to tell you again, and I don't want--I don't want to die without telling my Ammi. I don't want the last thing the angels write in my book to be a lie...
...I am Ms. Marvel.
Oh, beta...

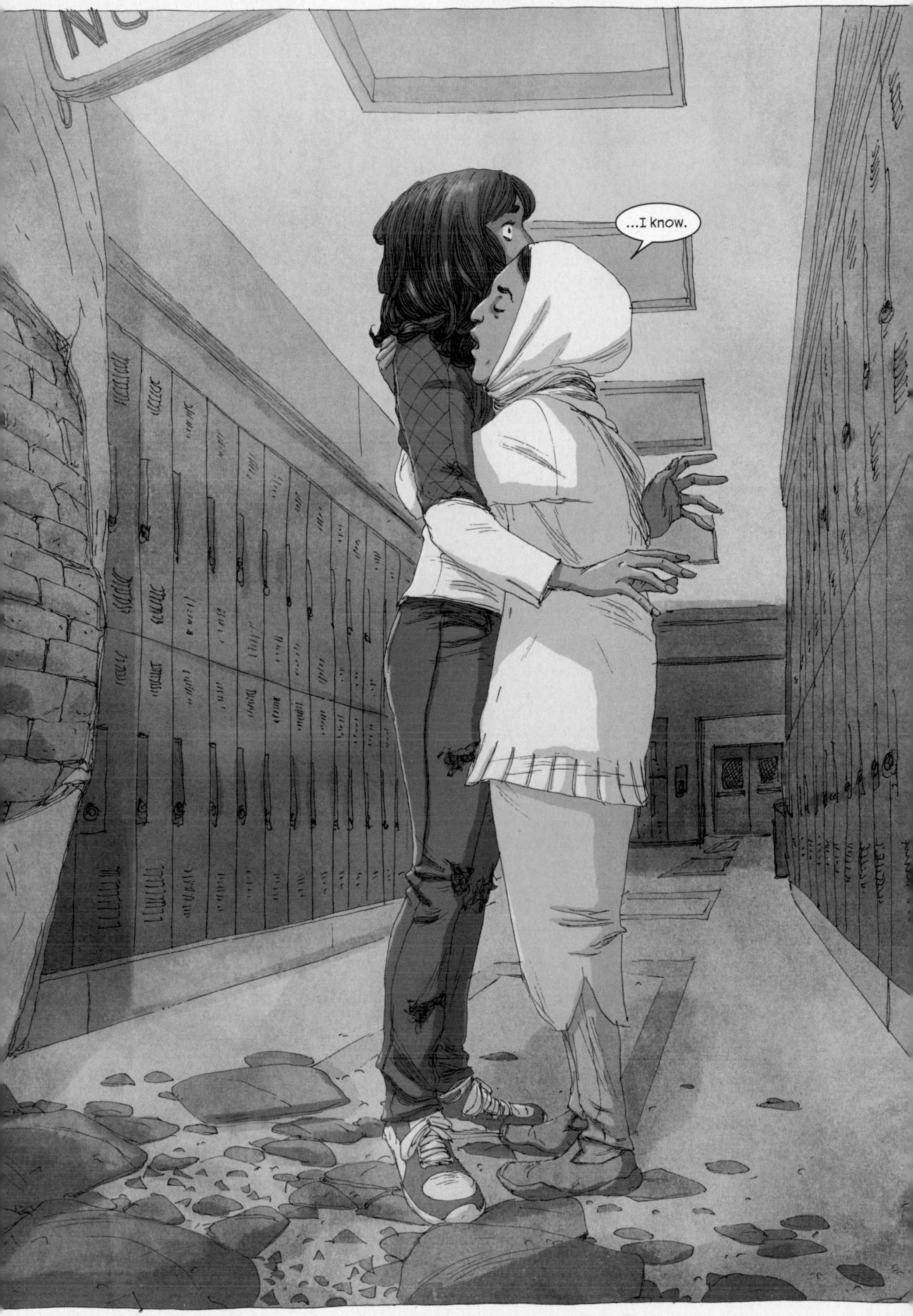
...I know.

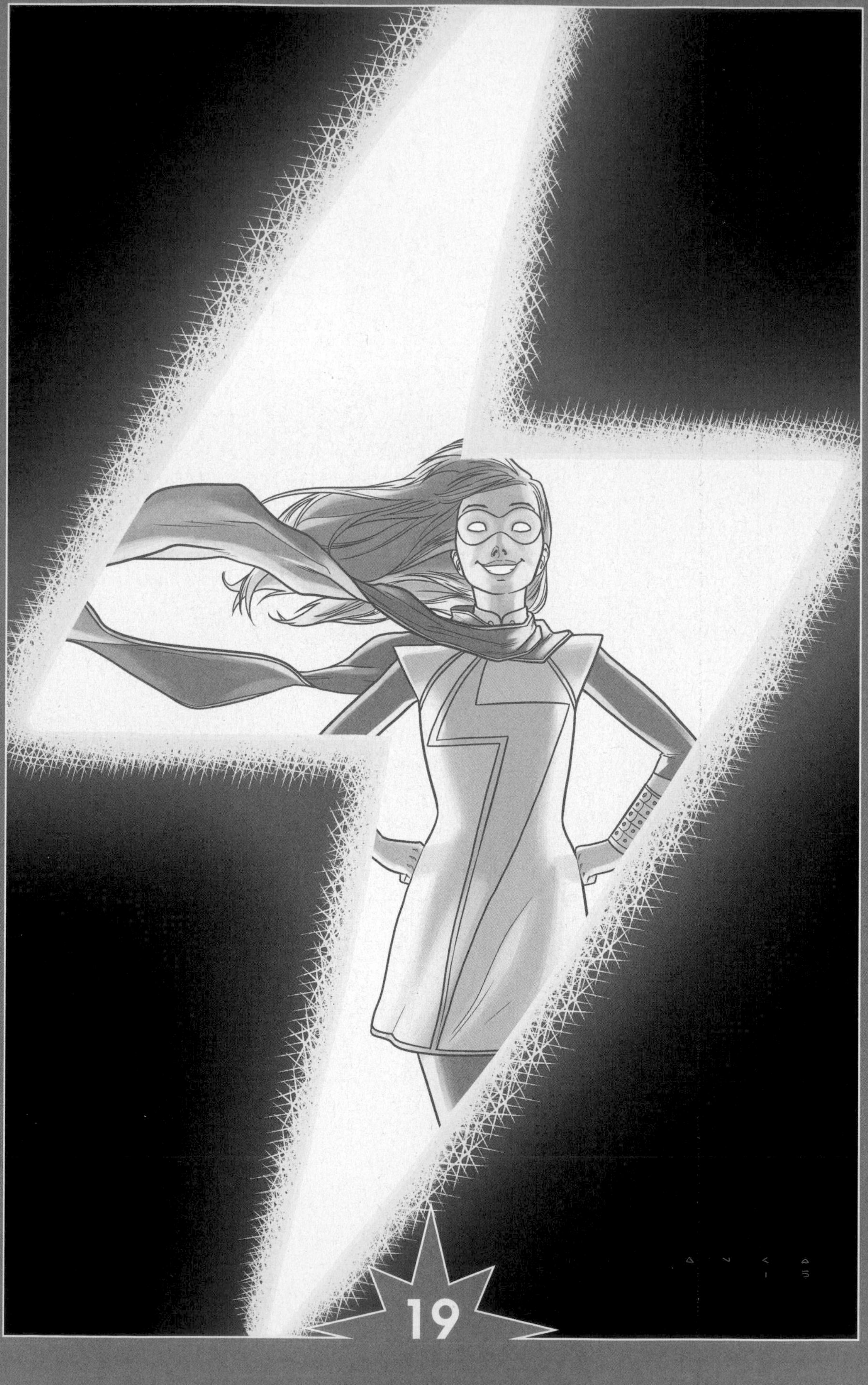
19

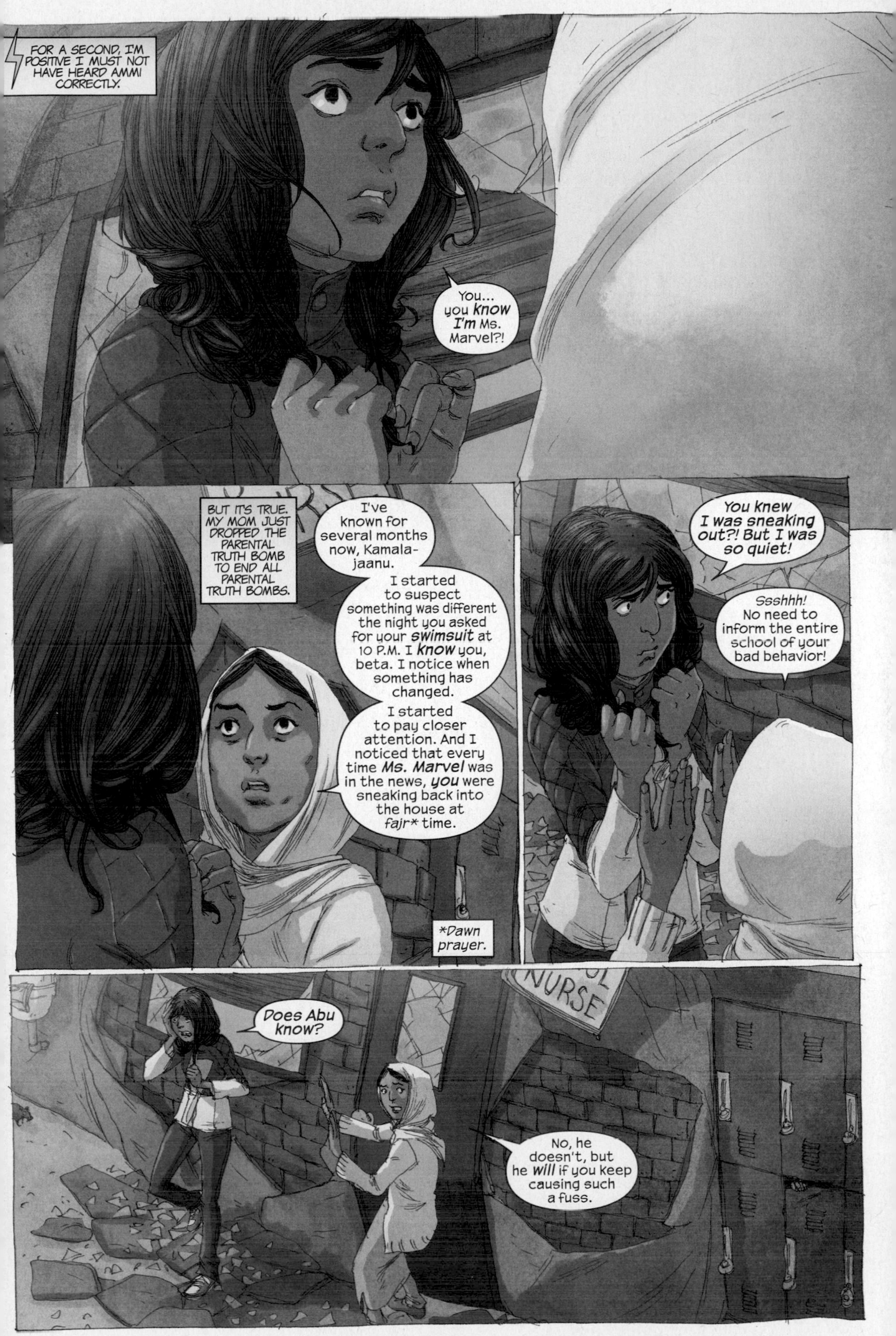

FOR A SECOND, I'M POSITIVE I MUST NOT HAVE HEARD AMMI CORRECTLY.
You... you know I'm Ms. Marvel?!
BUT IT'S TRUE. MY MOM JUST DROPPED THE PARENTAL TRUTH BOMB TO END ALL PARENTAL TRUTH BOMBS.
I've known for several months now, Kamala-jaanu.
I started to suspect something was different the night you asked for your swimsuit at 10 P.M. I know you, beta. I notice when something has changed.
I started to pay closer attention. And I noticed that every time Ms. Marvel was in the news, you were sneaking back into the house at fajr* time.
*Dawn prayer.
You knew I was sneaking out?! But I was so quiet!
Ssshhh! No need to inform the entire school of your bad behavior!
NURSE
Does Abu know?
No, he doesn't, but he will if you keep causing such a fuss.

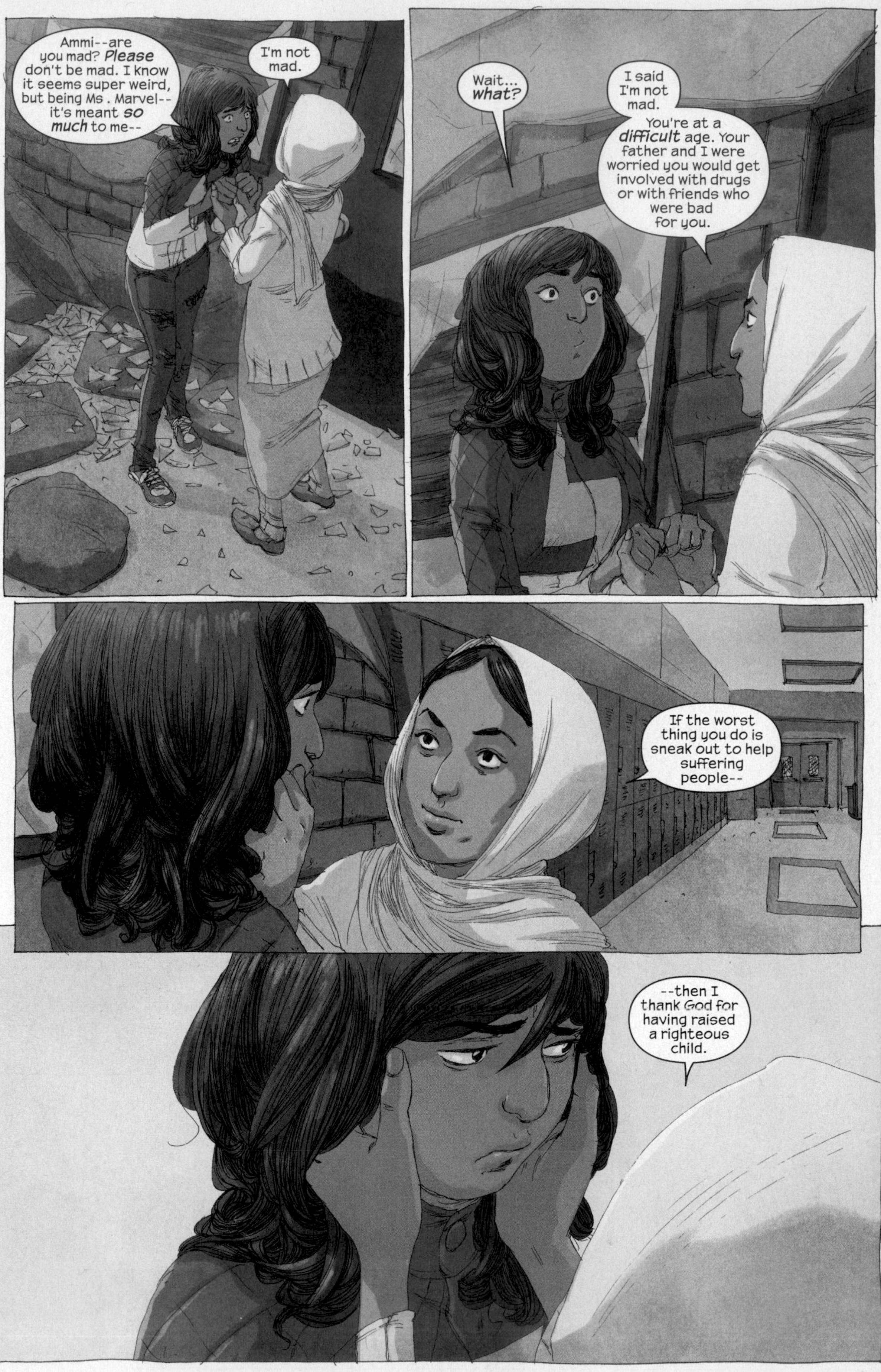
Ammi--are you mad? *Please* don't be mad. I know it seems super weird, but being Ms . Marvel-- it's meant *so much* to me--
I'm not mad.
Wait... *what?*
I said I'm not mad.
You're at a *difficult* age. Your father and I were worried you would get involved with drugs or with friends who were bad for you.
If the worst thing you do is sneak out to help suffering people--
--then I thank God for having raised a righteous child.

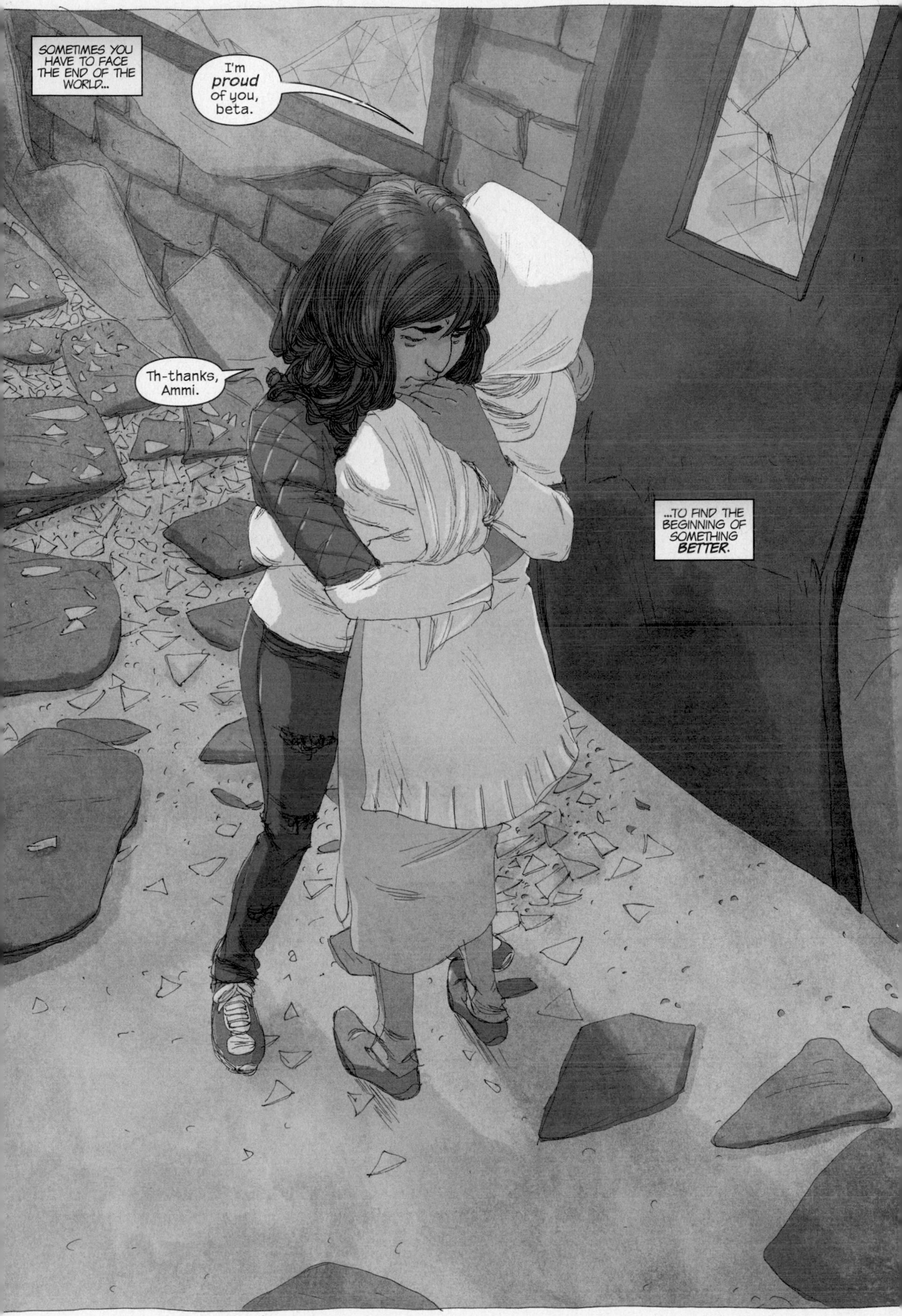
SOMETIMES YOU HAVE TO FACE THE END OF THE WORLD...
I'm *proud* of you, beta.
Th-thanks, Ammi.
...TO FIND THE BEGINNING OF SOMETHING ***BETTER.***

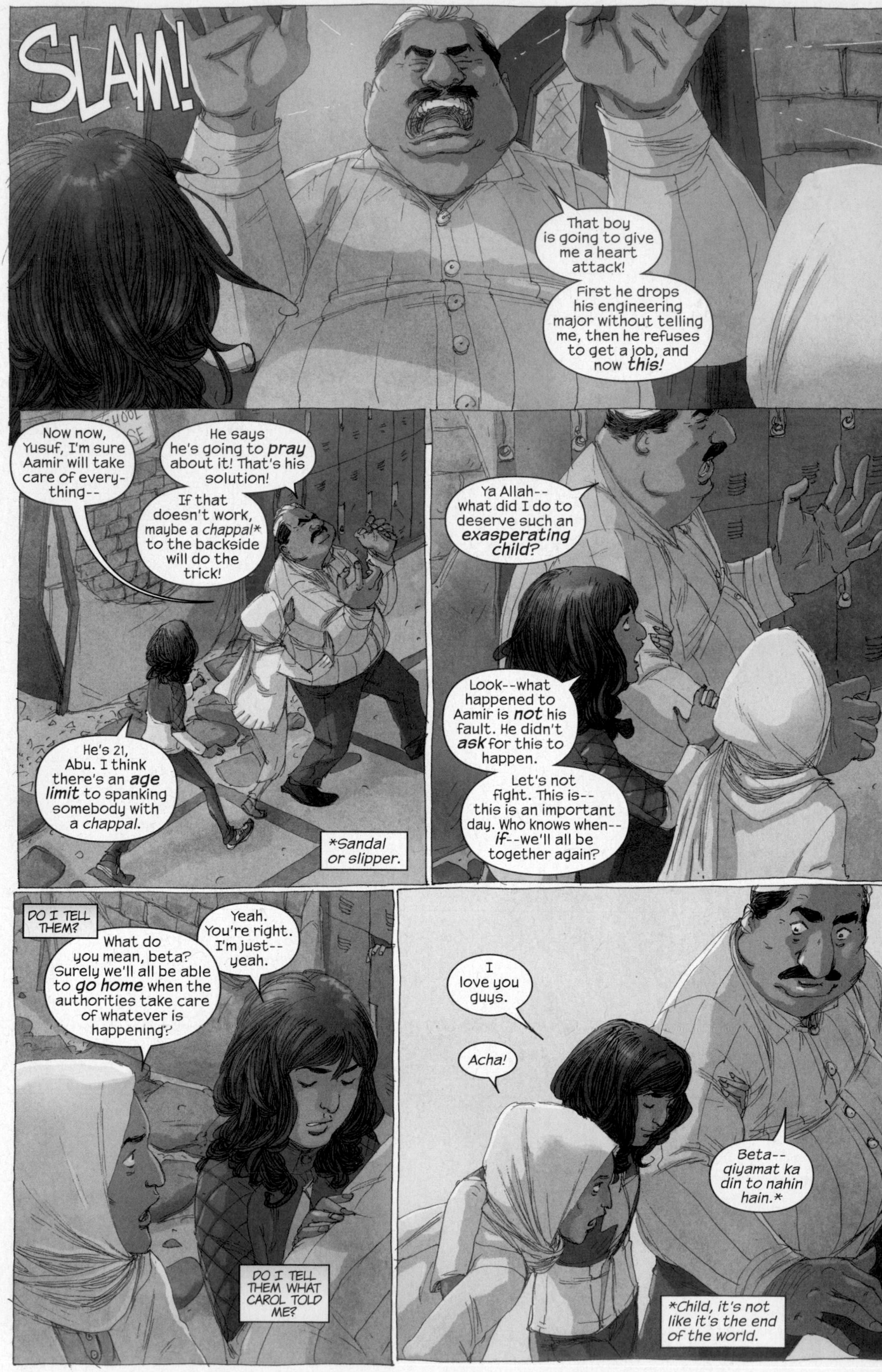

SLAM!
That boy is going to give me a heart attack!
First he drops his engineering major without telling me, then he refuses to get a job, and now this!
Now now, Yusuf, I'm sure Aamir will take care of every-thing--
He says he's going to pray about it! That's his solution!
If that doesn't work, maybe a chappal* to the backside will do the trick!
He's 21, Abu. I think there's an age limit to spanking somebody with a chappal.
*Sandal or slipper.
Ya Allah--what did I do to deserve such an exasperating child?
Look--what happened to Aamir is not his fault. He didn't ask for this to happen.
Let's not fight. This is--this is an important day. Who knows when--if--we'll all be together again?
DO I TELL THEM?
What do you mean, beta? Surely we'll all be able to go home when the authorities take care of whatever is happening?
Yeah. You're right. I'm just--yeah.
DO I TELL THEM WHAT CAROL TOLD ME?
I love you guys.
Acha!
Beta--qiyamat ka din to nahin hain.*
*Child, it's not like it's the end of the world.

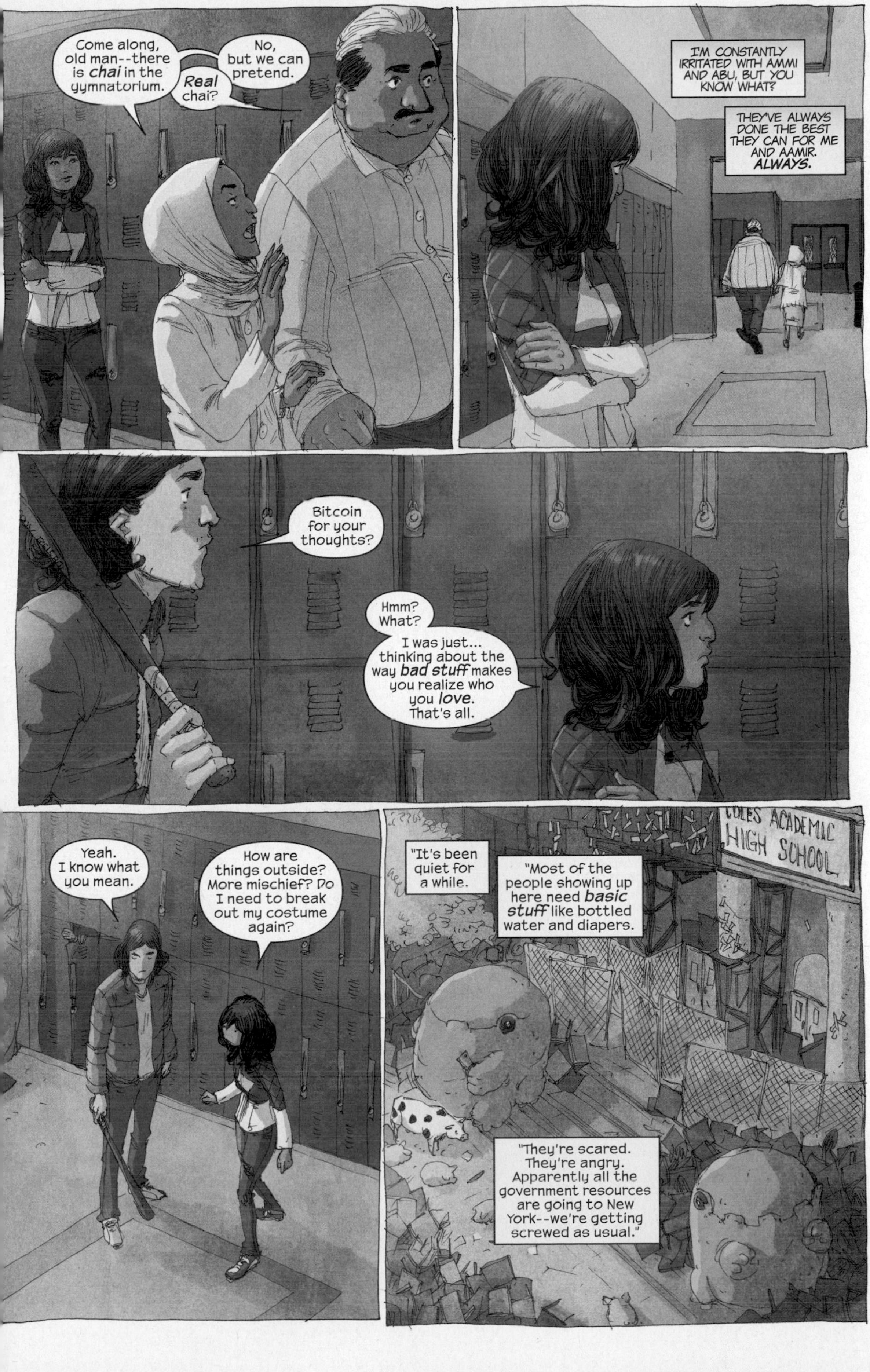
Come along, old man--there is chai in the gymnatorium.
No, but we can pretend.
Real chai?
I'M CONSTANTLY IRRITATED WITH AMMI AND ABU, BUT YOU KNOW WHAT?
THEY'VE ALWAYS DONE THE BEST THEY CAN FOR ME AND AAMIR. ALWAYS.
Bitcoin for your thoughts?
Hmm? What?
I was just... thinking about the way bad stuff makes you realize who you love. That's all.
Yeah. I know what you mean.
How are things outside? More mischief? Do I need to break out my costume again?
COLES ACADEMIC HIGH SCHOOL
"It's been quiet for a while.
"Most of the people showing up here need basic stuff like bottled water and diapers.
"They're scared. They're angry. Apparently all the government resources are going to New York--we're getting screwed as usual."

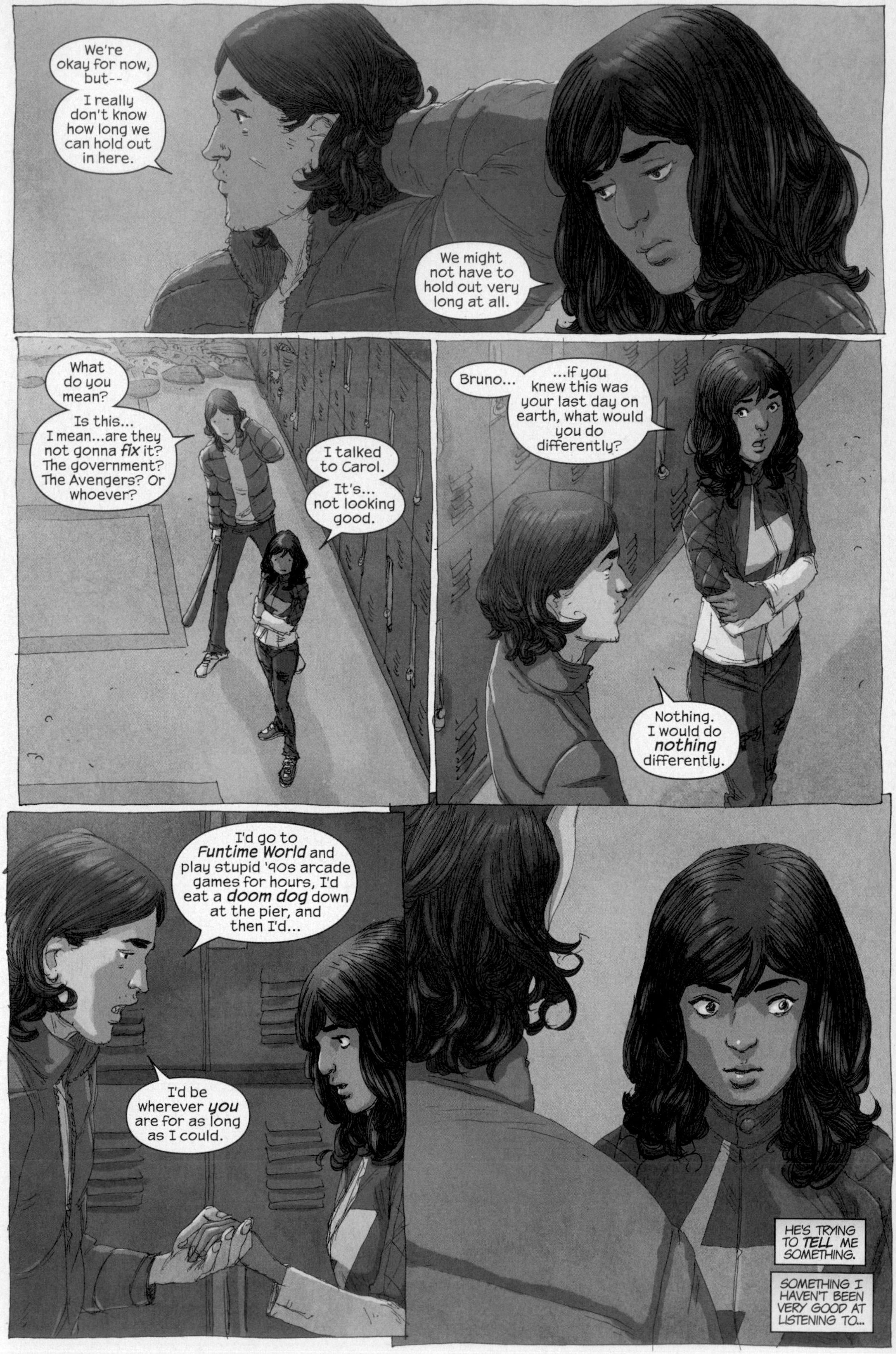
We're okay for now, but--
I really don't know how long we can hold out in here.
We might not have to hold out very long at all.
What do you mean?
Is this... I mean...are they not gonna *fix* it? The government? The Avengers? Or whoever?
I talked to Carol.
It's... not looking good.
Bruno...
...if you knew this was your last day on earth, what would you do differently?
Nothing. I would do ***nothing*** differently.
I'd go to ***Funtime World*** and play stupid '90s arcade games for hours, I'd eat a ***doom dog*** down at the pier, and then I'd...
I'd be wherever ***you*** are for as long as I could.
HE'S TRYING TO ***TELL*** ME SOMETHING.
SOMETHING I HAVEN'T BEEN VERY GOOD AT LISTENING TO...

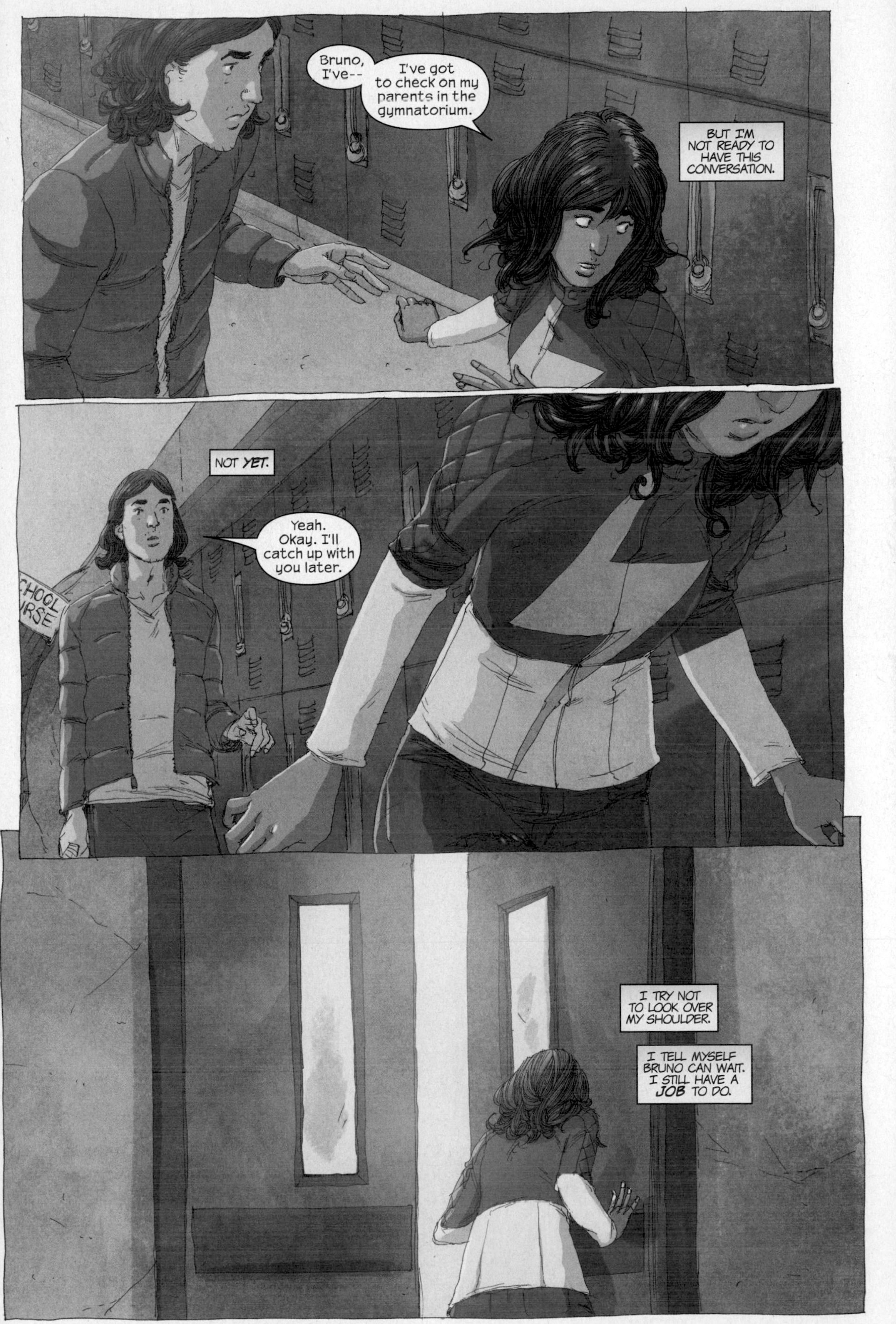
Bruno, I've--
I've got to check on my parents in the gymnatorium.
BUT I'M NOT READY TO HAVE THIS CONVERSATION.
NOT YET.
Yeah. Okay. I'll catch up with you later.
I TRY NOT TO LOOK OVER MY SHOULDER.
I TELL MYSELF BRUNO CAN WAIT. I STILL HAVE A JOB TO DO.

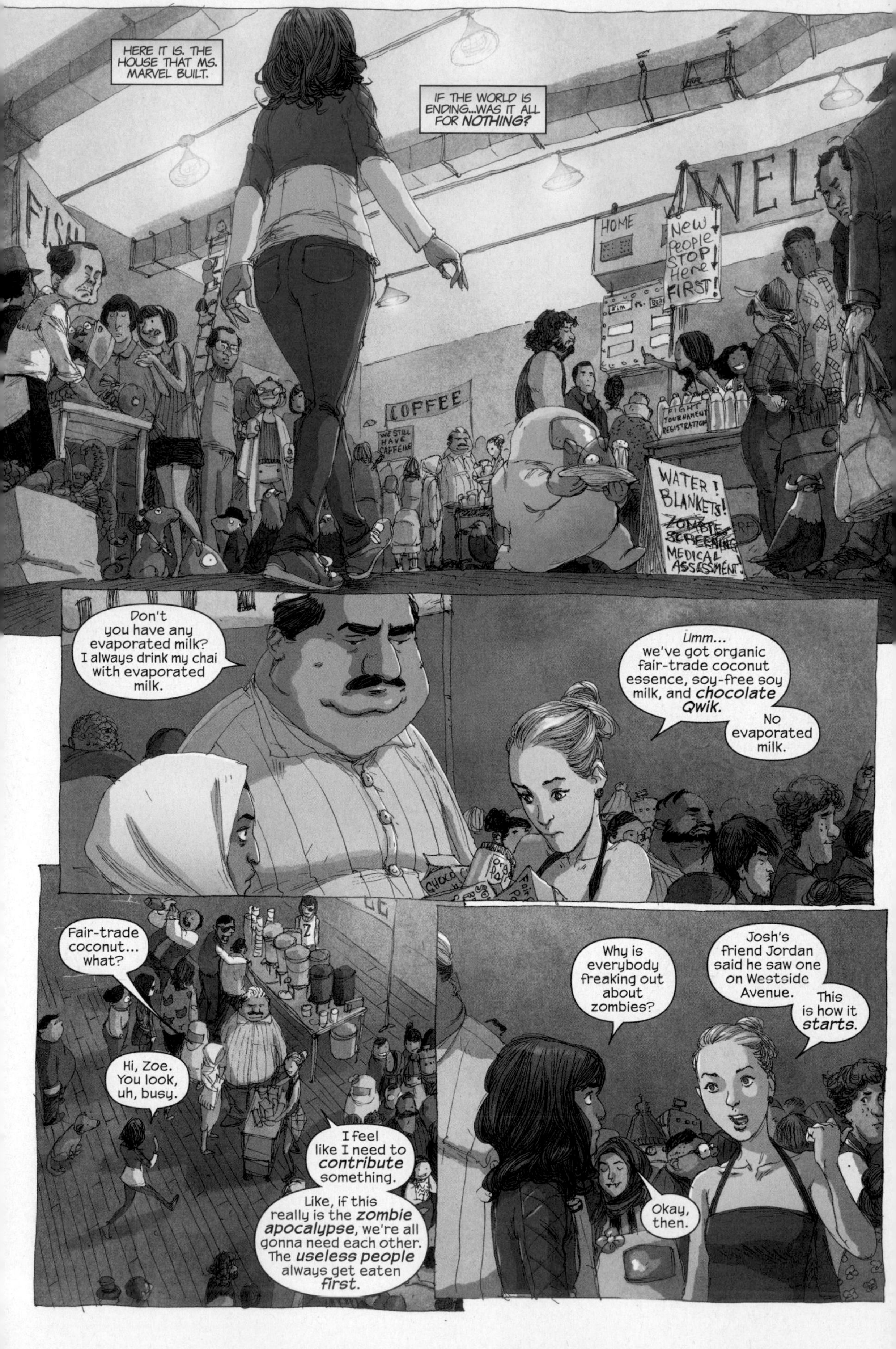
HERE IT IS. THE HOUSE THAT MS. MARVEL BUILT.
IF THE WORLD IS ENDING...WAS IT ALL FOR NOTHING?
FISH
COFFEE
WE STILL HAVE CAFFEINE
HOME
WEL
New People STOP Here FIRST!
FIGHT TOURNAMENT REGISTRATION
WATER! BLANKETS! ZOMBIE SCREENING MEDICAL ASSESSMENT!
Don't you have any evaporated milk? I always drink my chai with evaporated milk.
Umm... we've got organic fair-trade coconut essence, soy-free soy milk, and chocolate Qwik.
No evaporated milk.
Fair-trade coconut... what?
Hi, Zoe. You look, uh, busy.
I feel like I need to contribute something.
Like, if this really is the zombie apocalypse, we're all gonna need each other. The useless people always get eaten first.
Why is everybody freaking out about zombies?
Josh's friend Jordan said he saw one on Westside Avenue.
This is how it starts.
Okay, then.

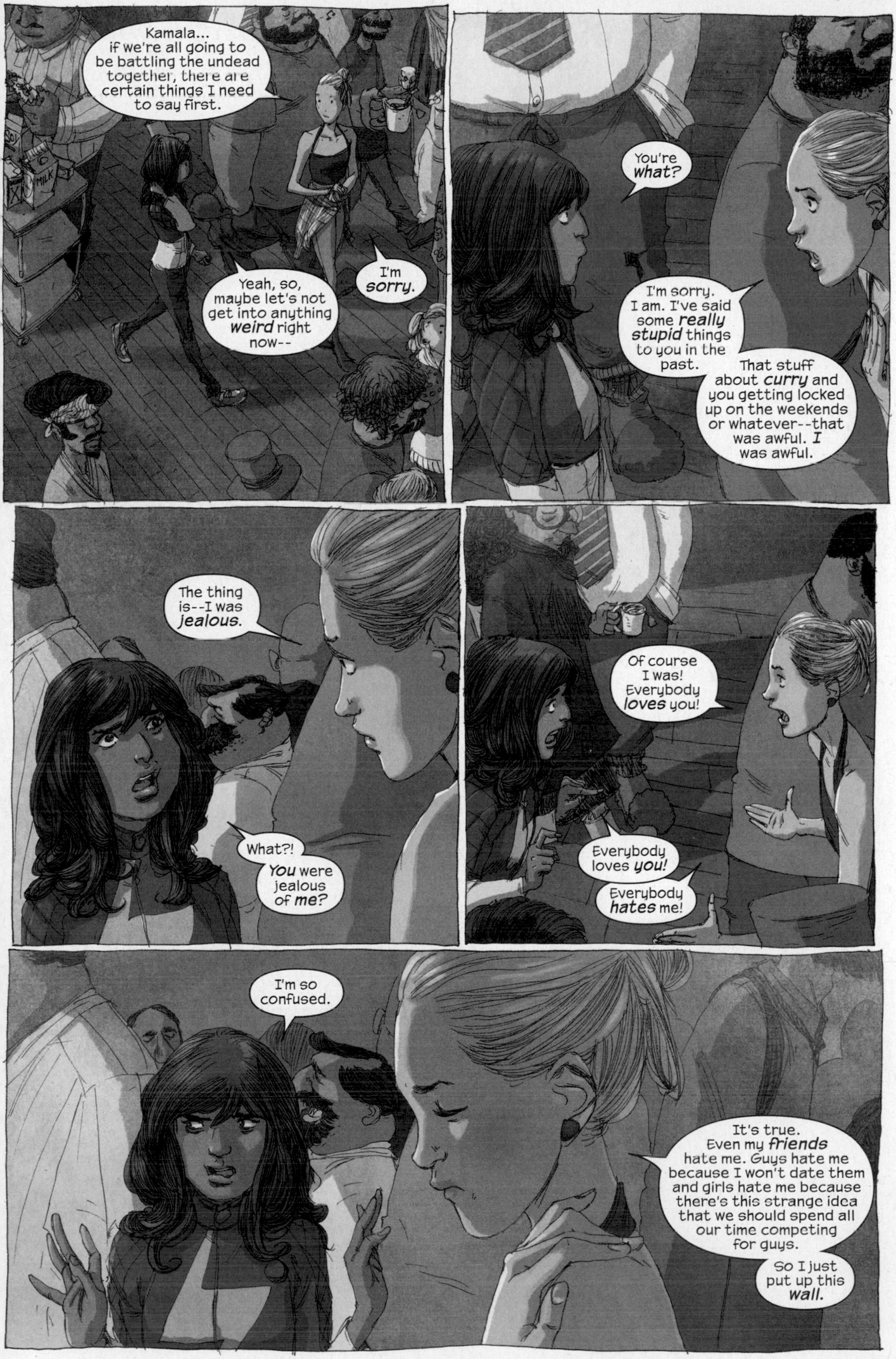

Kamala... if we're all going to be battling the undead together, there are certain things I need to say first.
Yeah, so, maybe let's not get into anything *weird* right now--
I'm *sorry.*
You're *what?*
I'm sorry. I am. I've said some *really stupid* things to you in the past.
That stuff about *curry* and you getting locked up on the weekends or whatever--that was awful. *I* was awful.
The thing is--I was *jealous.*
What?! *You* were jealous of *me?*
Of course I was! Everybody *loves* you!
Everybody loves *you!*
Everybody *hates* me!
I'm so confused.
It's true. Even my *friends* hate me. Guys hate me because I won't date them and girls hate me because there's this strange idea that we should spend all our time competing for guys.
So I just put up this *wall.*

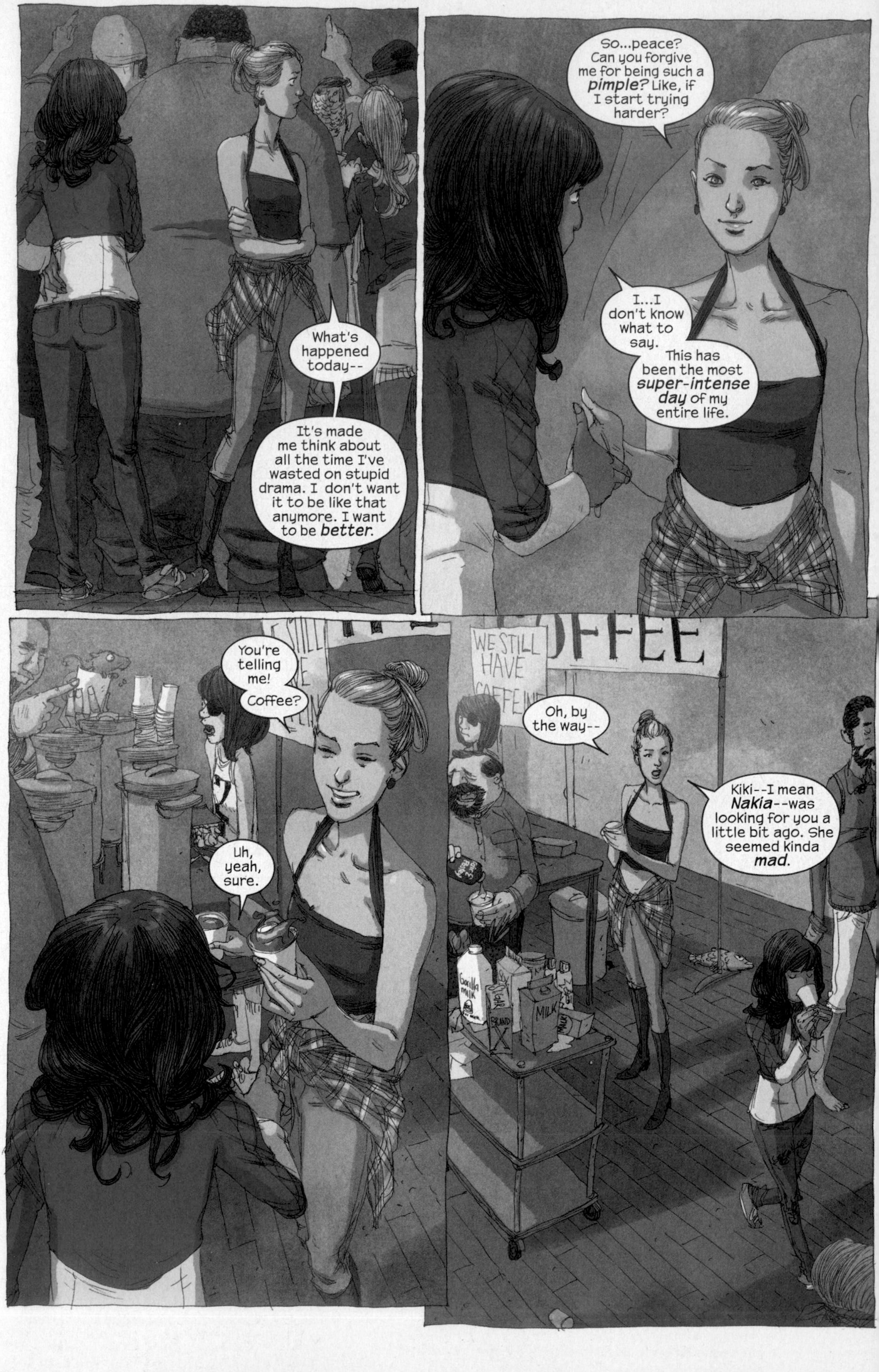
What's happened today--
It's made me think about all the time I've wasted on stupid drama. I don't want it to be like that anymore. I want to be *better*.
So...peace? Can you forgive me for being such a *pimple?* Like, if I start trying harder?
I...I don't know what to say.
This has been the most *super-intense day* of my entire life.
You're telling me!
Coffee?
Uh, yeah, sure.
COFFEE
WE STILL HAVE COFFEINE
Oh, by the way--
Kiki--I mean *Nakia*--was looking for you a little bit ago. She seemed kinda *mad*.
Gorilla MILK
MILK

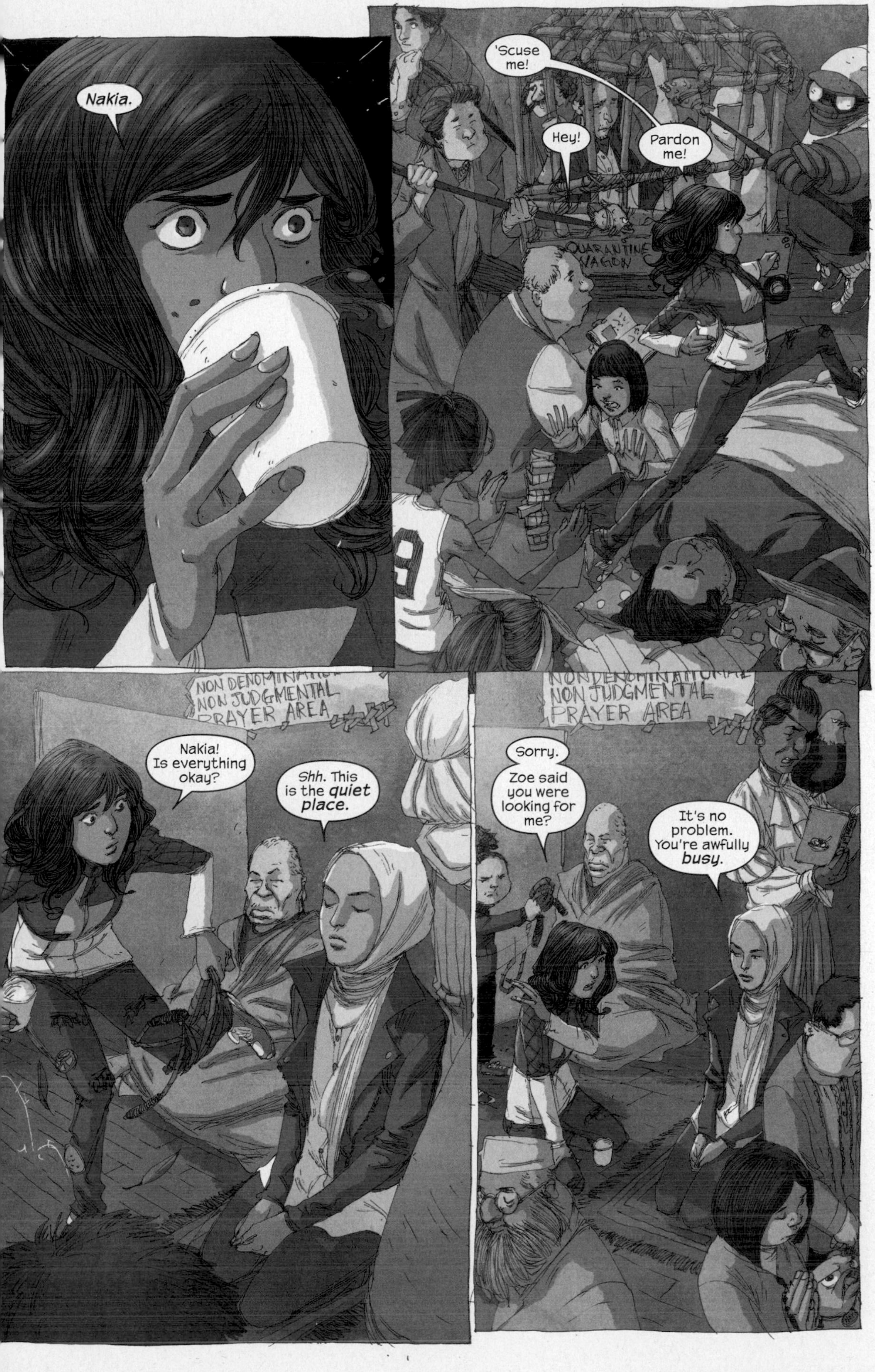
Nakia.
'Scuse me!
Hey!
Pardon me!
QUARANTINE WAGON
NON DENOMINATIONAL NON JUDGMENTAL PRAYER AREA
Nakia! Is everything okay?
Shh. This is the ***quiet place.***
NON DENOMINATIONAL NON JUDGMENTAL PRAYER AREA
Sorry.
Zoe said you were looking for me?
It's no problem. You're awfully ***busy.***

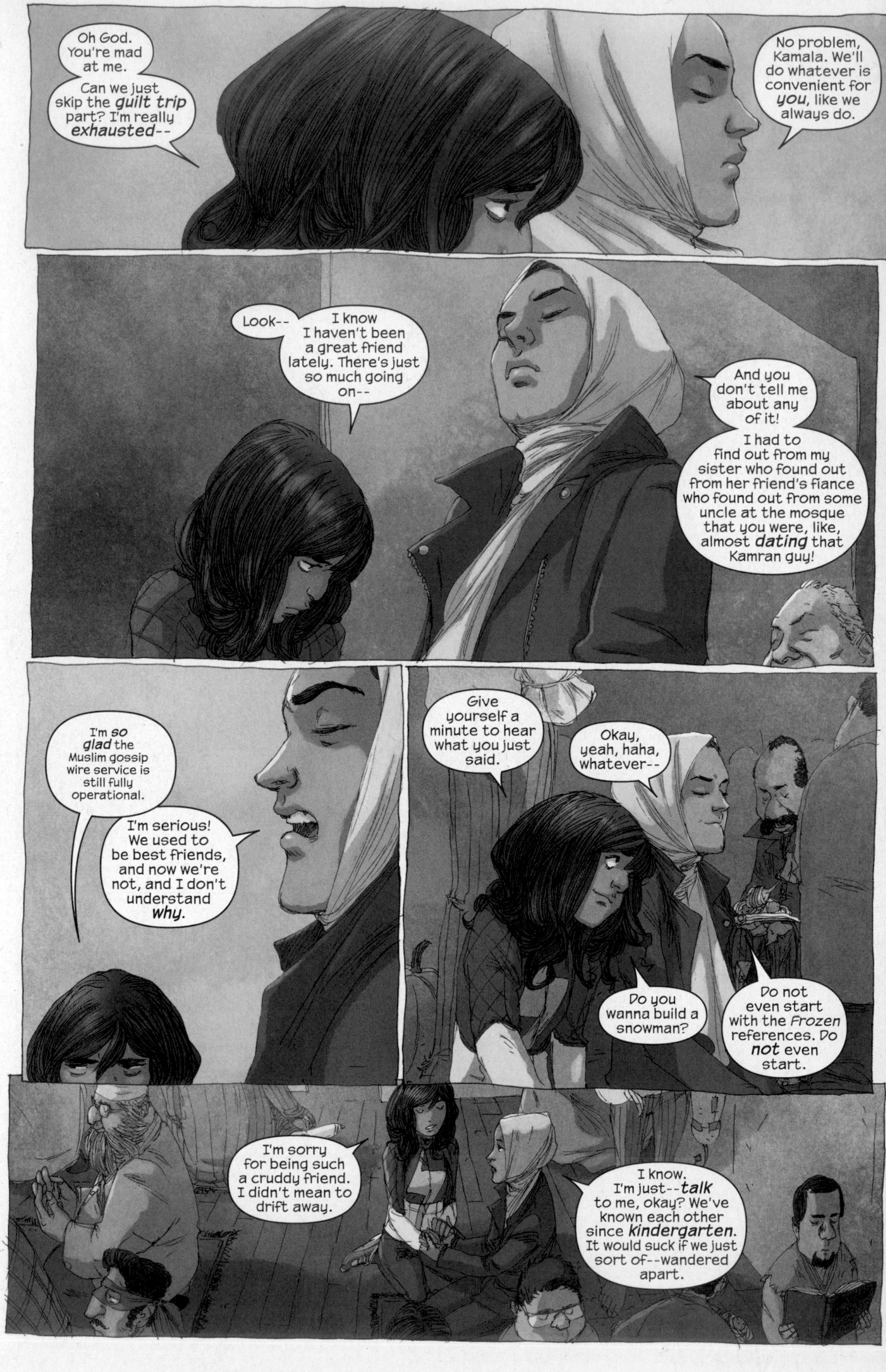
Oh God. You're mad at me.
Can we just skip the *guilt trip* part? I'm really *exhausted*--
No problem, Kamala. We'll do whatever is convenient for *you*, like we always do.
Look--
I know I haven't been a great friend lately. There's just so much going on--
And you don't tell me about any of it!
I had to find out from my sister who found out from her friend's fiance who found out from some uncle at the mosque that you were, like, almost *dating* that Kamran guy!
I'm *so glad* the Muslim gossip wire service is still fully operational.
I'm serious! We used to be best friends, and now we're not, and I don't understand *why*.
Give yourself a minute to hear what you just said.
Okay, yeah, haha, whatever--
Do you wanna build a snowman?
Do not even start with the *Frozen* references. Do *not* even start.
I'm sorry for being such a cruddy friend. I didn't mean to drift away.
I know. I'm just--*talk* to me, okay? We've known each other since *kindergarten*. It would suck if we just sort of--wandered apart.

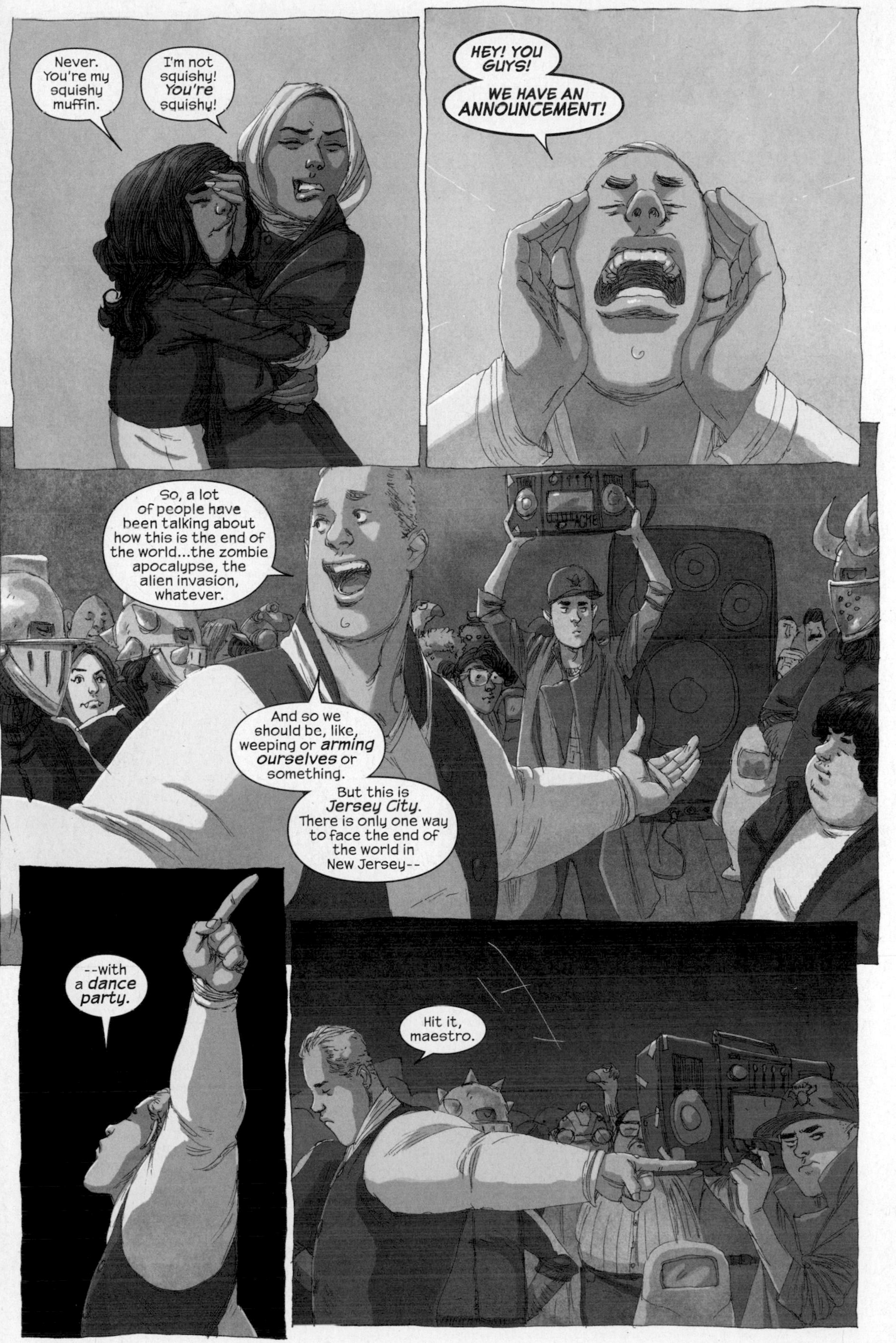

Never. You're my squishy muffin.
I'm not squishy! *You're* squishy!
HEY! YOU GUYS!
WE HAVE AN ANNOUNCEMENT!
So, a lot of people have been talking about how this is the end of the world...the zombie apocalypse, the alien invasion, whatever.
ACME
And so we should be, like, weeping or *arming ourselves* or something.
But this is *Jersey City*. There is only one way to face the end of the world in New Jersey--
--with a *dance party*.
Hit it, maestro.

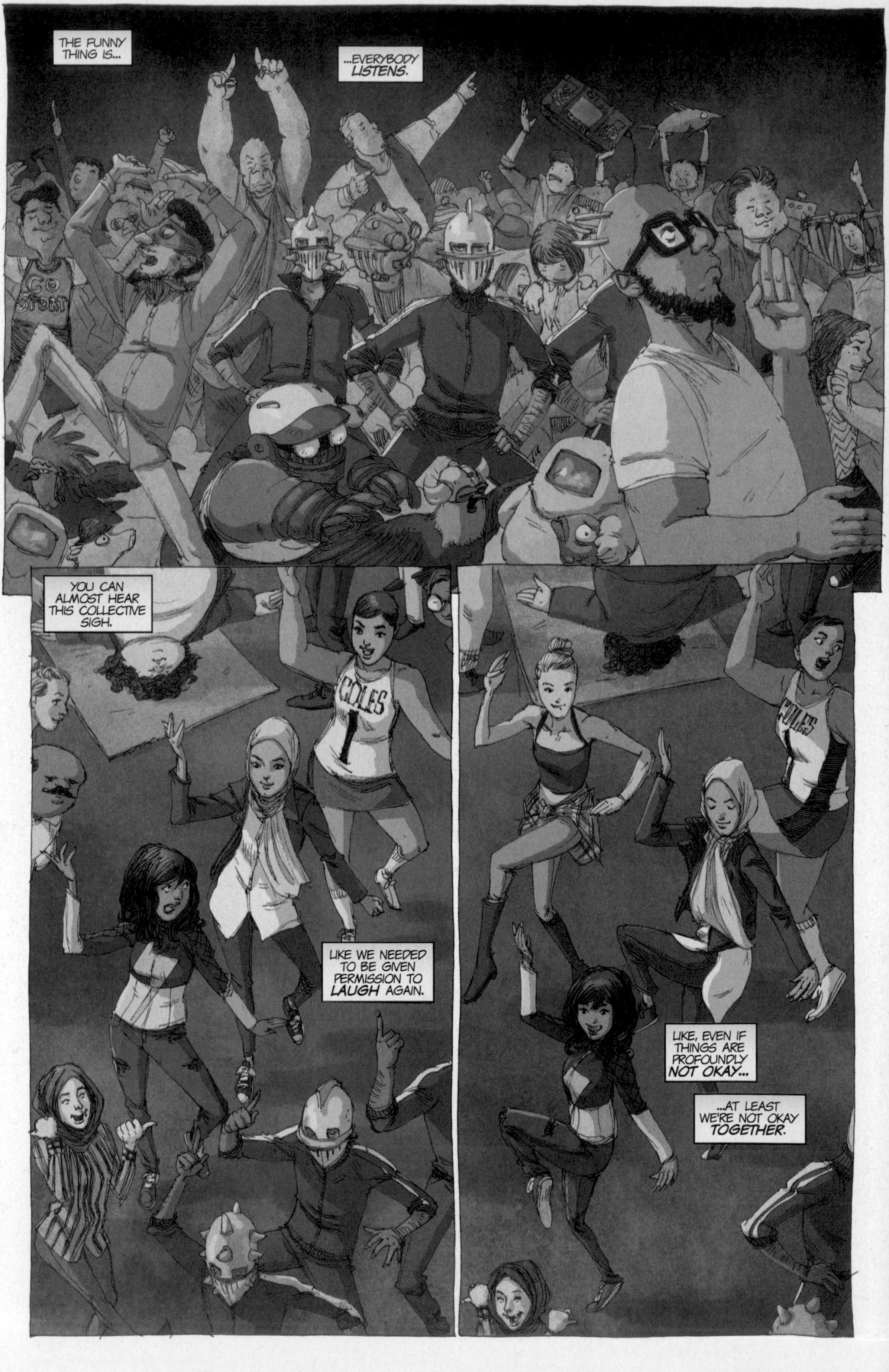
THE FUNNY THING IS...
...EVERYBODY LISTENS.
YOU CAN ALMOST HEAR THIS COLLECTIVE SIGH.
LIKE WE NEEDED TO BE GIVEN PERMISSION TO LAUGH AGAIN.
LIKE, EVEN IF THINGS ARE PROFOUNDLY NOT OKAY...
...AT LEAST WE'RE NOT OKAY TOGETHER.

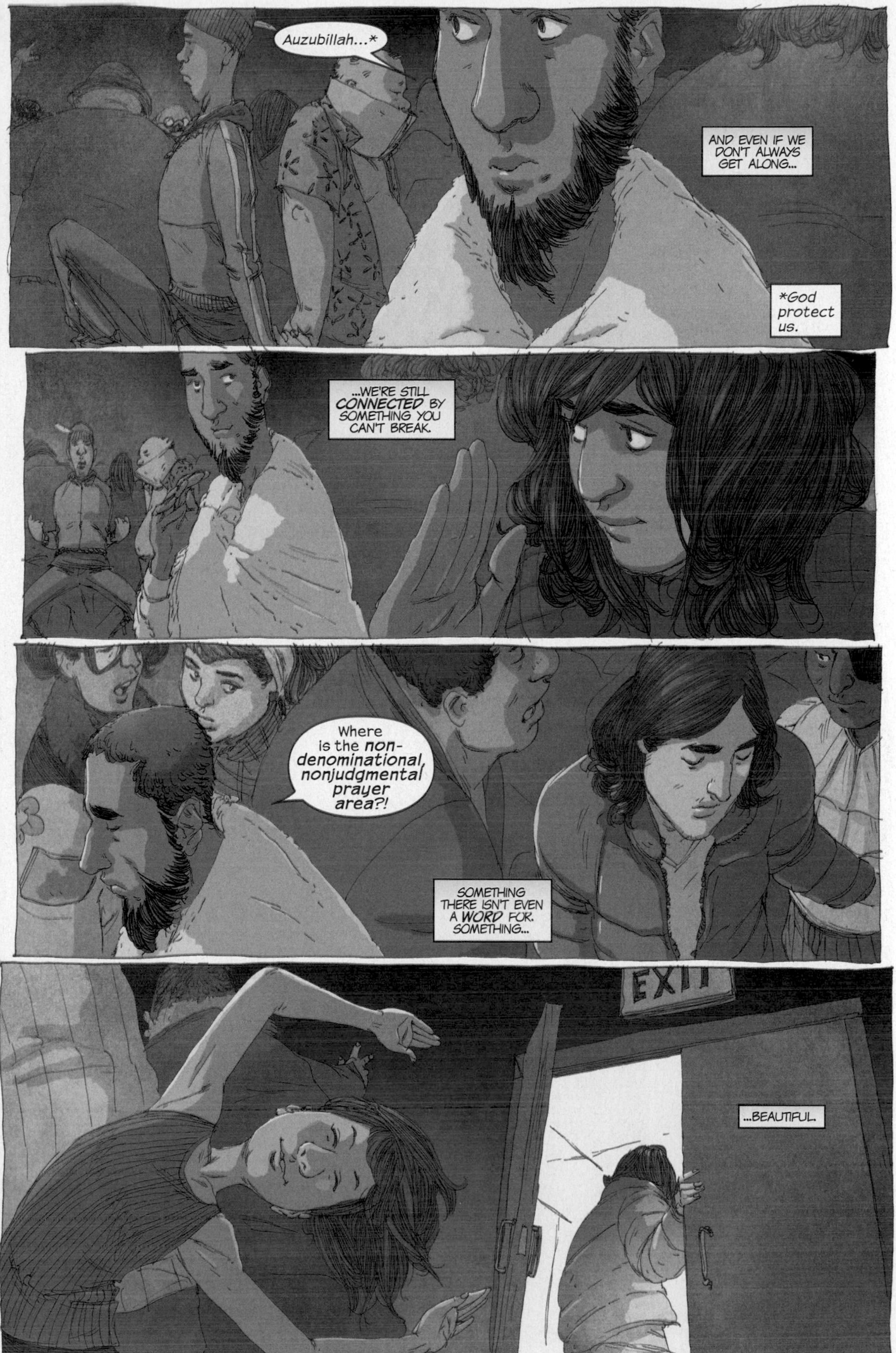
Auzubillah...*
AND EVEN IF WE DON'T ALWAYS GET ALONG...
*God protect us.
...WE'RE STILL CONNECTED BY SOMETHING YOU CAN'T BREAK.
Where is the non-denominational, nonjudgmental prayer area?!
SOMETHING THERE ISN'T EVEN A WORD FOR. SOMETHING...
EXIT
...BEAUTIFUL.

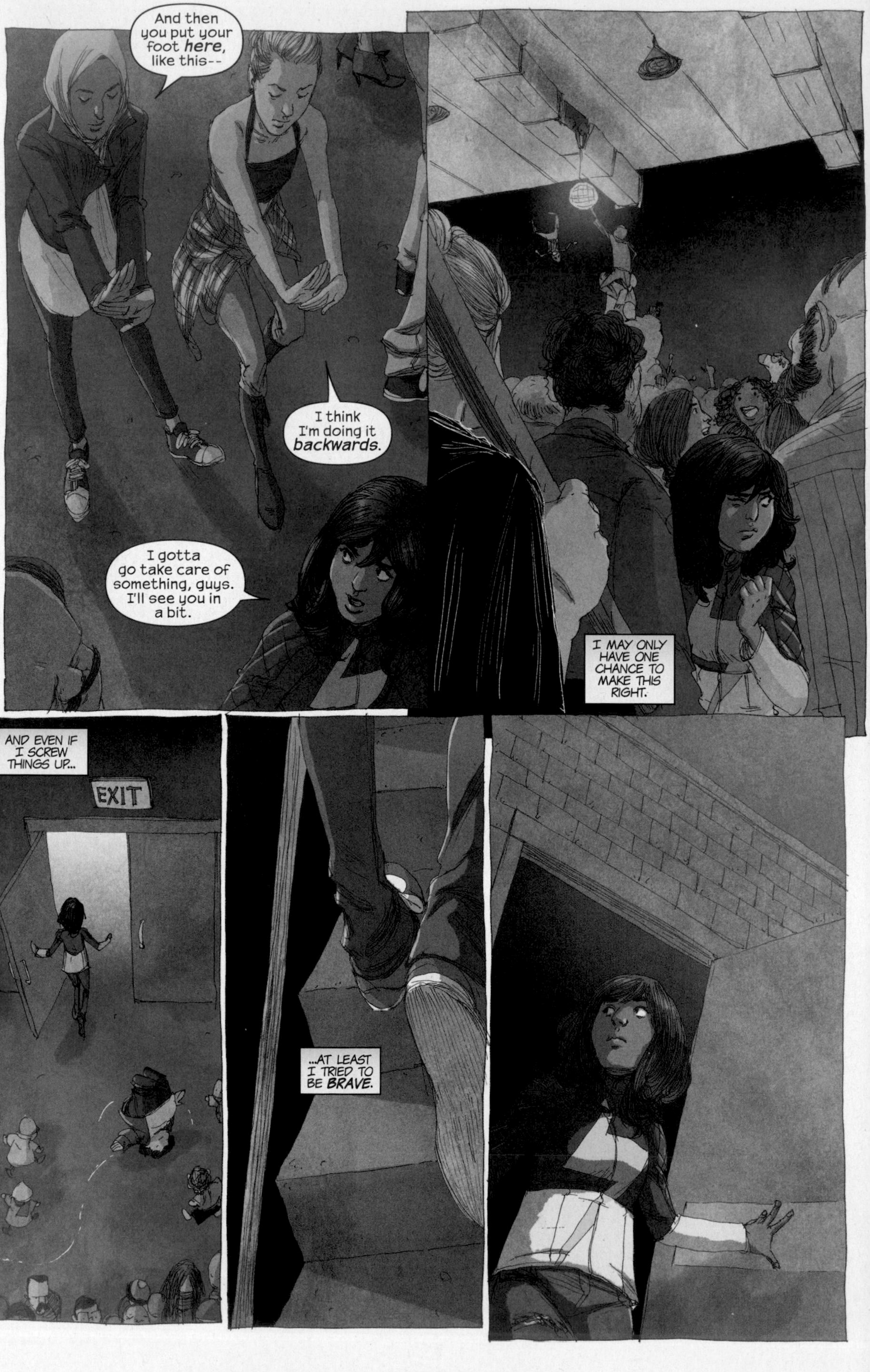
And then you put your foot *here*, like this--
I think I'm doing it *backwards*.
I gotta go take care of something, guys. I'll see you in a bit.
I MAY ONLY HAVE ONE CHANCE TO MAKE THIS RIGHT.
AND EVEN IF I SCREW THINGS UP...
EXIT
...AT LEAST I TRIED TO BE *BRAVE*.

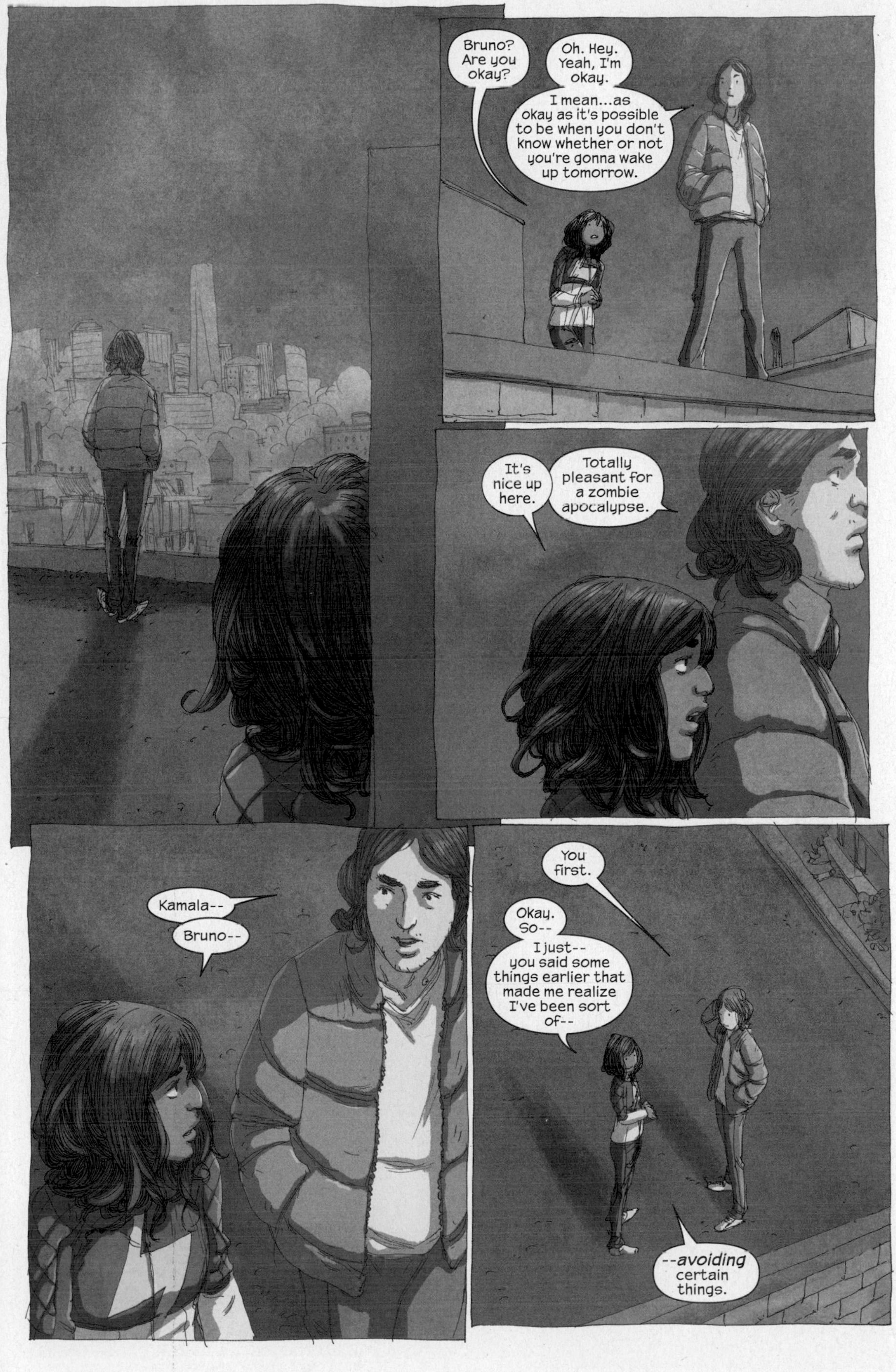
Bruno? Are you okay?
Oh. Hey. Yeah, I'm okay.
I mean...as okay as it's possible to be when you don't know whether or not you're gonna wake up tomorrow.
It's nice up here.
Totally pleasant for a zombie apocalypse.
Kamala--
Bruno--
You first.
Okay. So--
I just-- you said some things earlier that made me realize I've been sort of--
--*avoiding* certain things.

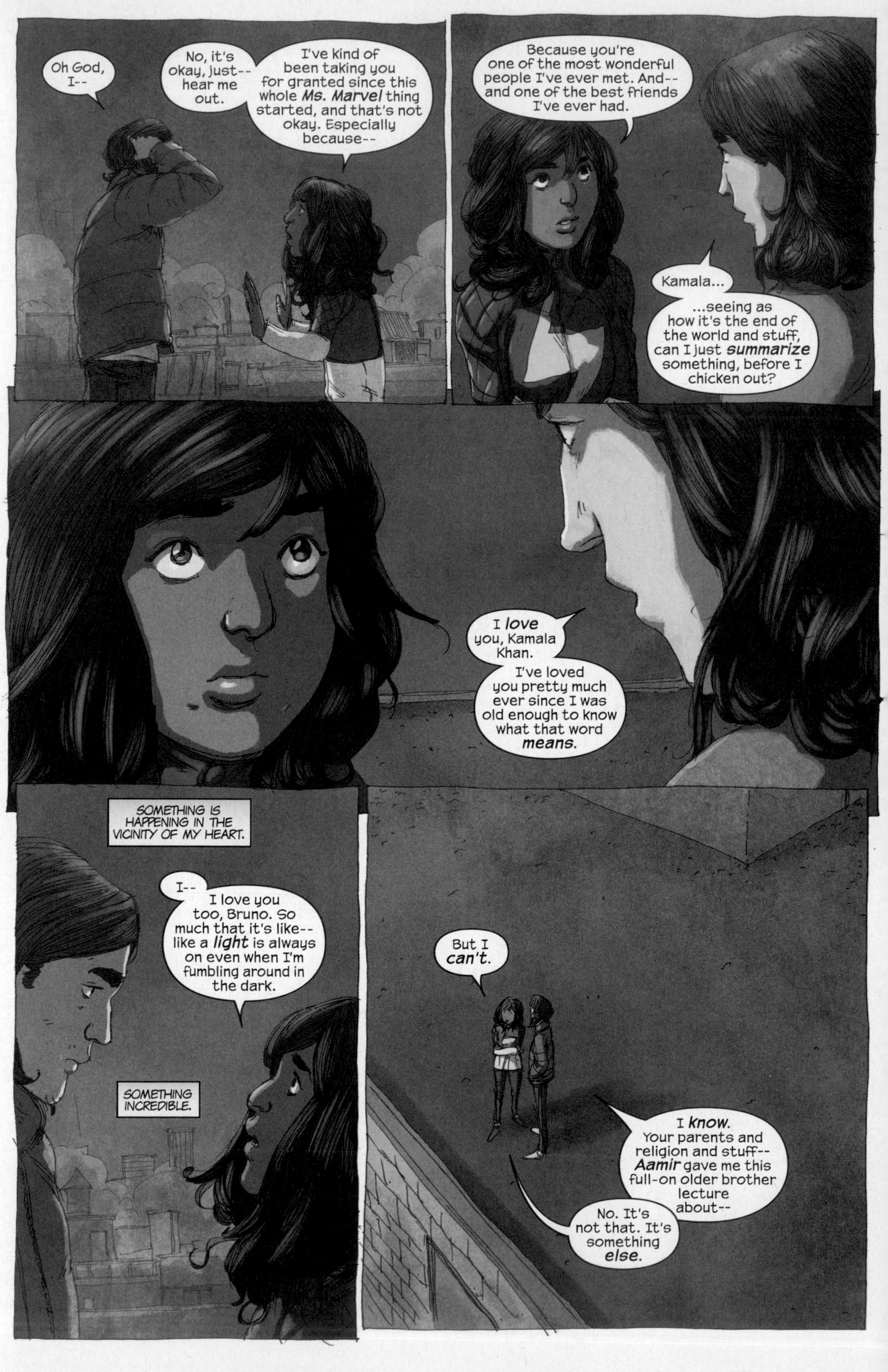
Oh God, I--
No, it's okay, just-- hear me out.
I've kind of been taking you for granted since this whole Ms. Marvel thing started, and that's not okay. Especially because--
Because you're one of the most wonderful people I've ever met. And-- and one of the best friends I've ever had.
Kamala...
...seeing as how it's the end of the world and stuff, can I just summarize something, before I chicken out?
I love you, Kamala Khan.
I've loved you pretty much ever since I was old enough to know what that word means.
SOMETHING IS HAPPENING IN THE VICINITY OF MY HEART.
I--
I love you too, Bruno. So much that it's like-- like a light is always on even when I'm fumbling around in the dark.
SOMETHING INCREDIBLE.
But I can't.
I know. Your parents and religion and stuff-- Aamir gave me this full-on older brother lecture about--
No. It's not that. It's something else.

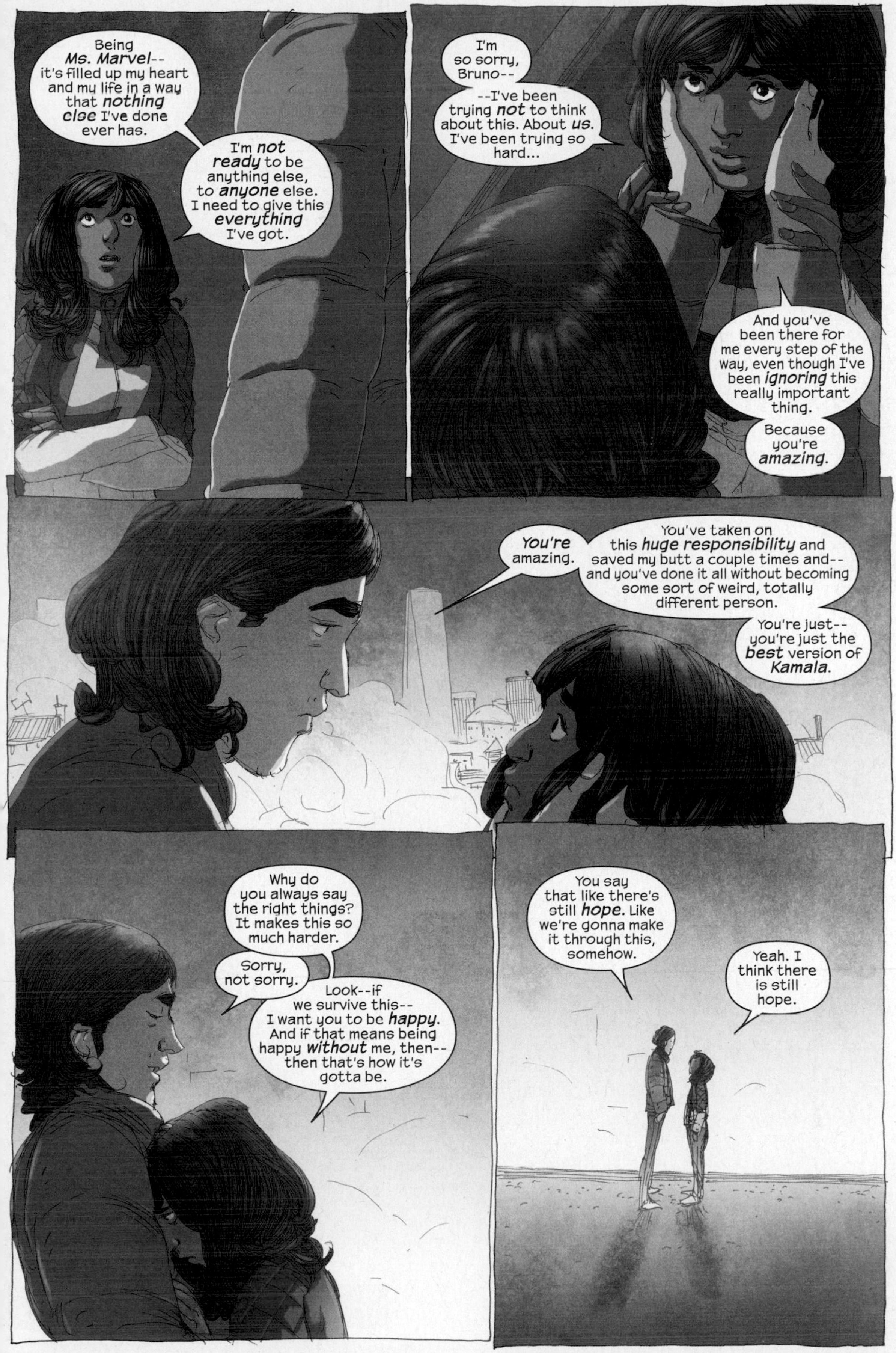
Being Ms. Marvel-- it's filled up my heart and my life in a way that nothing else I've done ever has.
I'm not ready to be anything else, to anyone else. I need to give this everything I've got.
I'm so sorry, Bruno--
--I've been trying not to think about this. About us. I've been trying so hard...
And you've been there for me every step of the way, even though I've been ignoring this really important thing.
Because you're amazing.
You're amazing.
You've taken on this huge responsibility and saved my butt a couple times and-- and you've done it all without becoming some sort of weird, totally different person.
You're just-- you're just the best version of Kamala.
Why do you always say the right things? It makes this so much harder.
Sorry, not sorry.
Look--if we survive this-- I want you to be happy. And if that means being happy without me, then-- then that's how it's gotta be.
You say that like there's still hope. Like we're gonna make it through this, somehow.
Yeah. I think there is still hope.

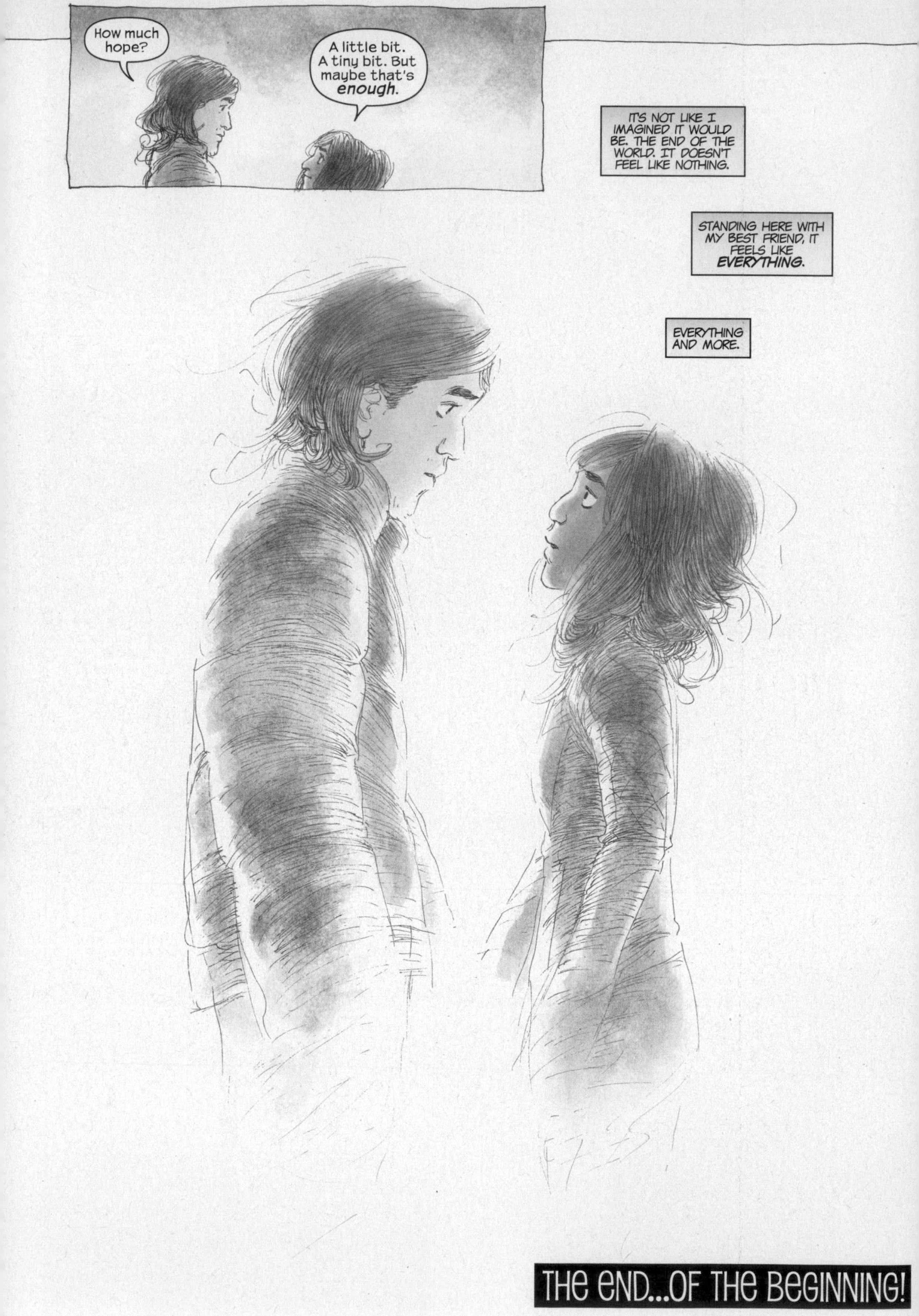

How much hope?
A little bit. A tiny bit. But maybe that's *enough*.
IT'S NOT LIKE I IMAGINED IT WOULD BE. THE END OF THE WORLD. IT DOESN'T FEEL LIKE NOTHING.
STANDING HERE WITH MY BEST FRIEND, IT FEELS LIKE *EVERYTHING*.
EVERYTHING AND MORE.
THE END...OF THE BEGINNING!

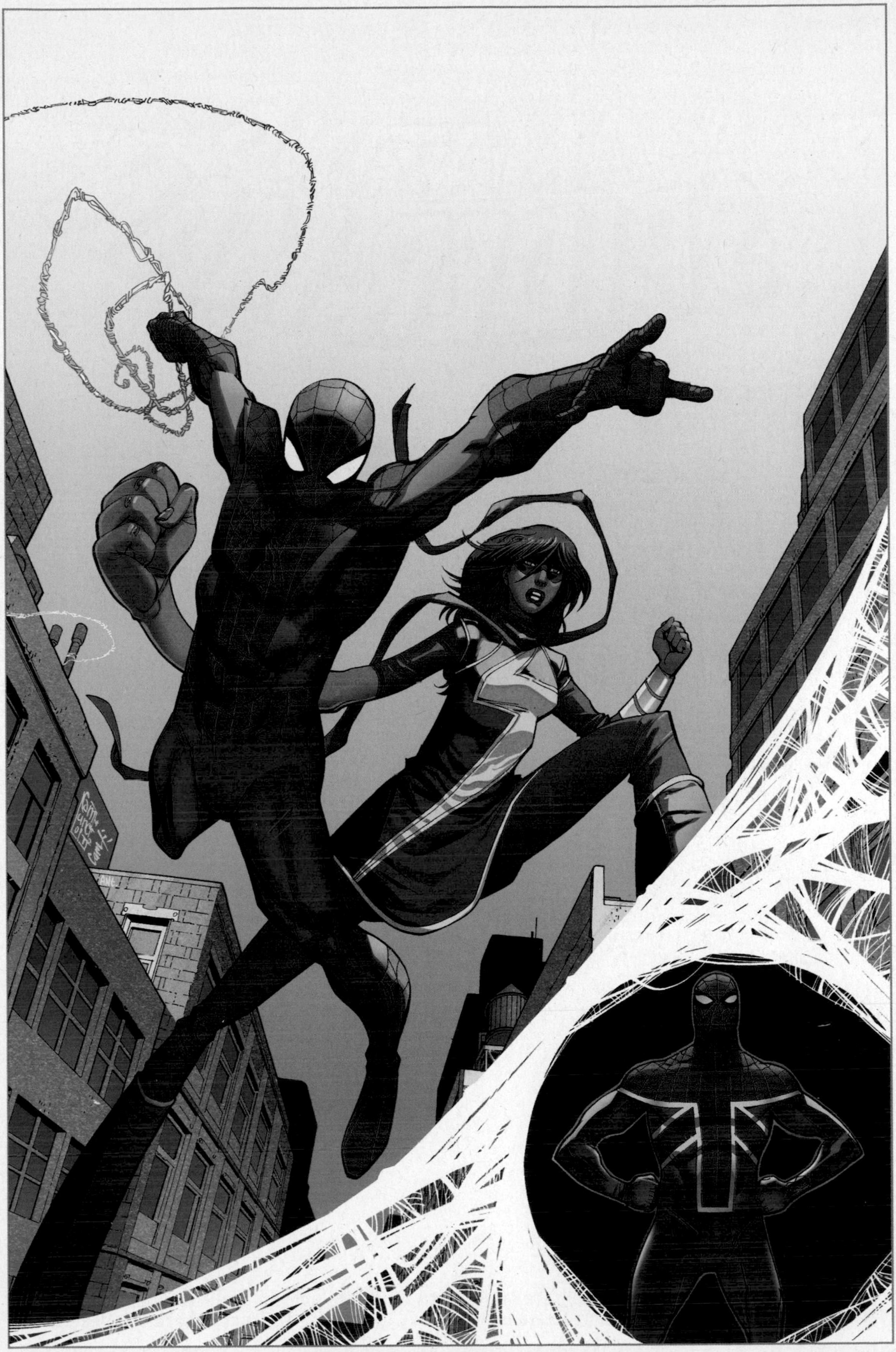

AMAZING SPIDER-MAN #7

Years ago, high school student PETER PARKER was bitten by a radioactive spider and gained the speed, agility, and proportional strength of a spider as well as the ability to stick to walls and a spider-sense that warned him of imminent danger. After learning that with great power there must also come great responsibility, he became the crime-fighting super hero…

the AMAZING SPIDER-MAN

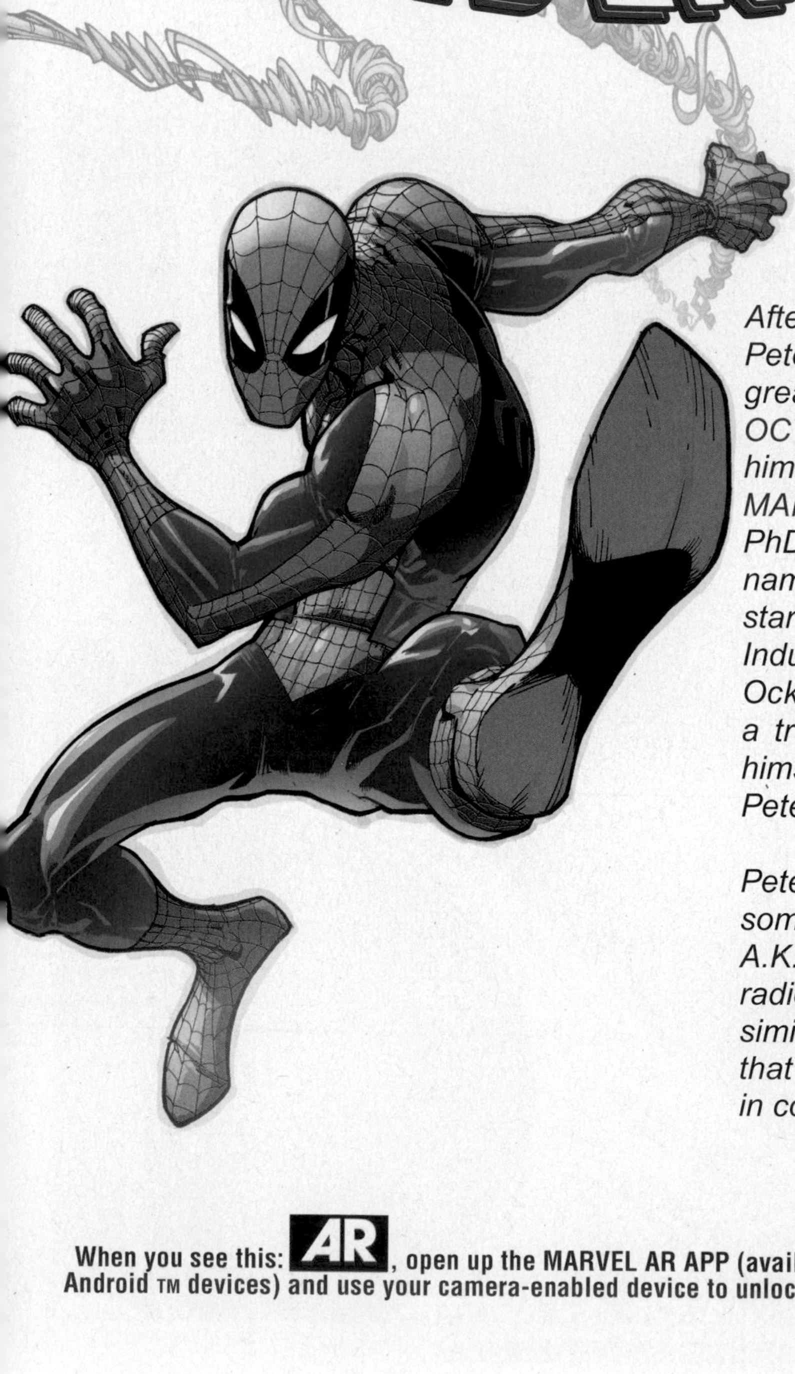

After swapping his mind into Peter's body, one of Spider-Man's greatest enemies, DOCTOR OCTOPUS, set out to prove himself the SUPERIOR SPIDER-MAN. He also completed Peter's PhD, fell in love with a woman named Anna Maria Marconi, and started his own company, "Parker Industries." But in the end Doc Ock realized that in order to be a true hero, he had to sacrifice himself and give control of Peter's body back to Peter.

Peter recently found out that someone else, Cindy Moon A.K.A. SILK, was bitten by his radioactive spider giving her similar powers to Peter. And that's not the only thing they have in common.

When you see this: AR, open up the MARVEL AR APP (available on applicable Apple ® iOS or Android TM devices) and use your camera-enabled device to unlock extra-special exclusive features!*

GREAT, NOT ONLY HAVEN'T I FOUND MY FAMILY, NOW I CAN'T FIND NETSCAPE! PETE, COULD YOU GIVE ME A HAND?

UH, SURE.

UH-OH.

TRIBECA.
THE APARTMENT OF PETER PARKER, ANNA MARIA MARCONI... AND, APPARENTLY, CINDY MOON.

9:23 A.M.

HERE, CINDY. FACEBOOK BARELY EXISTED LAST TIME YOU WERE ONLINE, BUT IT'S THE MOST POPULAR WAY TO...STAY...

...CLOSE...

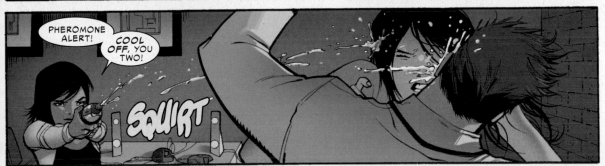

PHEROMONE ALERT! COOL OFF, YOU TWO!

SQUIRT

9:46.

BEHAVE!

9:58.

DOWN!

10:06.

THAT'S ENOUGH, ANNA!

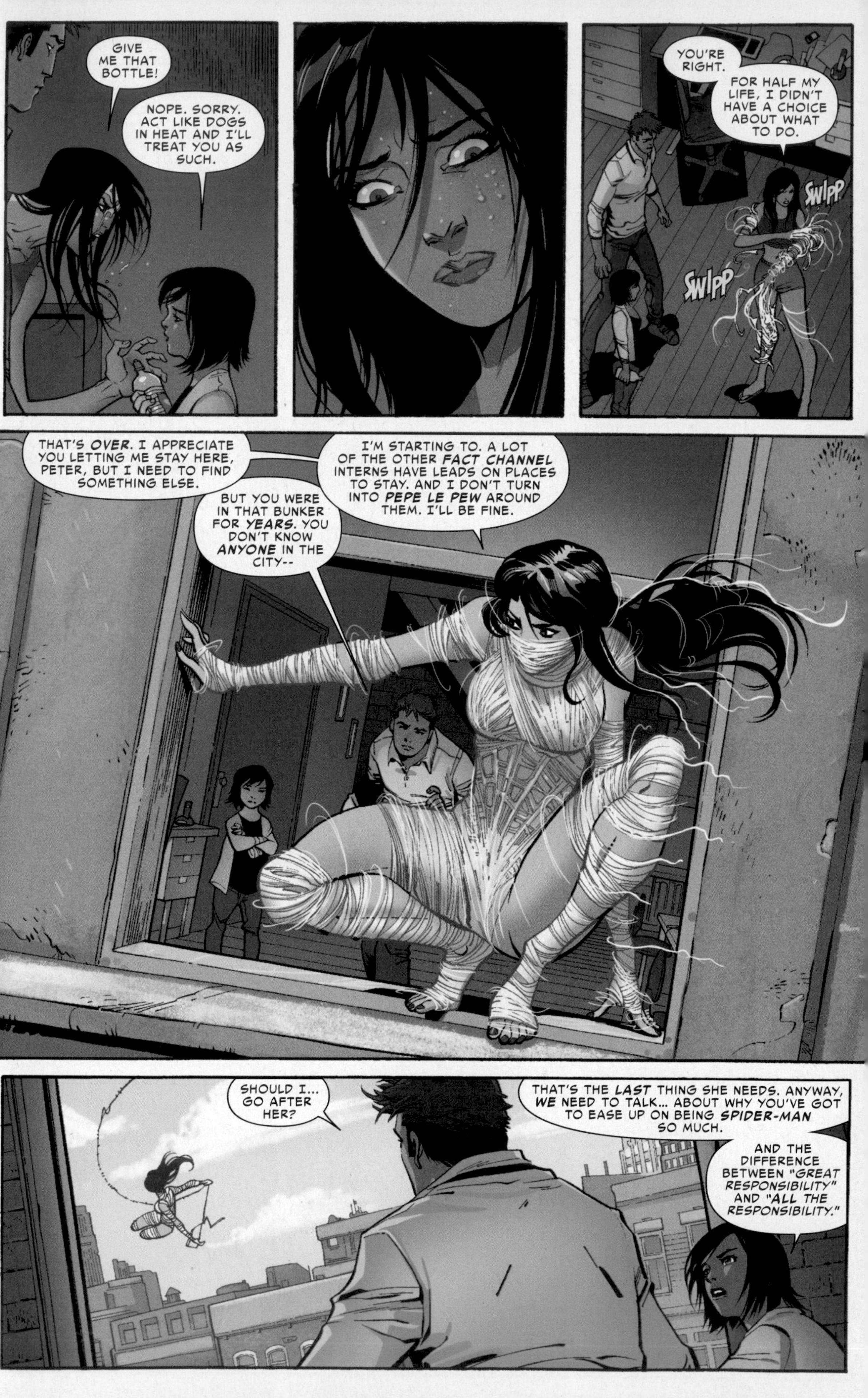
GIVE ME THAT BOTTLE!
NOPE. SORRY. ACT LIKE DOGS IN HEAT AND I'LL TREAT YOU AS SUCH.
YOU'RE RIGHT.
FOR HALF MY LIFE, I DIDN'T HAVE A CHOICE ABOUT WHAT TO DO.
SWIPP
SWIPP
THAT'S OVER. I APPRECIATE YOU LETTING ME STAY HERE, PETER, BUT I NEED TO FIND SOMETHING ELSE.
BUT YOU WERE IN THAT BUNKER FOR YEARS. YOU DON'T KNOW ANYONE IN THE CITY--
I'M STARTING TO. A LOT OF THE OTHER FACT CHANNEL INTERNS HAVE LEADS ON PLACES TO STAY. AND I DON'T TURN INTO PEPE LE PEW AROUND THEM. I'LL BE FINE.
SHOULD I... GO AFTER HER?
THAT'S THE LAST THING SHE NEEDS. ANYWAY, WE NEED TO TALK... ABOUT WHY YOU'VE GOT TO EASE UP ON BEING SPIDER-MAN SO MUCH.
AND THE DIFFERENCE BETWEEN "GREAT RESPONSIBILITY" AND "ALL THE RESPONSIBILITY."

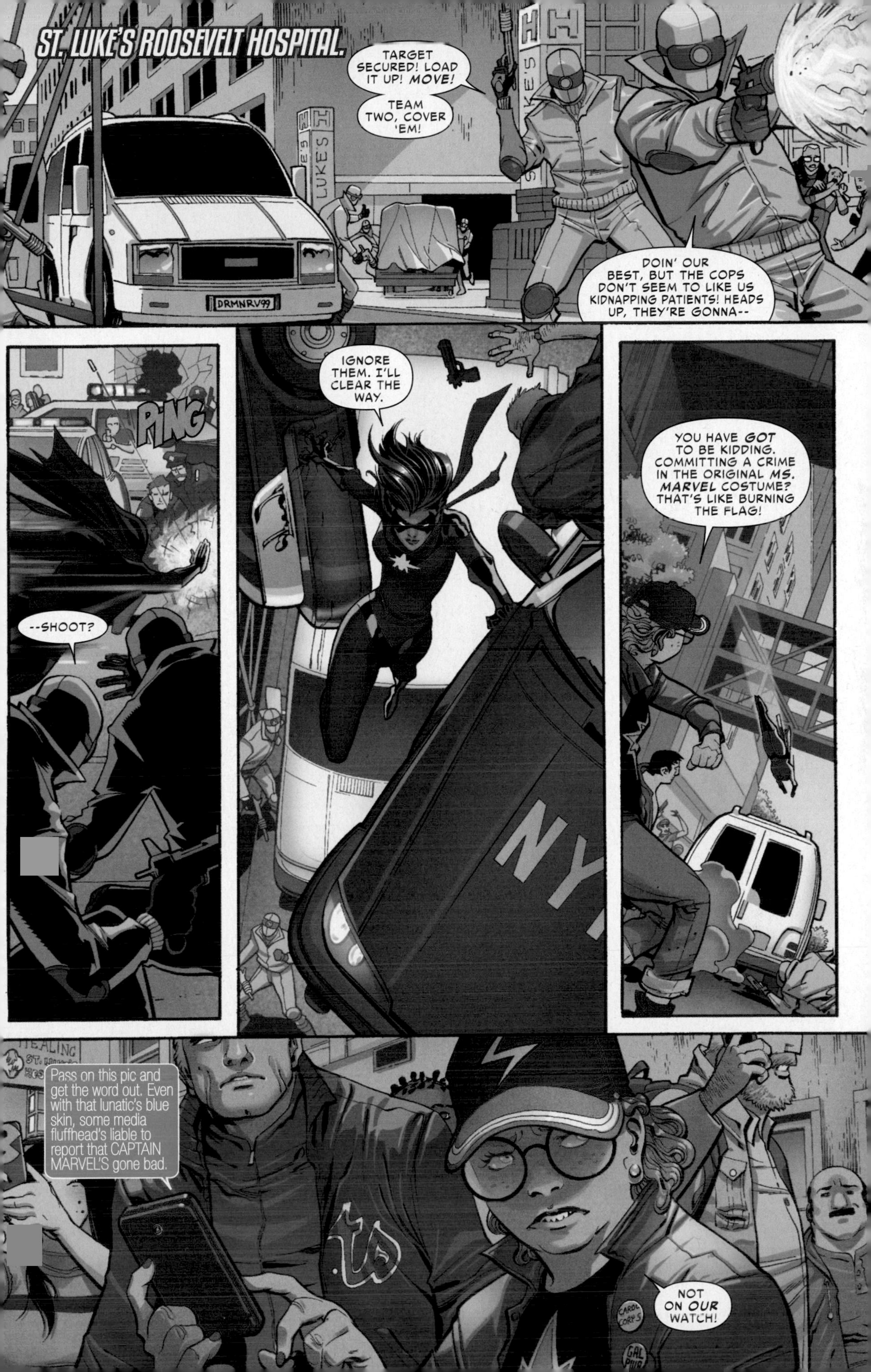

ST. LUKE'S ROOSEVELT HOSPITAL.
TARGET SECURED! LOAD IT UP! MOVE!
TEAM TWO, COVER 'EM!
DRMNRV99
DOIN' OUR BEST, BUT THE COPS DON'T SEEM TO LIKE US KIDNAPPING PATIENTS! HEADS UP, THEY'RE GONNA--
PING
--SHOOT?
IGNORE THEM. I'LL CLEAR THE WAY.
NY
YOU HAVE GOT TO BE KIDDING. COMMITTING A CRIME IN THE ORIGINAL MS. MARVEL COSTUME? THAT'S LIKE BURNING THE FLAG!
Pass on this pic and get the word out. Even with that lunatic's blue skin, some media fluffhead's liable to report that CAPTAIN MARVEL'S gone bad.
NOT ON OUR WATCH!
CAROL CORPS

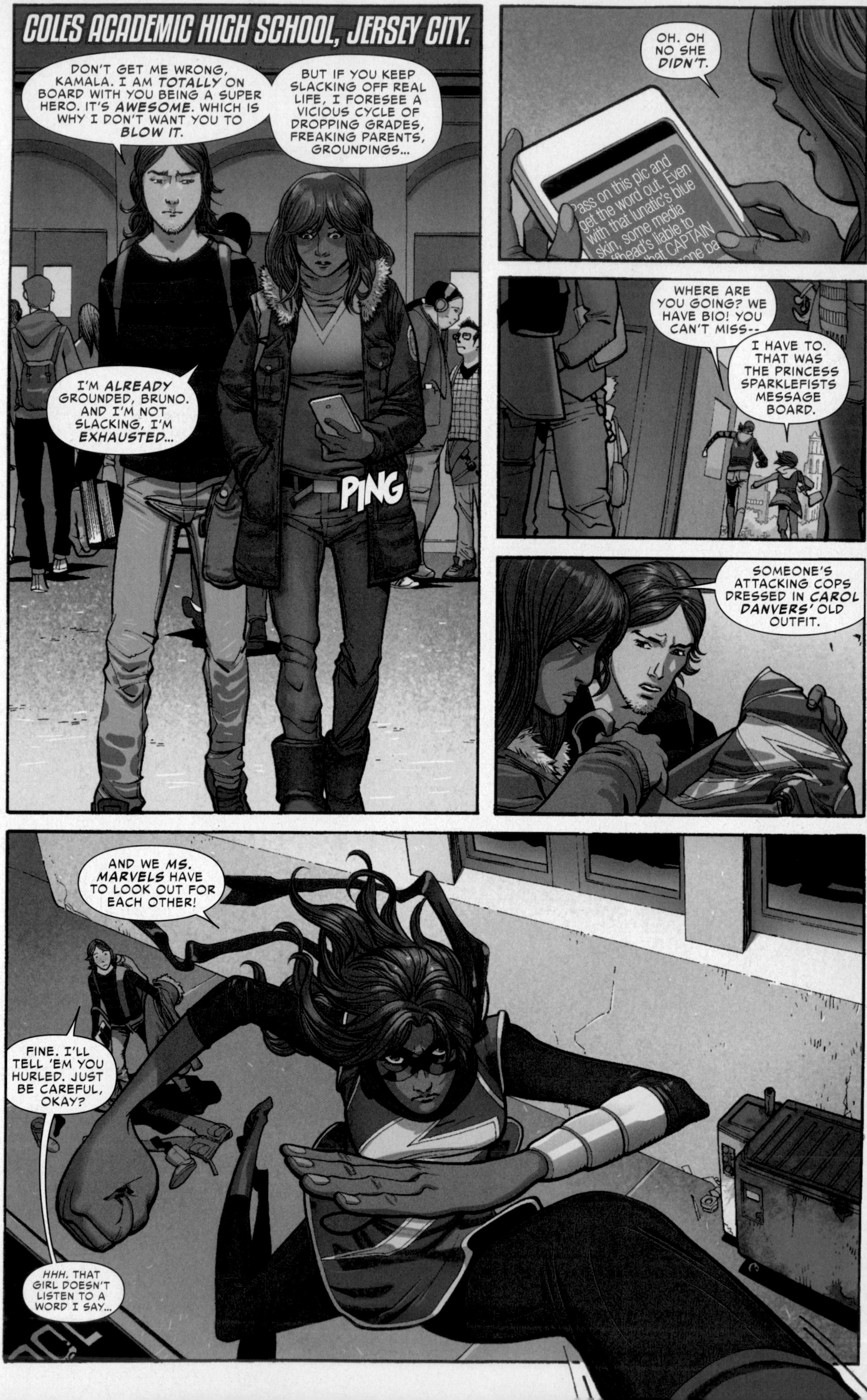
COLES ACADEMIC HIGH SCHOOL, JERSEY CITY.
DON'T GET ME WRONG, KAMALA. I AM TOTALLY ON BOARD WITH YOU BEING A SUPER HERO. IT'S AWESOME. WHICH IS WHY I DON'T WANT YOU TO BLOW IT.
BUT IF YOU KEEP SLACKING OFF REAL LIFE, I FORESEE A VICIOUS CYCLE OF DROPPING GRADES, FREAKING PARENTS, GROUNDINGS...
I'M ALREADY GROUNDED, BRUNO. AND I'M NOT SLACKING, I'M EXHAUSTED...
PING
OH. OH NO SHE DIDN'T.
Pass on this pic and get the word out. Even with that lunatic's blue skin, some media
WHERE ARE YOU GOING? WE HAVE BIO! YOU CAN'T MISS--
I HAVE TO. THAT WAS THE PRINCESS SPARKLEFISTS MESSAGE BOARD.
SOMEONE'S ATTACKING COPS DRESSED IN CAROL DANVERS' OLD OUTFIT.
AND WE MS. MARVELS HAVE TO LOOK OUT FOR EACH OTHER!
FINE. I'LL TELL 'EM YOU HURLED. JUST BE CAREFUL, OKAY?
HHH. THAT GIRL DOESN'T LISTEN TO A WORD I SAY...

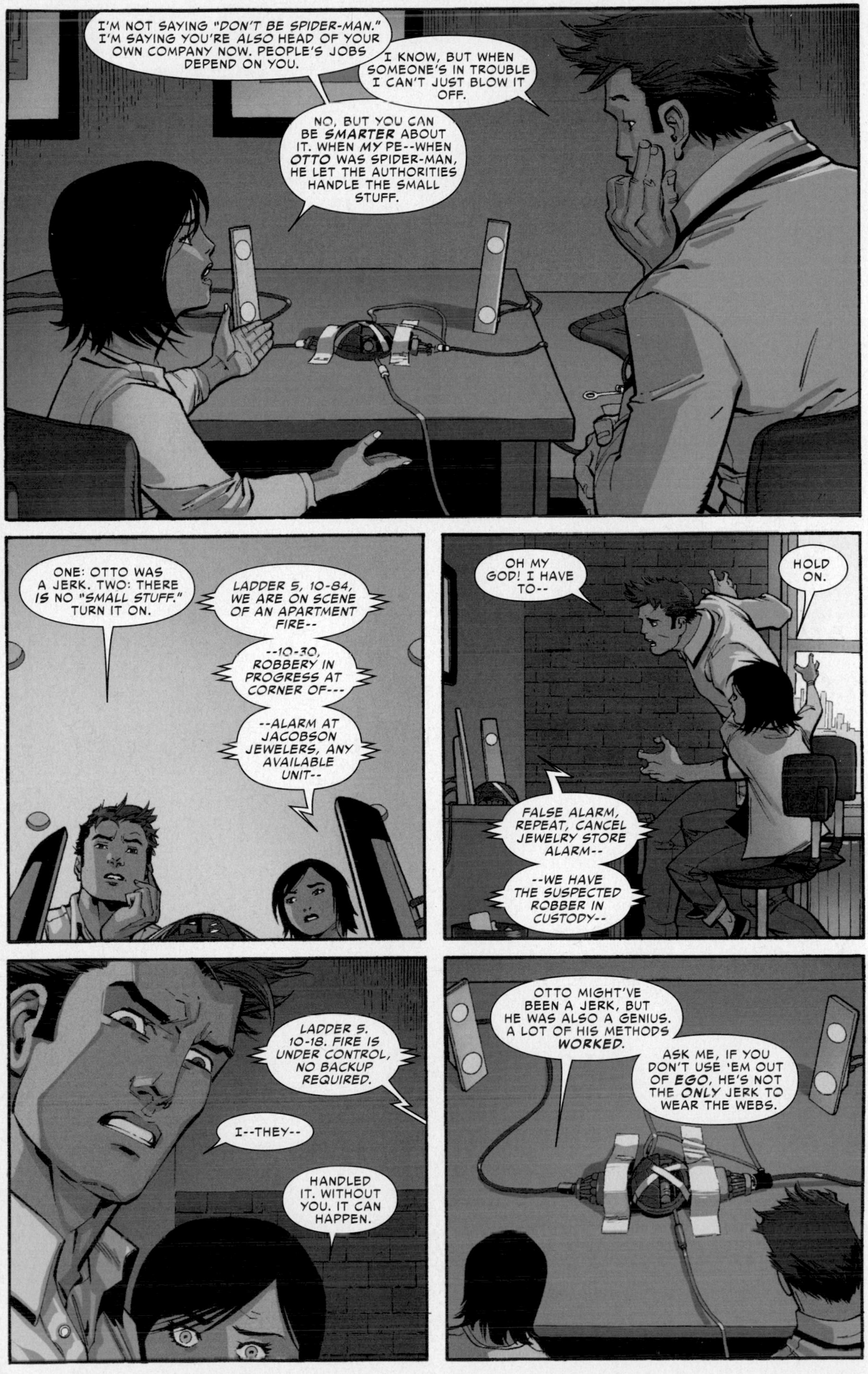
I'M NOT SAYING "DON'T BE SPIDER-MAN." I'M SAYING YOU'RE ALSO HEAD OF YOUR OWN COMPANY NOW. PEOPLE'S JOBS DEPEND ON YOU.
I KNOW, BUT WHEN SOMEONE'S IN TROUBLE I CAN'T JUST BLOW IT OFF.
NO, BUT YOU CAN BE SMARTER ABOUT IT. WHEN MY PE--WHEN OTTO WAS SPIDER-MAN, HE LET THE AUTHORITIES HANDLE THE SMALL STUFF.
ONE: OTTO WAS A JERK. TWO: THERE IS NO "SMALL STUFF." TURN IT ON.
LADDER 5, 10-84, WE ARE ON SCENE OF AN APARTMENT FIRE--
--10-30, ROBBERY IN PROGRESS AT CORNER OF---
--ALARM AT JACOBSON JEWELERS, ANY AVAILABLE UNIT--
OH MY GOD! I HAVE TO--
HOLD ON.
FALSE ALARM, REPEAT, CANCEL JEWELRY STORE ALARM--
--WE HAVE THE SUSPECTED ROBBER IN CUSTODY--
LADDER 5. 10-18. FIRE IS UNDER CONTROL, NO BACKUP REQUIRED.
I--THEY--
HANDLED IT. WITHOUT YOU. IT CAN HAPPEN.
OTTO MIGHT'VE BEEN A JERK, BUT HE WAS ALSO A GENIUS. A LOT OF HIS METHODS WORKED.
ASK ME, IF YOU DON'T USE 'EM OUT OF EGO, HE'S NOT THE ONLY JERK TO WEAR THE WEBS.

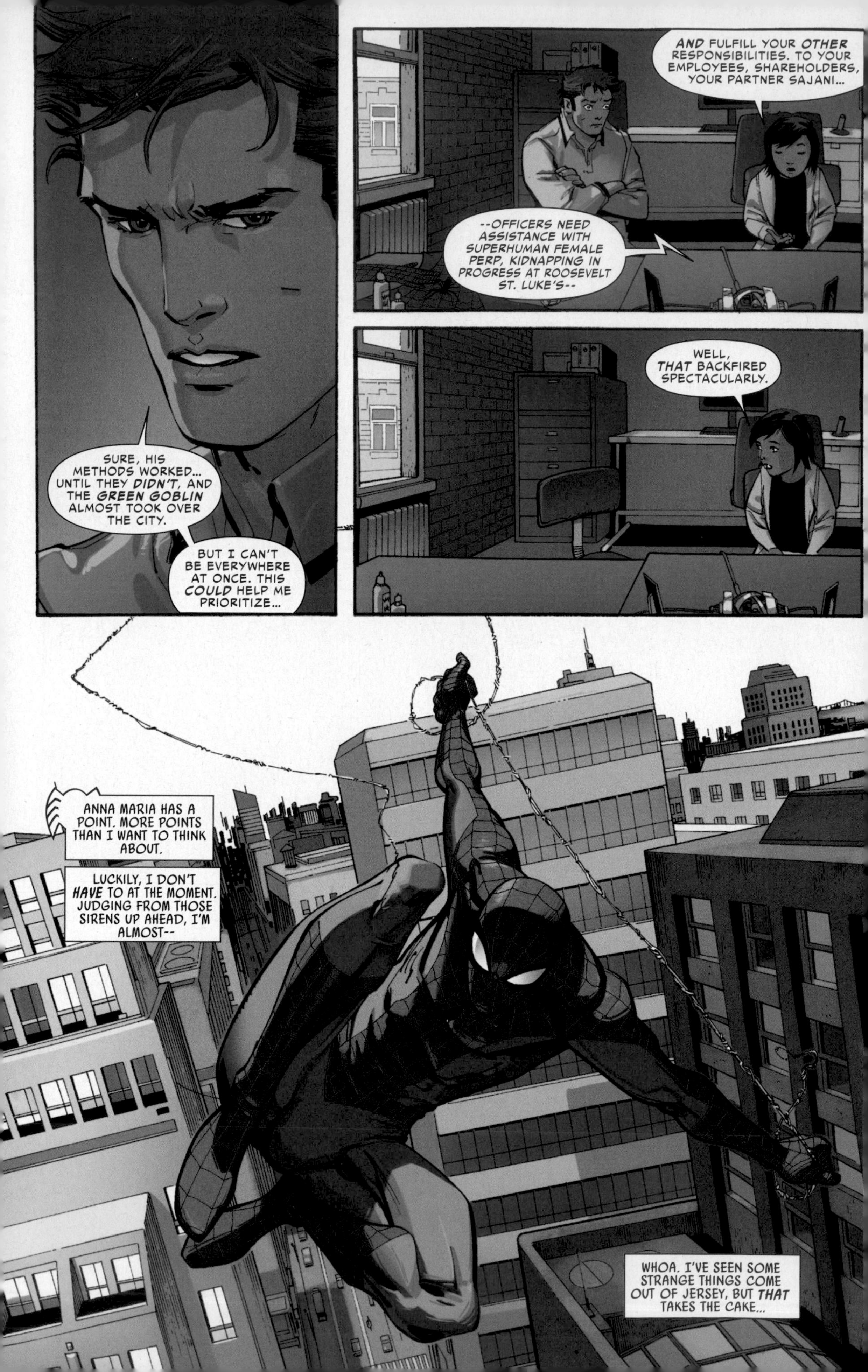
SURE, HIS METHODS WORKED... UNTIL THEY DIDN'T, AND THE GREEN GOBLIN ALMOST TOOK OVER THE CITY.
BUT I CAN'T BE EVERYWHERE AT ONCE. THIS COULD HELP ME PRIORITIZE...
AND FULFILL YOUR OTHER RESPONSIBILITIES. TO YOUR EMPLOYEES, SHAREHOLDERS, YOUR PARTNER SAJANI...
--OFFICERS NEED ASSISTANCE WITH SUPERHUMAN FEMALE PERP, KIDNAPPING IN PROGRESS AT ROOSEVELT ST. LUKE'S--
WELL, THAT BACKFIRED SPECTACULARLY.
ANNA MARIA HAS A POINT. MORE POINTS THAN I WANT TO THINK ABOUT.
LUCKILY, I DON'T HAVE TO AT THE MOMENT. JUDGING FROM THOSE SIRENS UP AHEAD, I'M ALMOST--
WHOA. I'VE SEEN SOME STRANGE THINGS COME OUT OF JERSEY, BUT THAT TAKES THE CAKE...

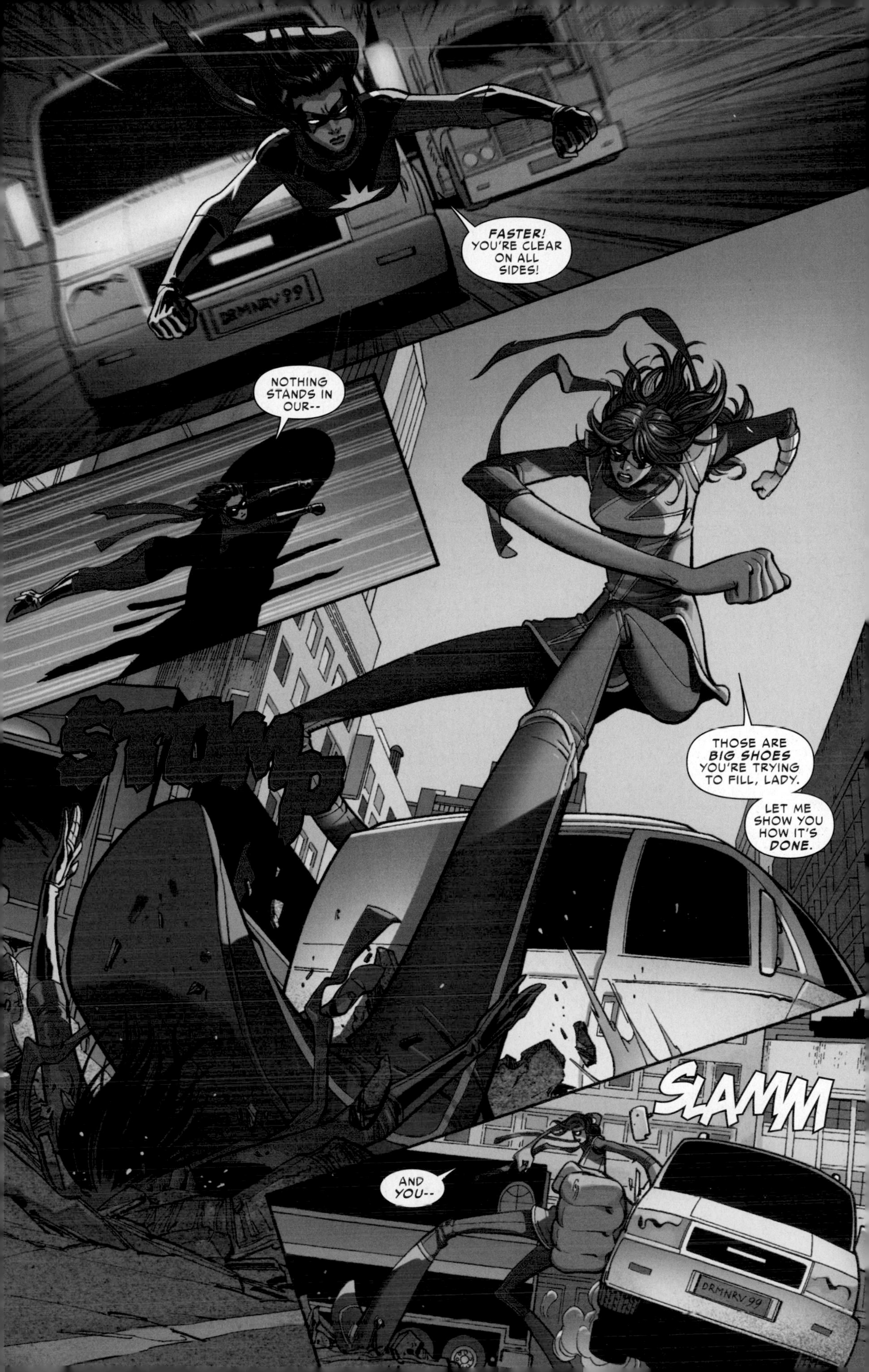
FASTER! YOU'RE CLEAR ON ALL SIDES!
DRMNRV 99
NOTHING STANDS IN OUR--
STOMP
THOSE ARE BIG SHOES YOU'RE TRYING TO FILL, LADY.
LET ME SHOW YOU HOW IT'S DONE.
SLAMM
AND YOU--
DRMNRV 99

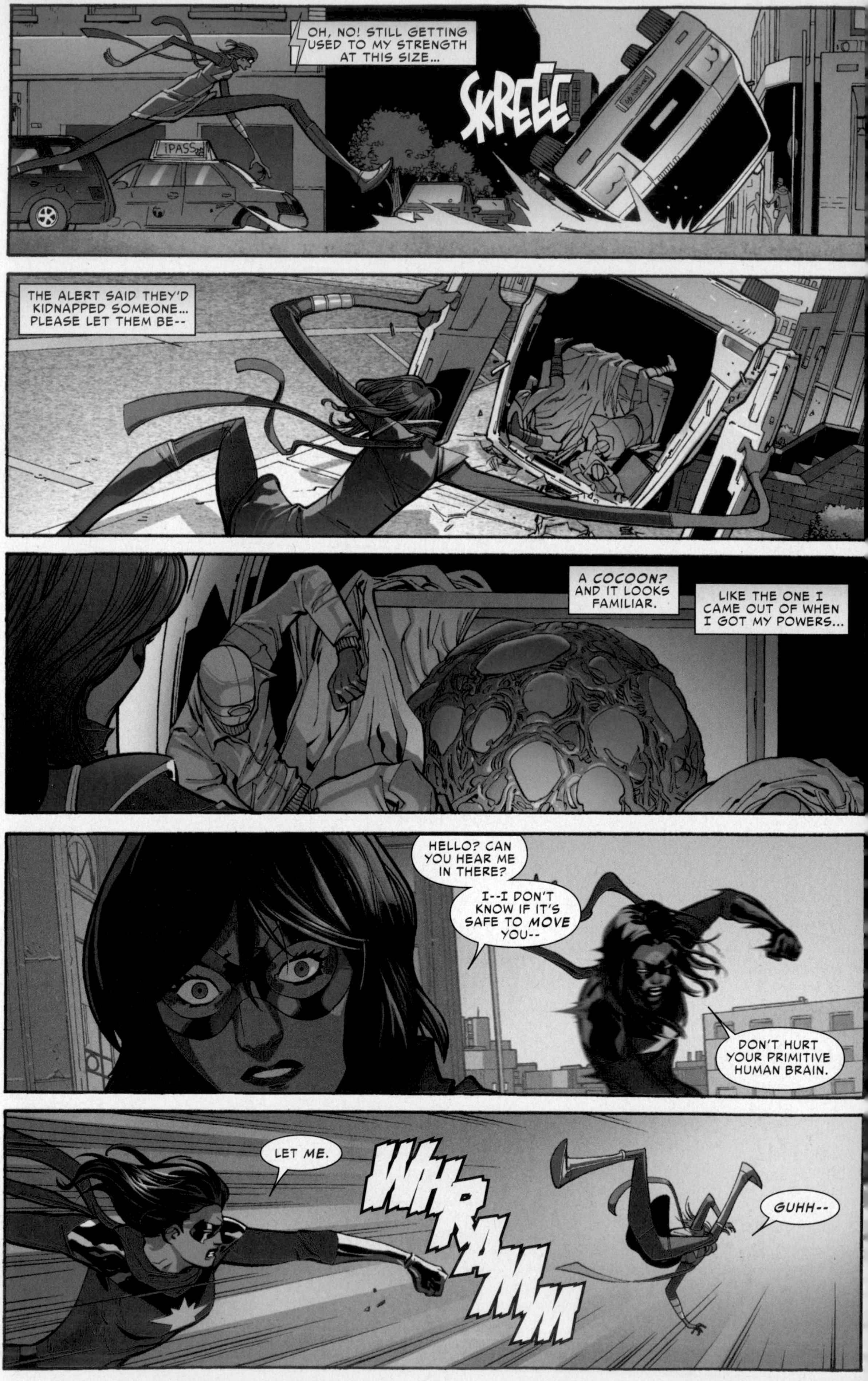

OH, NO! STILL GETTING USED TO MY STRENGTH AT THIS SIZE...
SKREEE
iPASS
THE ALERT SAID THEY'D KIDNAPPED SOMEONE... PLEASE LET THEM BE--
A COCOON? AND IT LOOKS FAMILIAR.
LIKE THE ONE I CAME OUT OF WHEN I GOT MY POWERS...
HELLO? CAN YOU HEAR ME IN THERE?
I--I DON'T KNOW IF IT'S SAFE TO MOVE YOU--
DON'T HURT YOUR PRIMITIVE HUMAN BRAIN.
LET ME.
WHRAMMM
GUHH--

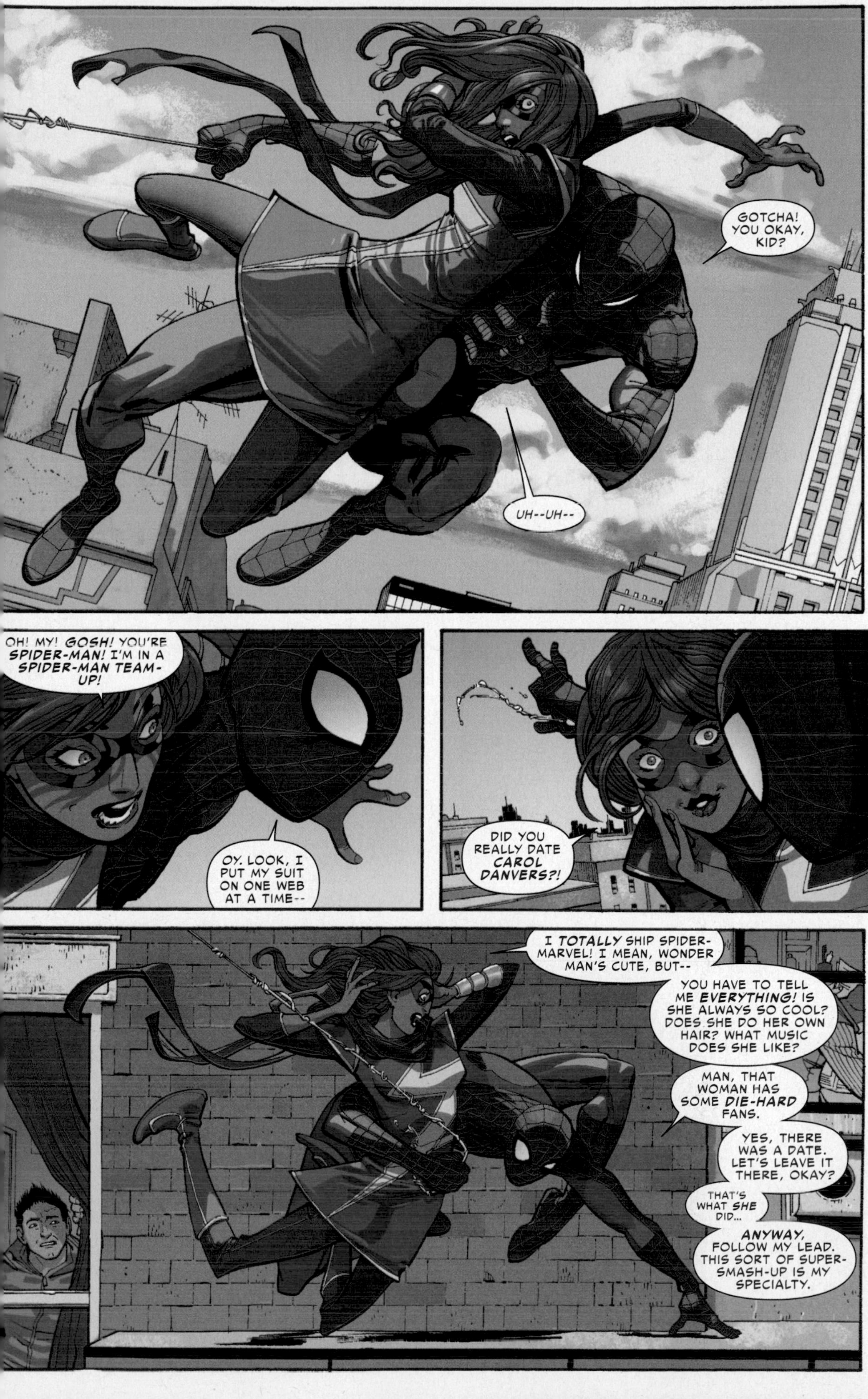

GOTCHA! YOU OKAY, KID?
UH--UH--
OH! MY! GOSH! YOU'RE SPIDER-MAN! I'M IN A SPIDER-MAN TEAM-UP!
OY. LOOK, I PUT MY SUIT ON ONE WEB AT A TIME--
DID YOU REALLY DATE CAROL DANVERS?!
I TOTALLY SHIP SPIDER-MARVEL! I MEAN, WONDER MAN'S CUTE, BUT--
YOU HAVE TO TELL ME EVERYTHING! IS SHE ALWAYS SO COOL? DOES SHE DO HER OWN HAIR? WHAT MUSIC DOES SHE LIKE?
MAN, THAT WOMAN HAS SOME DIE-HARD FANS.
YES, THERE WAS A DATE. LET'S LEAVE IT THERE, OKAY?
THAT'S WHAT SHE DID...
ANYWAY, FOLLOW MY LEAD. THIS SORT OF SUPER-SMASH-UP IS MY SPECIALTY.

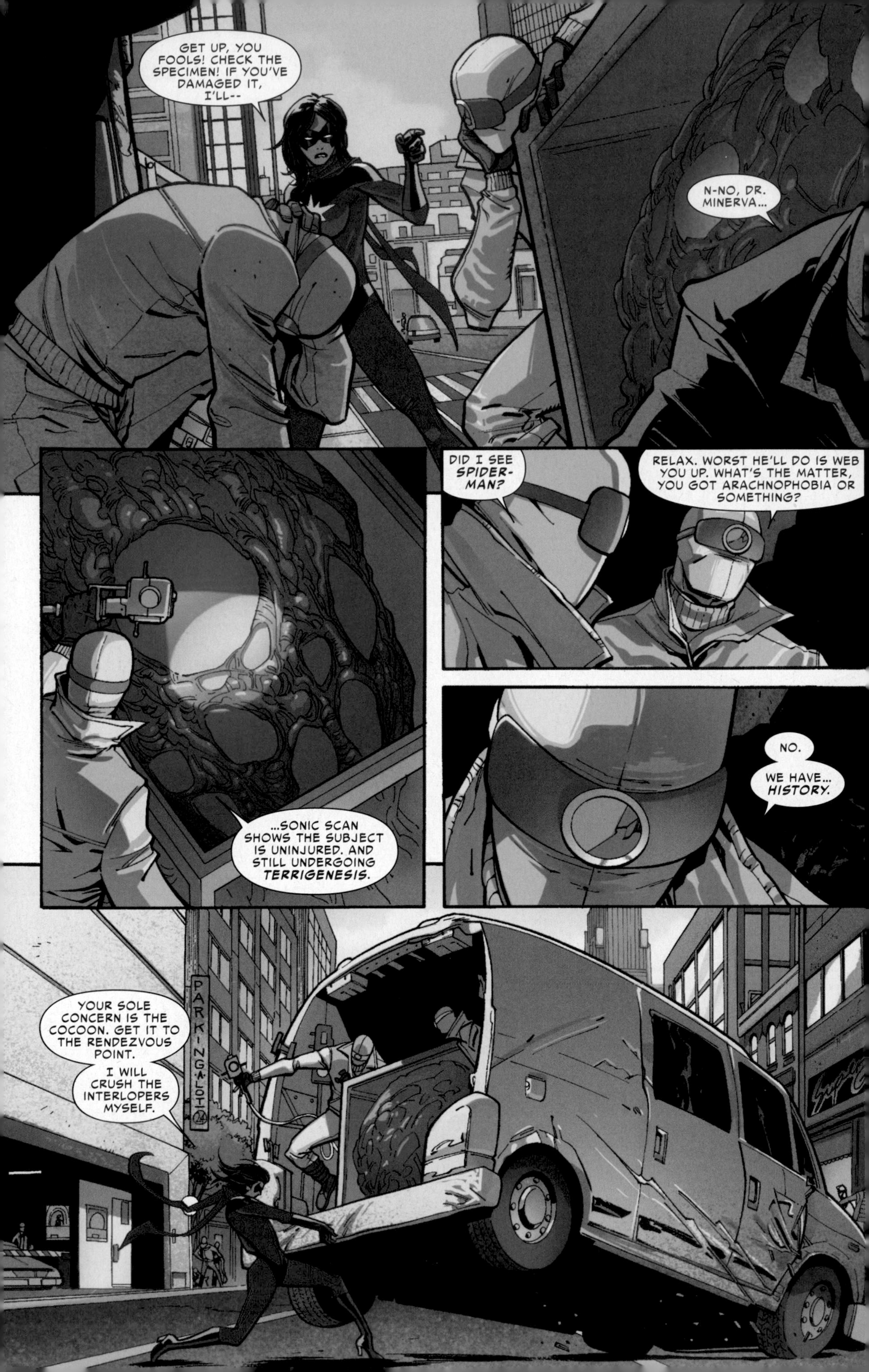
GET UP, YOU FOOLS! CHECK THE SPECIMEN! IF YOU'VE DAMAGED IT, I'LL--
N-NO, DR. MINERVA...
...SONIC SCAN SHOWS THE SUBJECT IS UNINJURED. AND STILL UNDERGOING TERRIGENESIS.
DID I SEE SPIDER-MAN?
RELAX. WORST HE'LL DO IS WEB YOU UP. WHAT'S THE MATTER, YOU GOT ARACHNOPHOBIA OR SOMETHING?
NO.
WE HAVE... HISTORY.
YOUR SOLE CONCERN IS THE COCOON. GET IT TO THE RENDEZVOUS POINT.
I WILL CRUSH THE INTERLOPERS MYSELF.
PARKING LOT

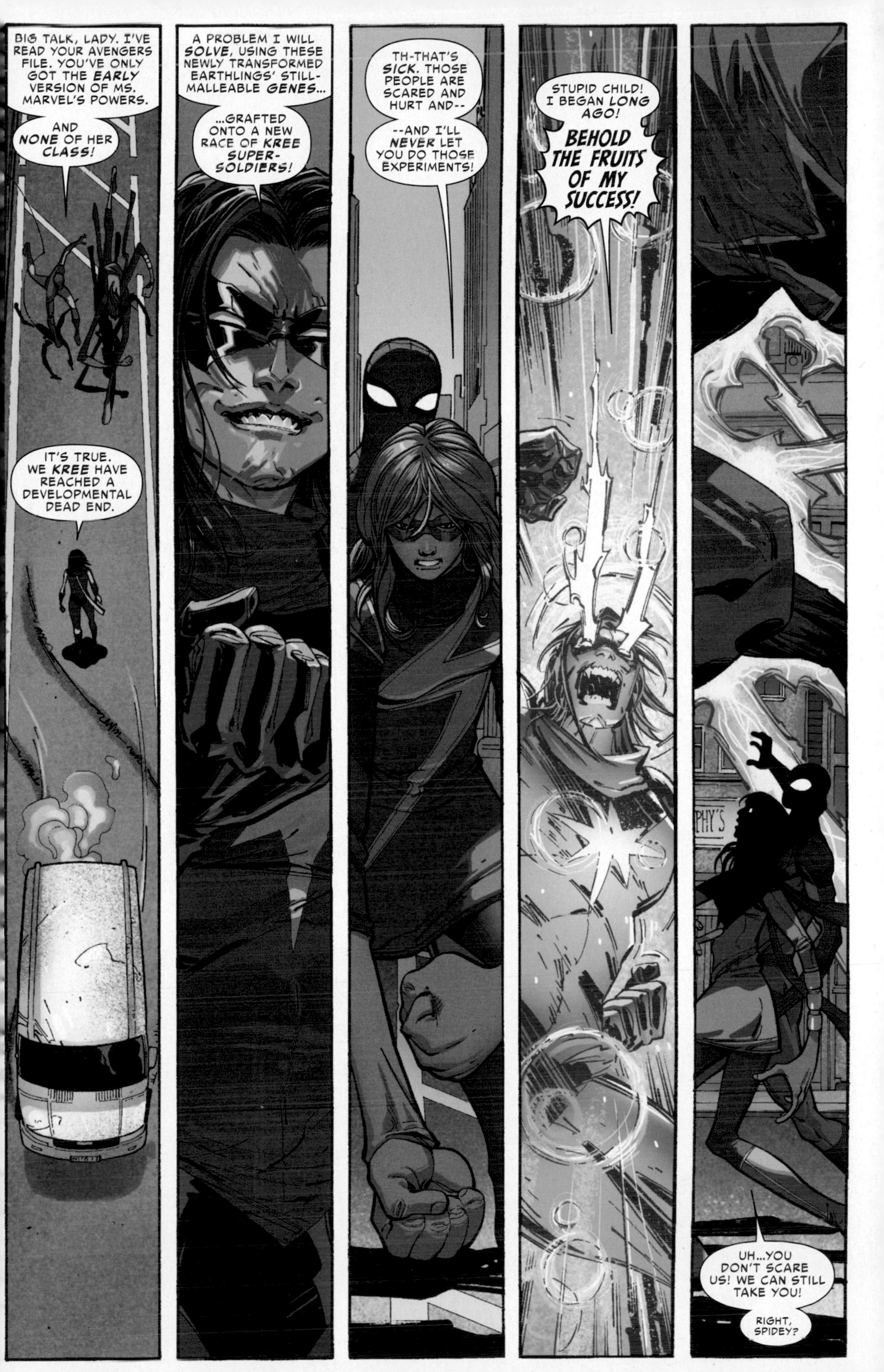

BIG TALK, LADY. I'VE READ YOUR AVENGERS FILE. YOU'VE ONLY GOT THE EARLY VERSION OF MS. MARVEL'S POWERS.
AND NONE OF HER CLASS!
IT'S TRUE. WE KREE HAVE REACHED A DEVELOPMENTAL DEAD END.
A PROBLEM I WILL SOLVE, USING THESE NEWLY TRANSFORMED EARTHLINGS' STILL-MALLEABLE GENES...
...GRAFTED ONTO A NEW RACE OF KREE SUPER-SOLDIERS!
TH-THAT'S SICK. THOSE PEOPLE ARE SCARED AND HURT AND--
--AND I'LL NEVER LET YOU DO THOSE EXPERIMENTS!
STUPID CHILD! I BEGAN LONG AGO!
BEHOLD THE FRUITS OF MY SUCCESS!
UH...YOU DON'T SCARE US! WE CAN STILL TAKE YOU!
RIGHT, SPIDEY?

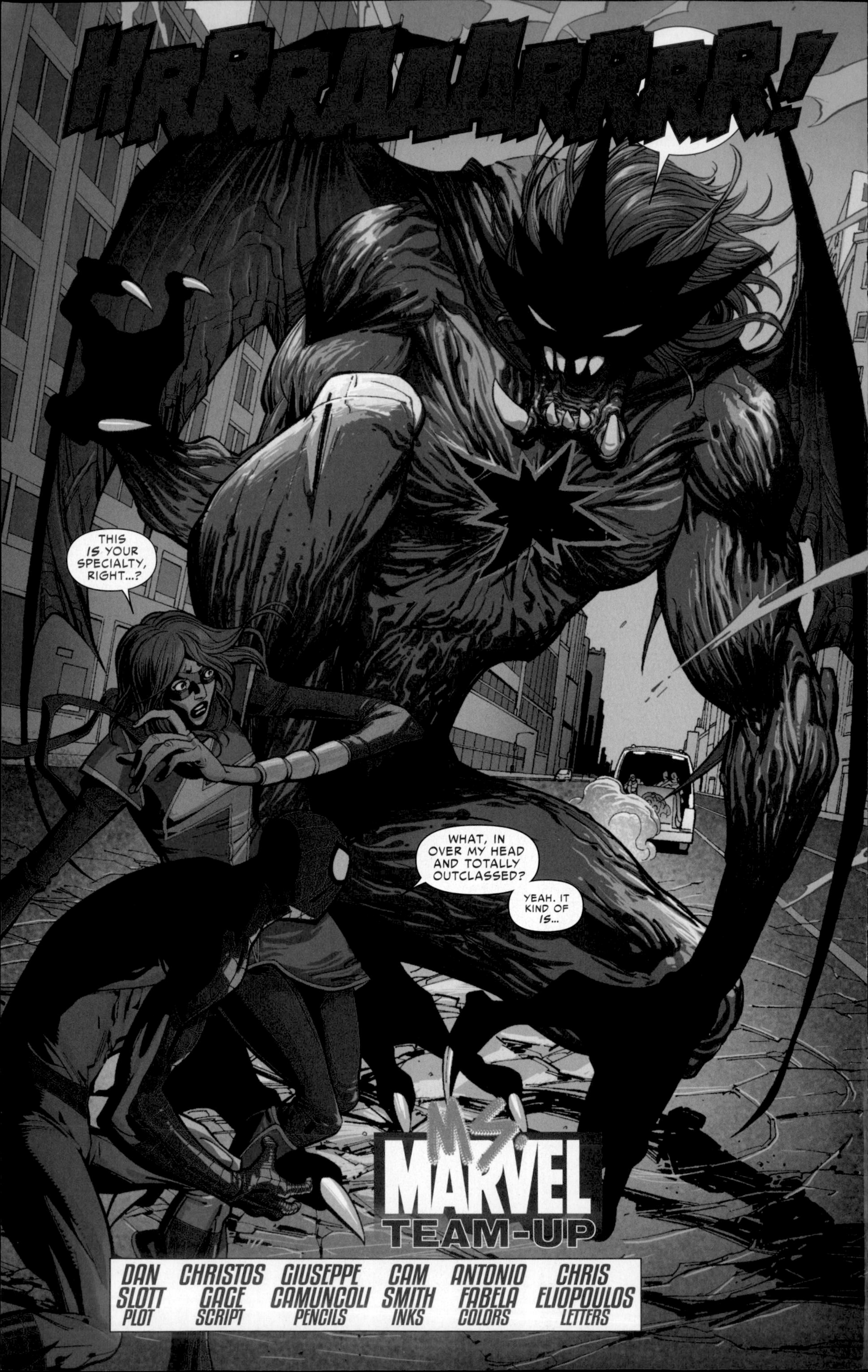
HRRAAARRRR!
THIS IS YOUR SPECIALTY, RIGHT...?
WHAT, IN OVER MY HEAD AND TOTALLY OUTCLASSED?
YEAH. IT KIND OF IS...
MS. MARVEL TEAM-UP
DAN SLOTT PLOT
CHRISTOS GAGE SCRIPT
GIUSEPPE CAMUNCOLI PENCILS
CAM SMITH INKS
ANTONIO FABELA COLORS
CHRIS ELIOPOULOS LETTERS

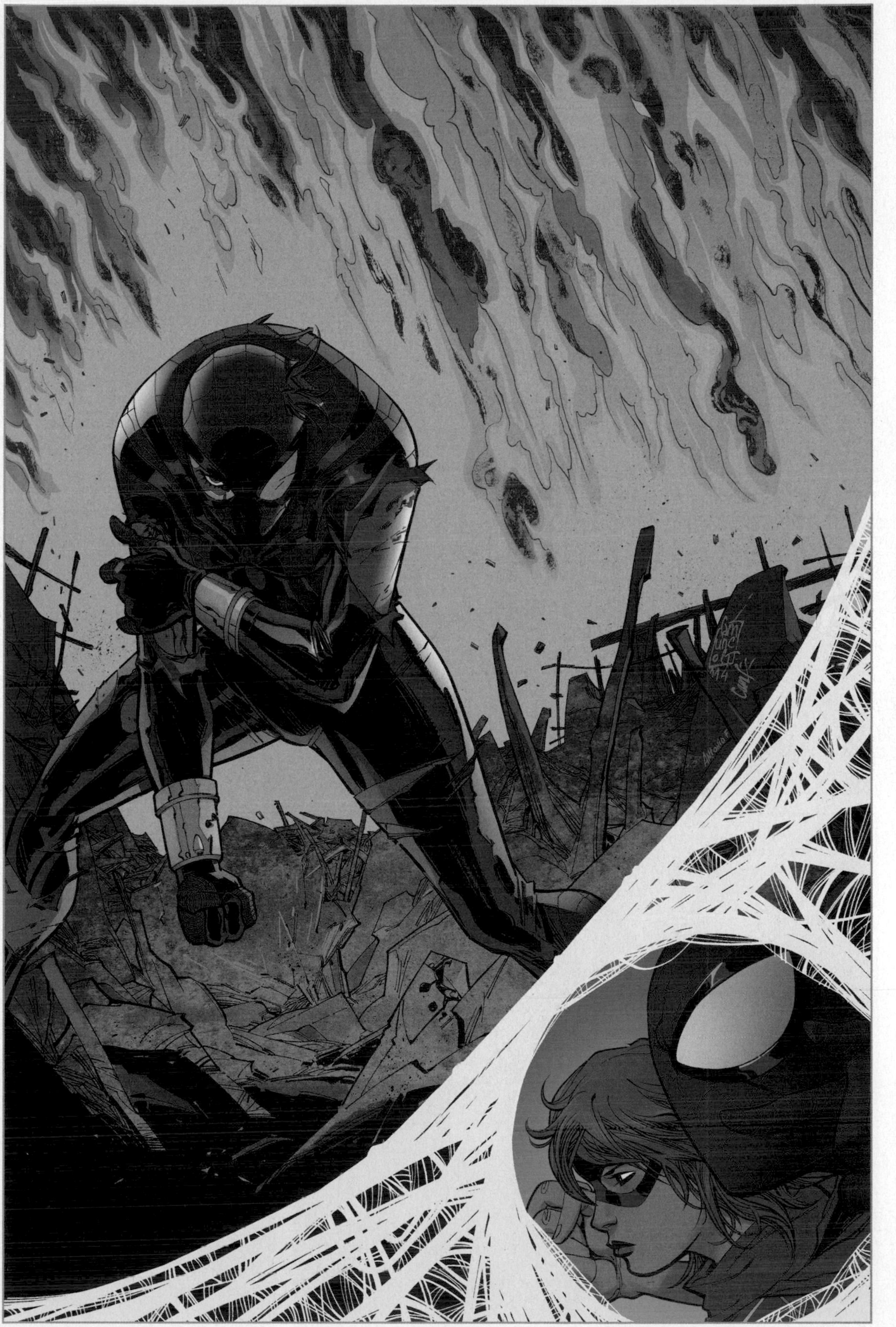

AMAZING SPIDER-MAN #8

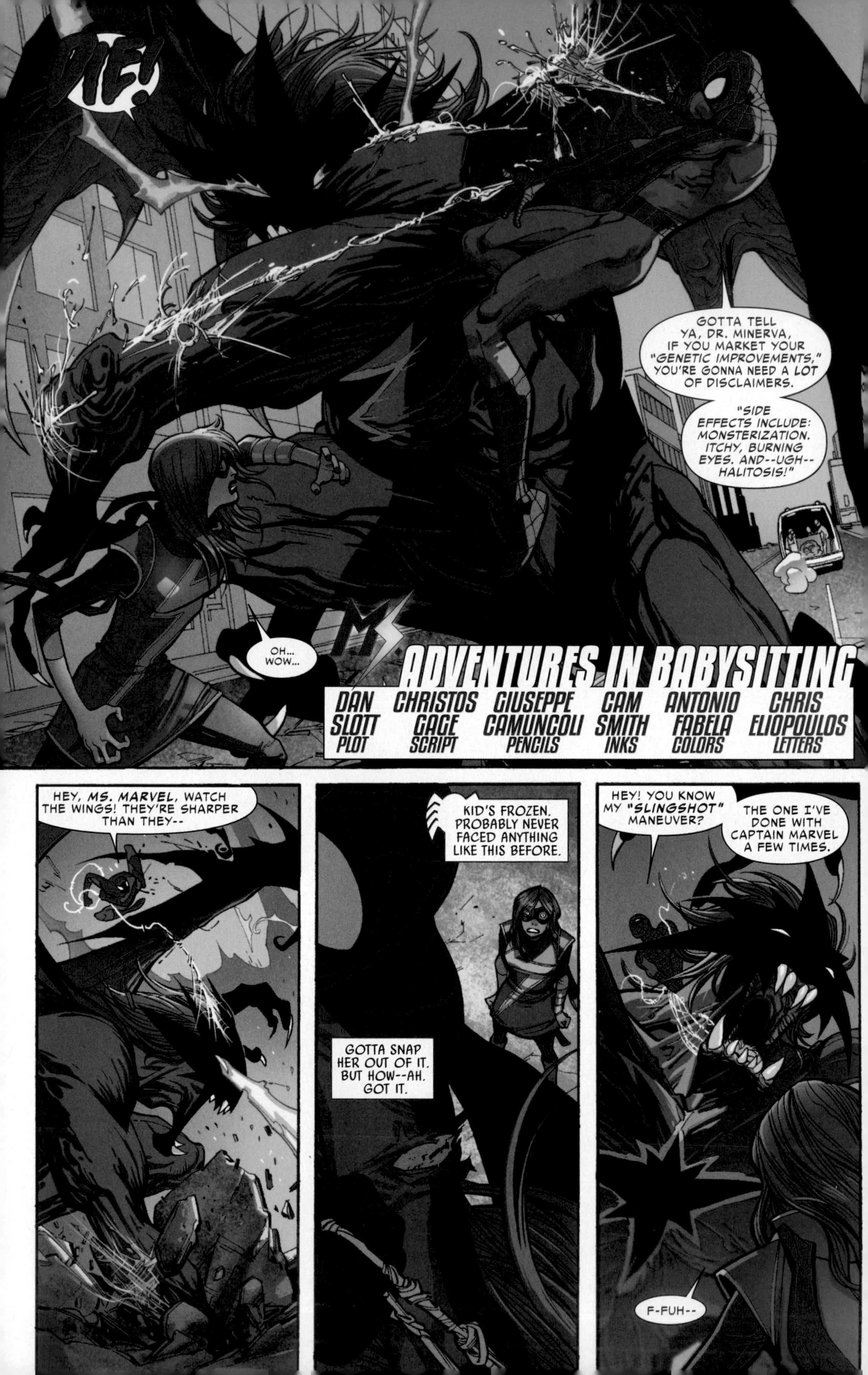
DIE!
GOTTA TELL YA, DR. MINERVA, IF YOU MARKET YOUR "GENETIC IMPROVEMENTS," YOU'RE GONNA NEED A LOT OF DISCLAIMERS.
"SIDE EFFECTS INCLUDE: MONSTERIZATION. ITCHY, BURNING EYES. AND--UGH--HALITOSIS!"
OH... WOW...
ADVENTURES IN BABYSITTING
DAN SLOTT PLOT
CHRISTOS GAGE SCRIPT
GIUSEPPE CAMUNCOLI PENCILS
CAM SMITH INKS
ANTONIO FABELA COLORS
CHRIS ELIOPOULOS LETTERS
HEY, MS. MARVEL, WATCH THE WINGS! THEY'RE SHARPER THAN THEY--
KID'S FROZEN. PROBABLY NEVER FACED ANYTHING LIKE THIS BEFORE.
GOTTA SNAP HER OUT OF IT. BUT HOW--AH. GOT IT.
HEY! YOU KNOW MY "SLINGSHOT" MANEUVER?
THE ONE I'VE DONE WITH CAPTAIN MARVEL A FEW TIMES.
F-FUH--

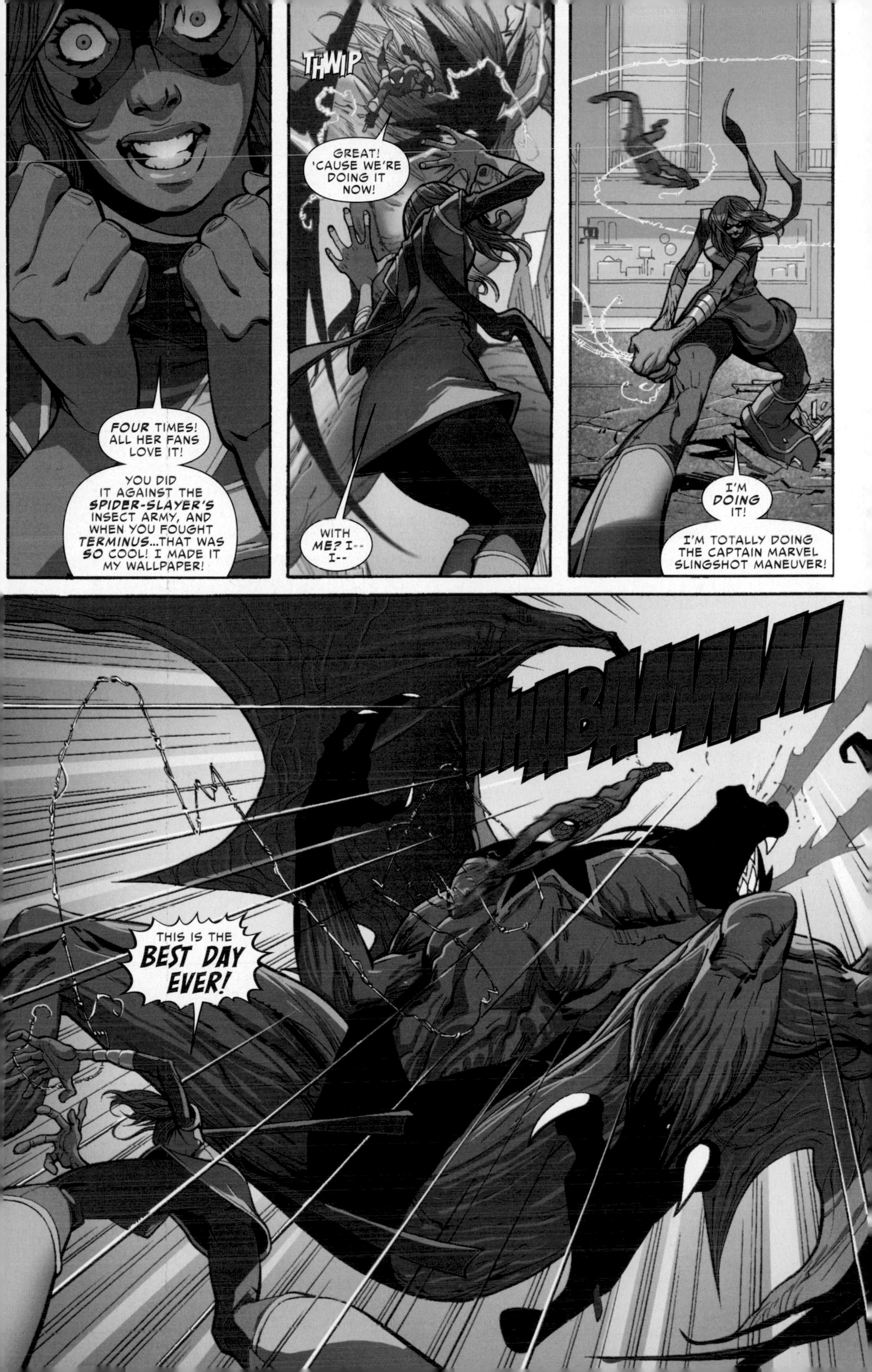
FOUR TIMES! ALL HER FANS LOVE IT!
YOU DID IT AGAINST THE SPIDER-SLAYER'S INSECT ARMY, AND WHEN YOU FOUGHT TERMINUS...THAT WAS SO COOL! I MADE IT MY WALLPAPER!
THWIP
GREAT! 'CAUSE WE'RE DOING IT NOW!
WITH ME? I-- I--
I'M DOING IT!
I'M TOTALLY DOING THE CAPTAIN MARVEL SLINGSHOT MANEUVER!
WHABAMMMM
THIS IS THE BEST DAY EVER!

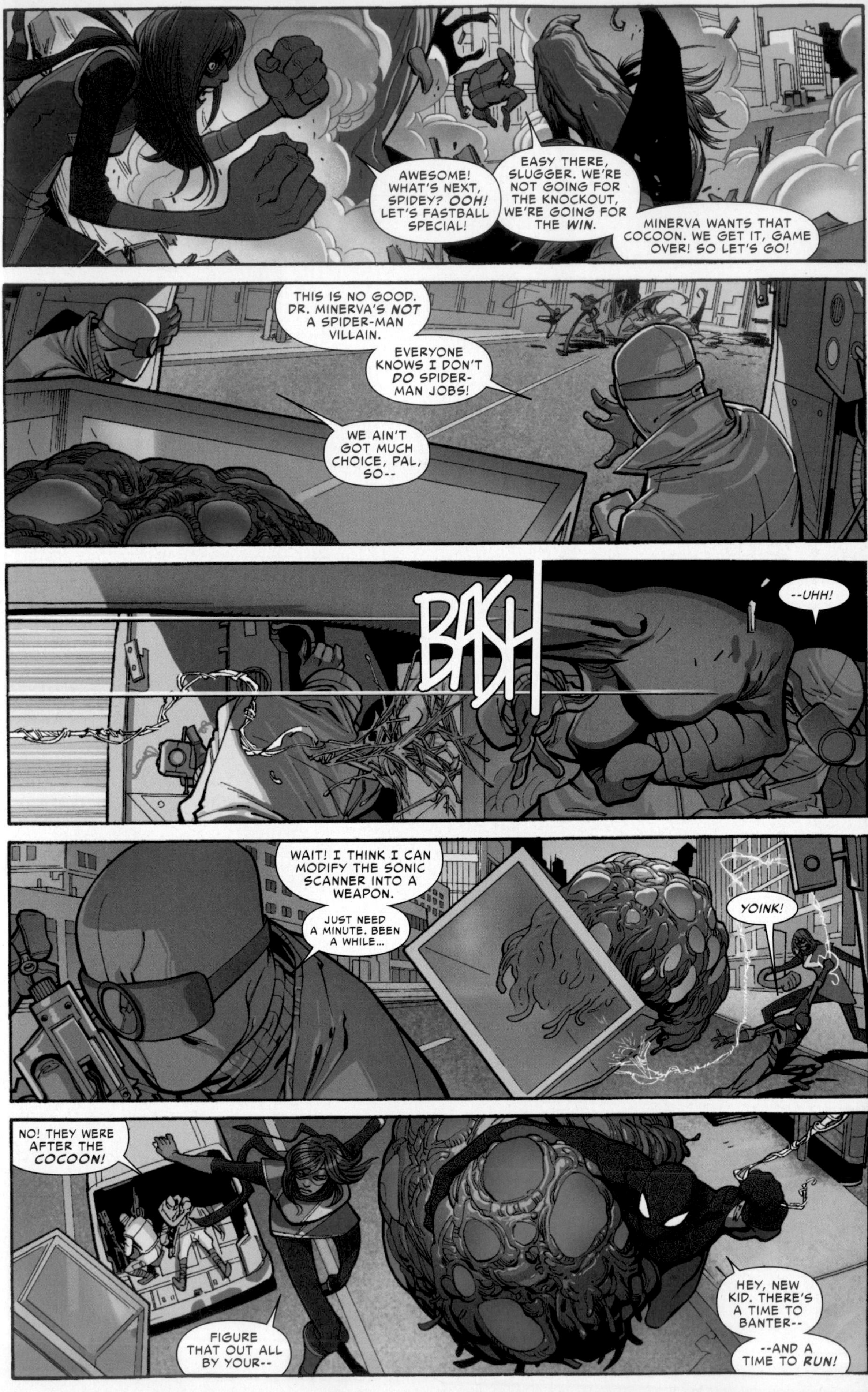
AWESOME! WHAT'S NEXT, SPIDEY? OOH! LET'S FASTBALL SPECIAL!
EASY THERE, SLUGGER. WE'RE NOT GOING FOR THE KNOCKOUT, WE'RE GOING FOR THE WIN.
MINERVA WANTS THAT COCOON. WE GET IT, GAME OVER! SO LET'S GO!
THIS IS NO GOOD. DR. MINERVA'S NOT A SPIDER-MAN VILLAIN.
EVERYONE KNOWS I DON'T DO SPIDER-MAN JOBS!
WE AIN'T GOT MUCH CHOICE, PAL, SO--
BASH
--UHH!
WAIT! I THINK I CAN MODIFY THE SONIC SCANNER INTO A WEAPON.
JUST NEED A MINUTE. BEEN A WHILE...
YOINK!
NO! THEY WERE AFTER THE COCOON!
FIGURE THAT OUT ALL BY YOUR--
HEY, NEW KID. THERE'S A TIME TO BANTER--
--AND A TIME TO RUN!

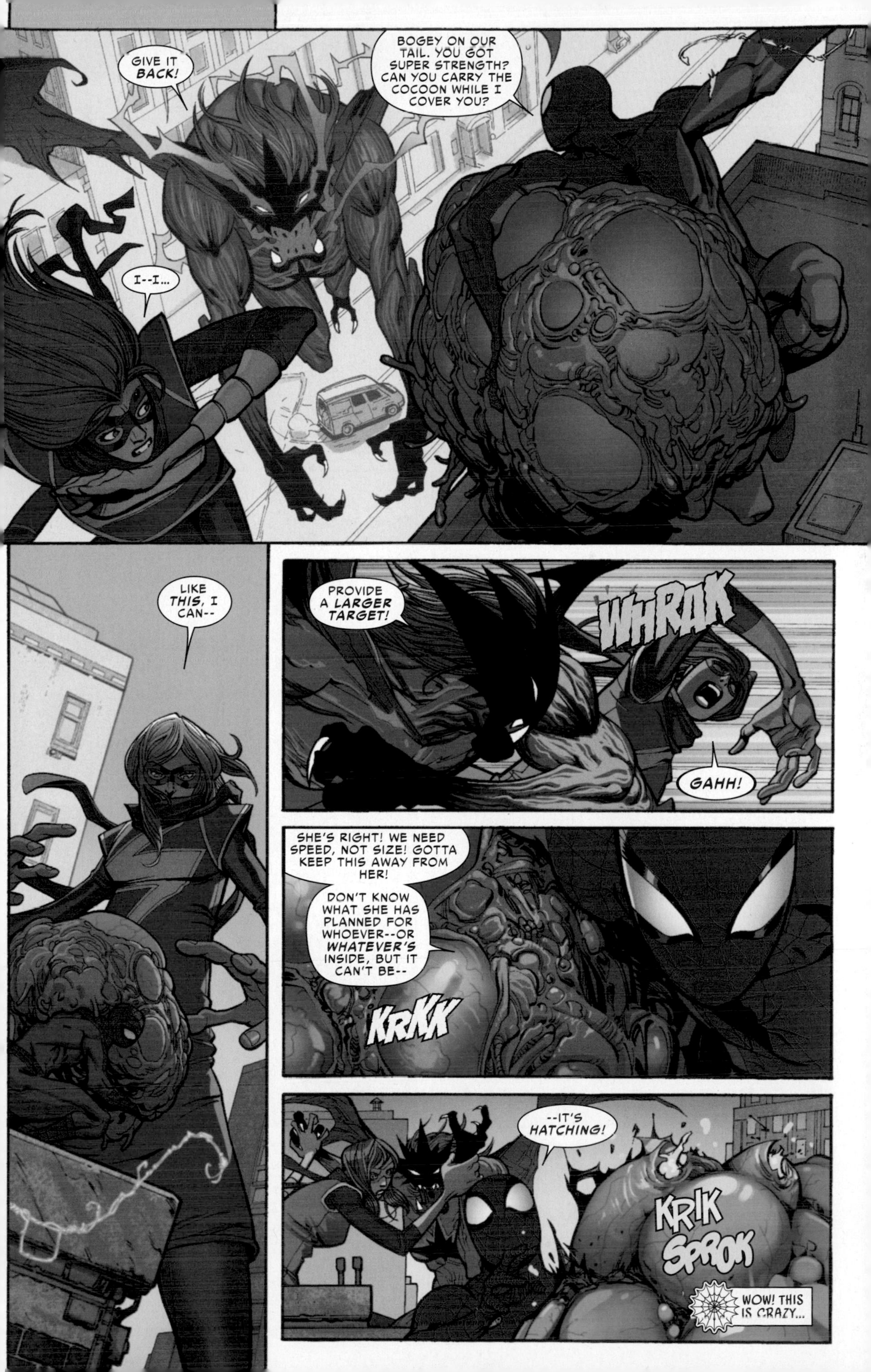
GIVE IT BACK!
BOGEY ON OUR TAIL. YOU GOT SUPER STRENGTH? CAN YOU CARRY THE COCOON WHILE I COVER YOU?
I--I...
LIKE THIS, I CAN--
PROVIDE A LARGER TARGET!
WHRAK
GAHH!
SHE'S RIGHT! WE NEED SPEED, NOT SIZE! GOTTA KEEP THIS AWAY FROM HER!
DON'T KNOW WHAT SHE HAS PLANNED FOR WHOEVER--OR WHATEVER'S INSIDE, BUT IT CAN'T BE--
KRKK
--IT'S HATCHING!
KRIK
SPROK
WOW! THIS IS CRAZY...

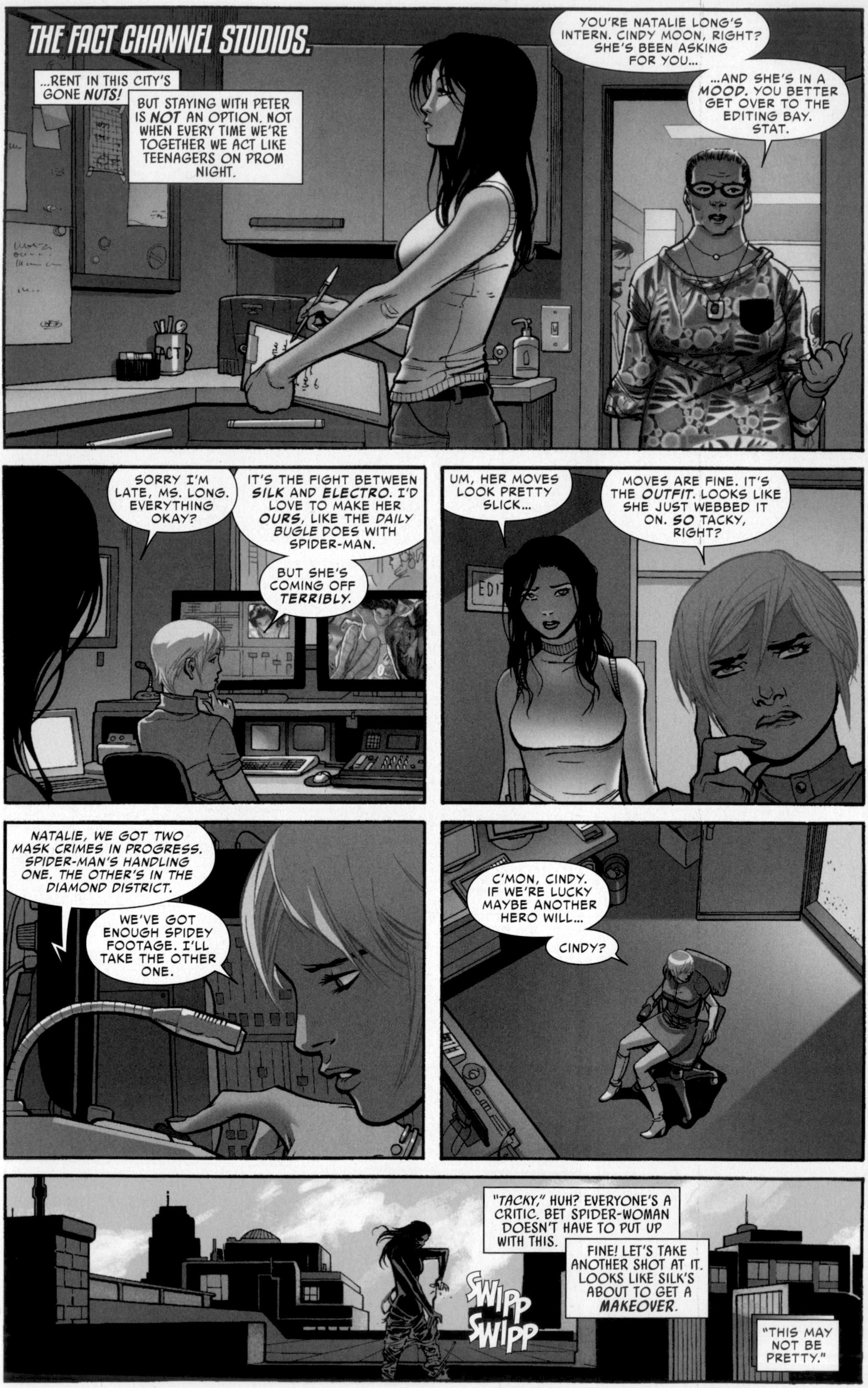
THE FACT CHANNEL STUDIOS.
...RENT IN THIS CITY'S GONE NUTS!
BUT STAYING WITH PETER IS NOT AN OPTION. NOT WHEN EVERY TIME WE'RE TOGETHER WE ACT LIKE TEENAGERS ON PROM NIGHT.
YOU'RE NATALIE LONG'S INTERN. CINDY MOON, RIGHT? SHE'S BEEN ASKING FOR YOU...
...AND SHE'S IN A MOOD. YOU BETTER GET OVER TO THE EDITING BAY. STAT.
SORRY I'M LATE, MS. LONG. EVERYTHING OKAY?
IT'S THE FIGHT BETWEEN SILK AND ELECTRO. I'D LOVE TO MAKE HER OURS, LIKE THE DAILY BUGLE DOES WITH SPIDER-MAN.
BUT SHE'S COMING OFF TERRIBLY.
UM, HER MOVES LOOK PRETTY SLICK...
MOVES ARE FINE. IT'S THE OUTFIT. LOOKS LIKE SHE JUST WEBBED IT ON. SO TACKY, RIGHT?
NATALIE, WE GOT TWO MASK CRIMES IN PROGRESS. SPIDER-MAN'S HANDLING ONE. THE OTHER'S IN THE DIAMOND DISTRICT.
WE'VE GOT ENOUGH SPIDEY FOOTAGE. I'LL TAKE THE OTHER ONE.
C'MON, CINDY. IF WE'RE LUCKY MAYBE ANOTHER HERO WILL...
CINDY?
"TACKY," HUH? EVERYONE'S A CRITIC. BET SPIDER-WOMAN DOESN'T HAVE TO PUT UP WITH THIS.
FINE! LET'S TAKE ANOTHER SHOT AT IT. LOOKS LIKE SILK'S ABOUT TO GET A MAKEOVER.
SWIPP
SWIPP
"THIS MAY NOT BE PRETTY."

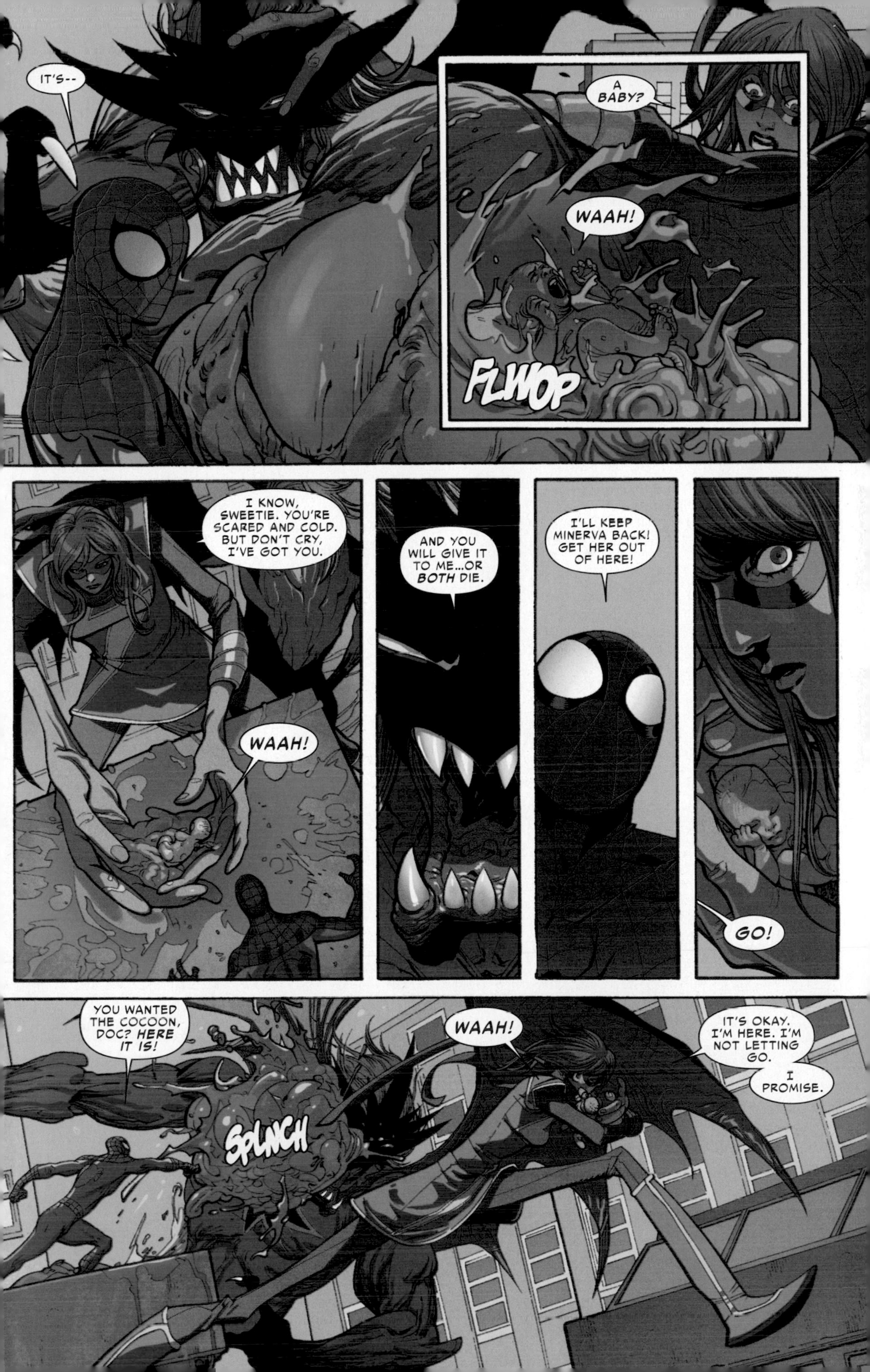
IT'S--
A BABY?
WAAH!
FLWOP
I KNOW, SWEETIE. YOU'RE SCARED AND COLD. BUT DON'T CRY, I'VE GOT YOU.
WAAH!
AND YOU WILL GIVE IT TO ME...OR BOTH DIE.
I'LL KEEP MINERVA BACK! GET HER OUT OF HERE!
GO!
YOU WANTED THE COCOON, DOC? HERE IT IS!
SPLNCH
WAAH!
IT'S OKAY. I'M HERE. I'M NOT LETTING GO.
I PROMISE.

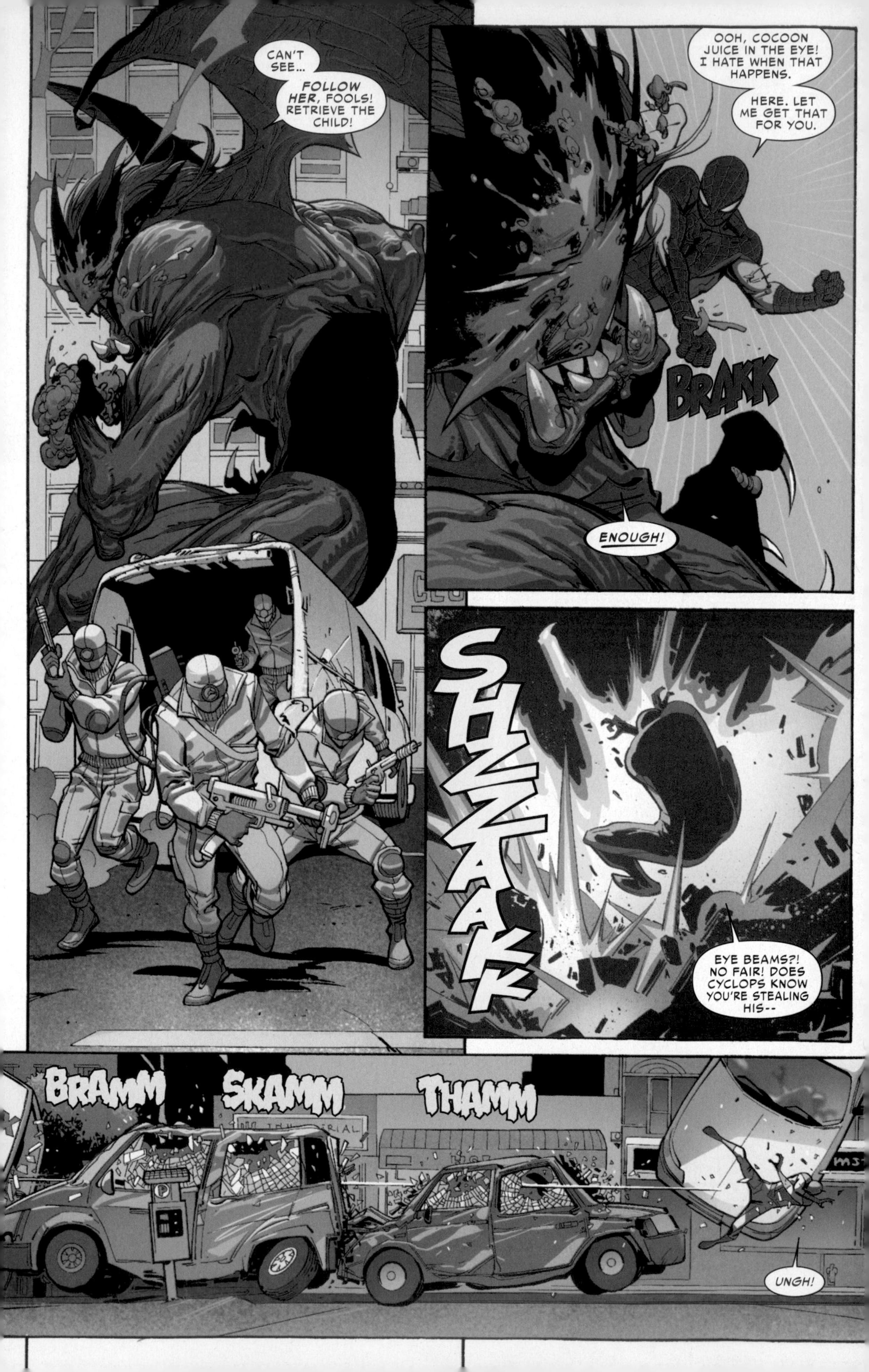
CAN'T SEE... FOLLOW HER, FOOLS! RETRIEVE THE CHILD!
OOH, COCOON JUICE IN THE EYE! I HATE WHEN THAT HAPPENS.
HERE. LET ME GET THAT FOR YOU.
BRAKK
ENOUGH!
SHZZAAKK
EYE BEAMS?! NO FAIR! DOES CYCLOPS KNOW YOU'RE STEALING HIS--
BRAMM
SKAMM
THAMM
UNGH!

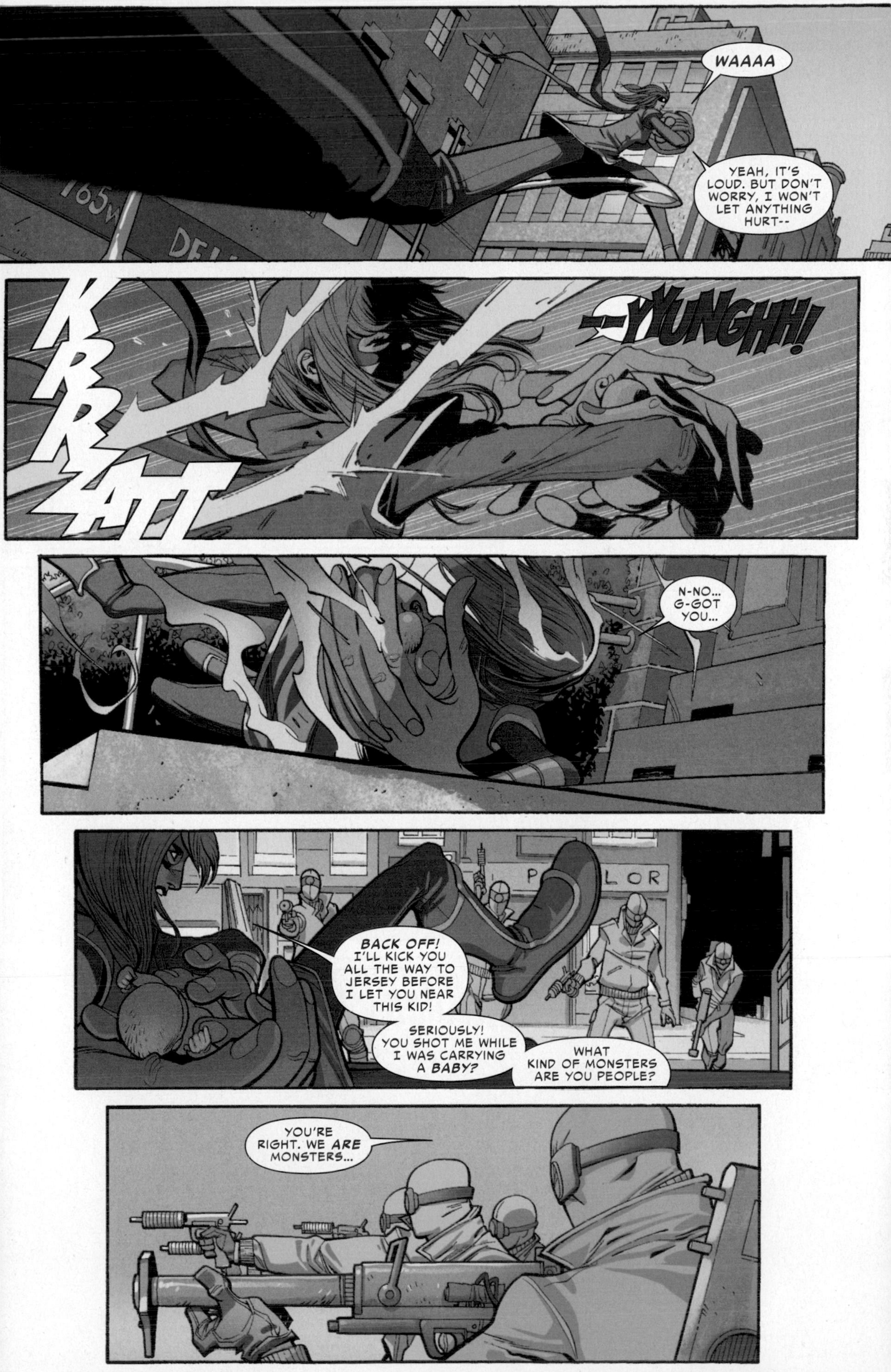

WAAAA
YEAH, IT'S LOUD. BUT DON'T WORRY, I WON'T LET ANYTHING HURT--
KRRZATT
--YYUNGHH!
N-NO... G-GOT YOU...
PARLOR
BACK OFF! I'LL KICK YOU ALL THE WAY TO JERSEY BEFORE I LET YOU NEAR THIS KID!
SERIOUSLY! YOU SHOT ME WHILE I WAS CARRYING A BABY?
WHAT KIND OF MONSTERS ARE YOU PEOPLE?
YOU'RE RIGHT. WE ARE MONSTERS...

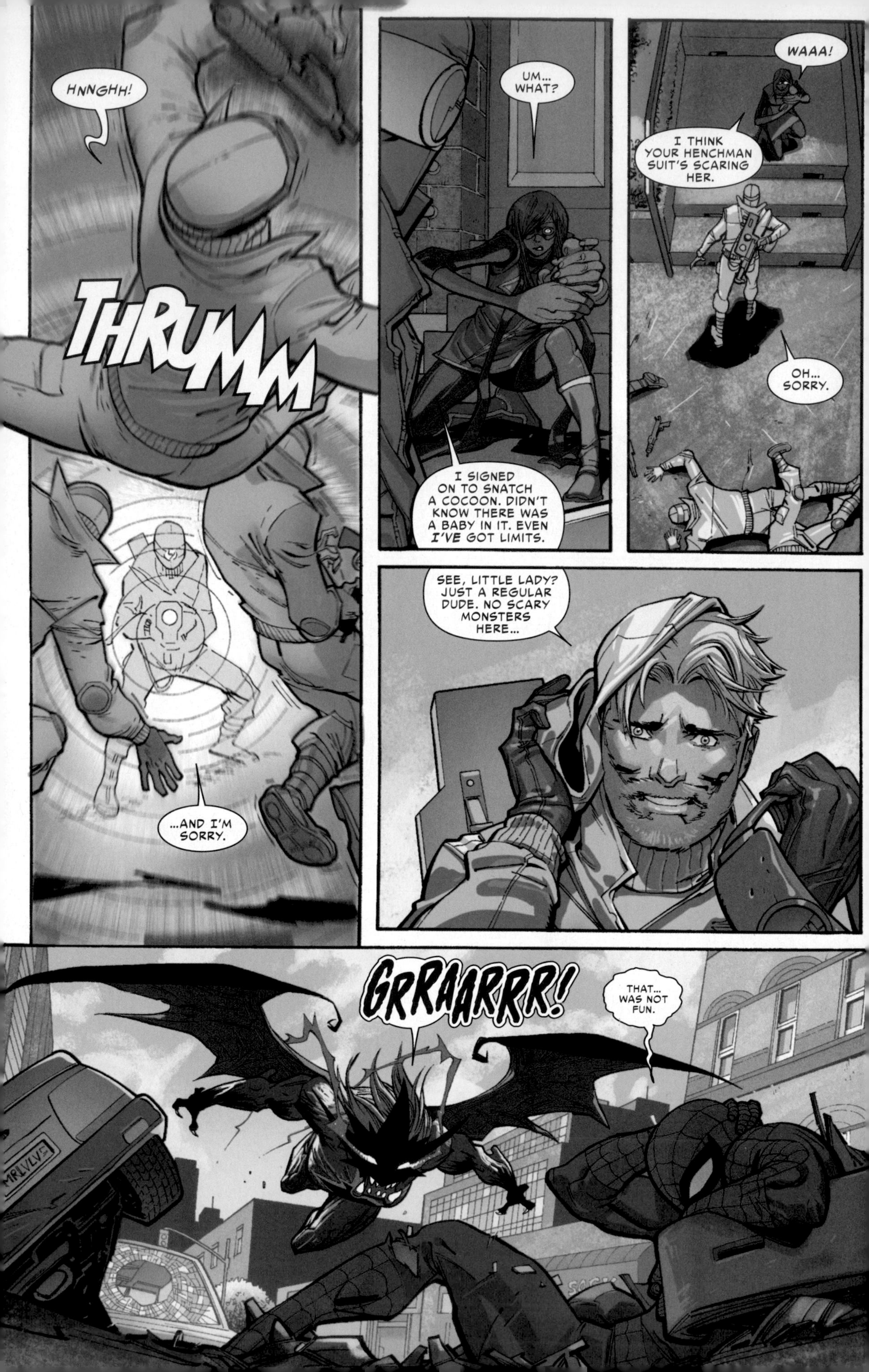
HNNGHH!
THRUMMM
...AND I'M SORRY.
UM... WHAT?
I SIGNED ON TO SNATCH A COCOON. DIDN'T KNOW THERE WAS A BABY IN IT. EVEN I'VE GOT LIMITS.
WAAA!
I THINK YOUR HENCHMAN SUIT'S SCARING HER.
OH... SORRY.
SEE, LITTLE LADY? JUST A REGULAR DUDE. NO SCARY MONSTERS HERE...
GRRAARRR!
THAT... WAS NOT FUN.
MRLVLVS

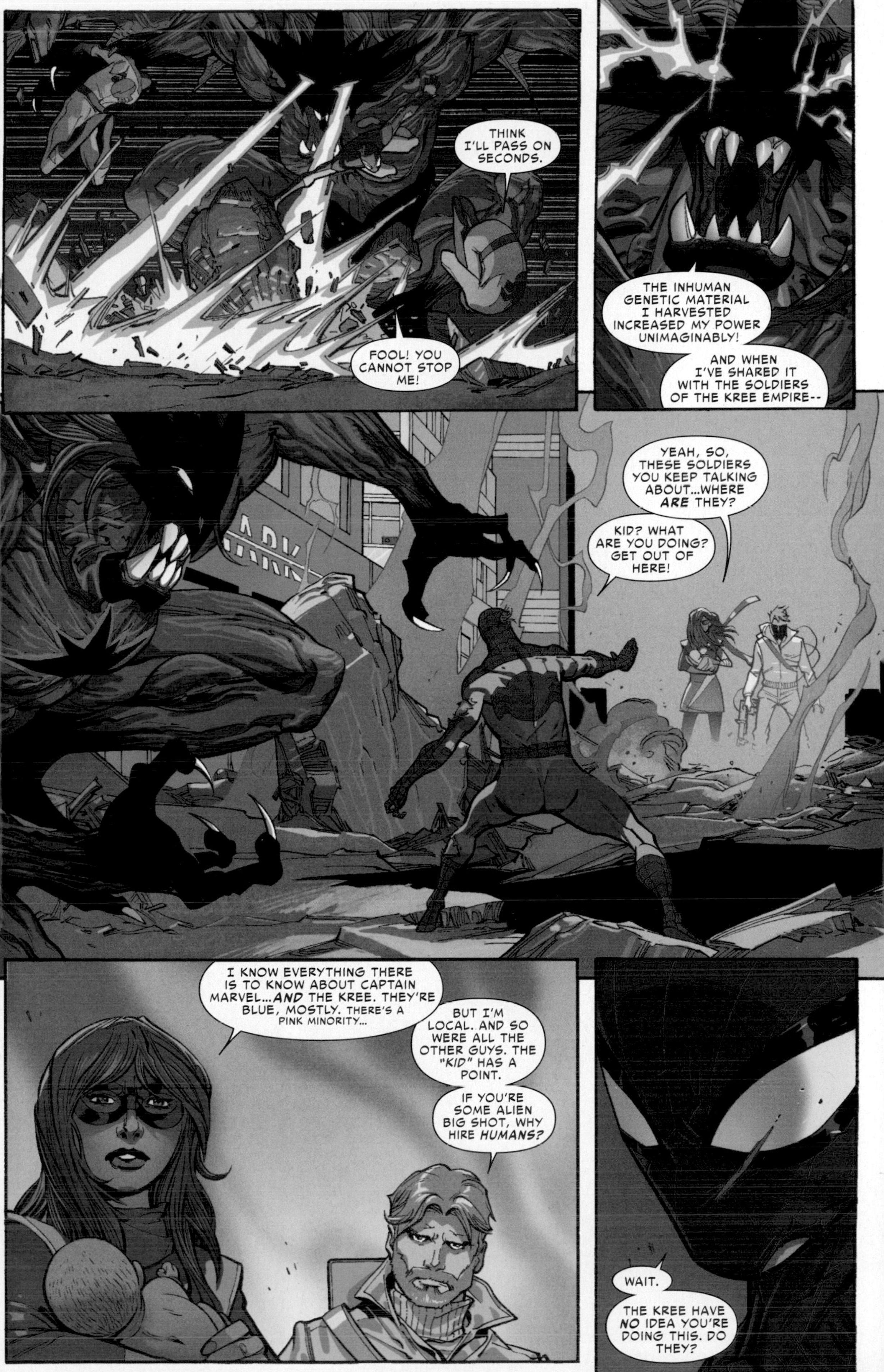
THINK I'LL PASS ON SECONDS.
FOOL! YOU CANNOT STOP ME!
THE INHUMAN GENETIC MATERIAL I HARVESTED INCREASED MY POWER UNIMAGINABLY!
AND WHEN I'VE SHARED IT WITH THE SOLDIERS OF THE KREE EMPIRE--
YEAH, SO, THESE SOLDIERS YOU KEEP TALKING ABOUT...WHERE *ARE* THEY?
KID? WHAT ARE YOU DOING? GET OUT OF HERE!
I KNOW EVERYTHING THERE IS TO KNOW ABOUT CAPTAIN MARVEL...*AND* THE KREE. THEY'RE BLUE, MOSTLY. THERE'S A PINK MINORITY...
BUT I'M LOCAL. AND SO WERE ALL THE OTHER GUYS. THE "*KID*" HAS A POINT.
IF YOU'RE SOME ALIEN BIG SHOT, WHY HIRE *HUMANS?*
WAIT.
THE KREE HAVE *NO* IDEA YOU'RE DOING THIS. DO THEY?

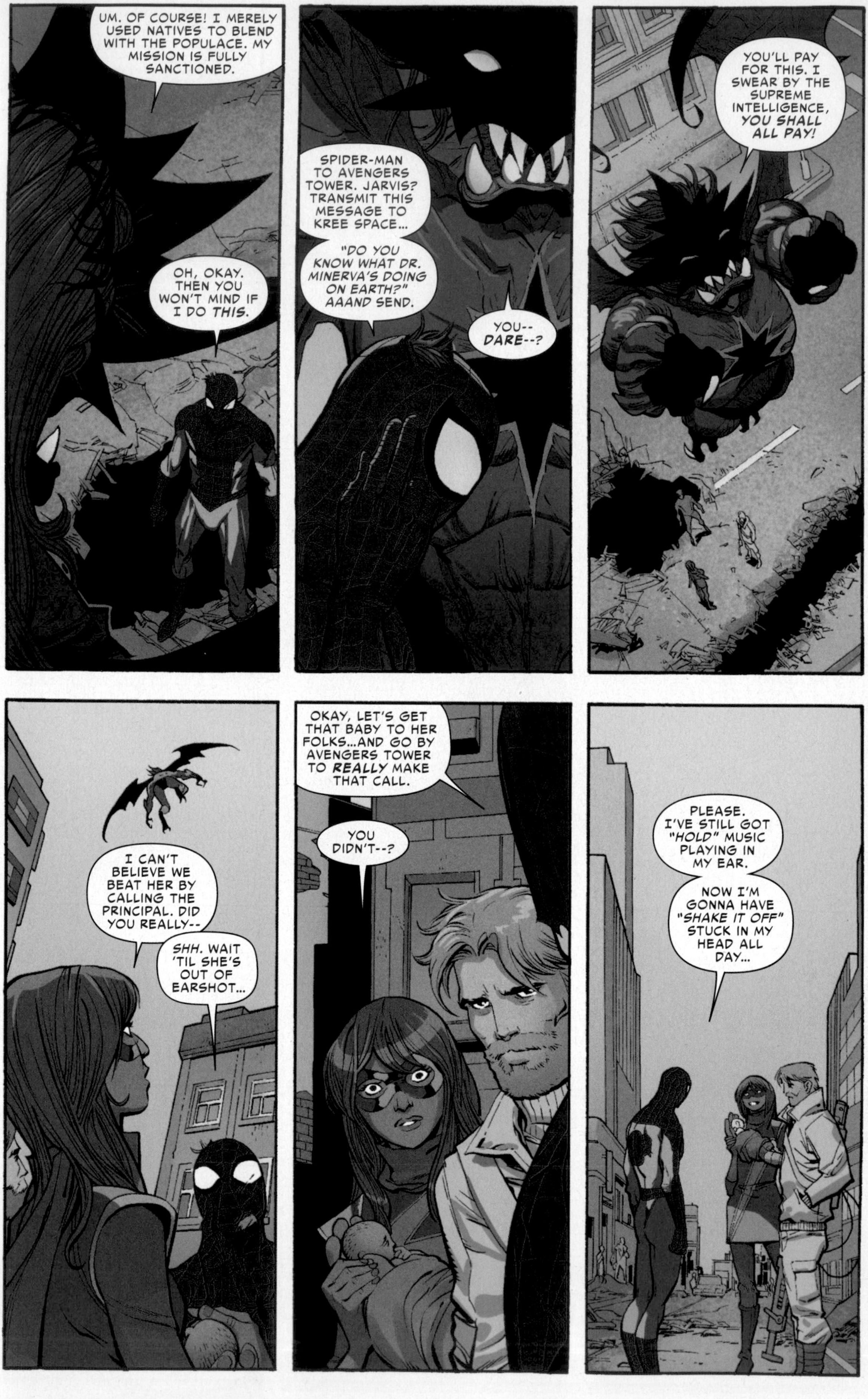

UM. OF COURSE! I MERELY USED NATIVES TO BLEND WITH THE POPULACE. MY MISSION IS FULLY SANCTIONED.
OH, OKAY. THEN YOU WON'T MIND IF I DO *THIS*.
SPIDER-MAN TO AVENGERS TOWER. JARVIS? TRANSMIT THIS MESSAGE TO KREE SPACE...
"DO YOU KNOW WHAT DR. MINERVA'S DOING ON EARTH?" AAAND SEND.
YOU-- *DARE*--?
YOU'LL PAY FOR THIS. I SWEAR BY THE SUPREME INTELLIGENCE, *YOU SHALL ALL PAY!*
I CAN'T BELIEVE WE BEAT HER BY CALLING THE PRINCIPAL. DID YOU REALLY--
SHH. WAIT 'TIL SHE'S OUT OF EARSHOT...
OKAY, LET'S GET THAT BABY TO HER FOLKS...AND GO BY AVENGERS TOWER TO *REALLY* MAKE THAT CALL.
YOU DIDN'T--?
PLEASE. I'VE STILL GOT "*HOLD*" MUSIC PLAYING IN MY EAR.
NOW I'M GONNA HAVE "*SHAKE IT OFF*" STUCK IN MY HEAD ALL DAY...

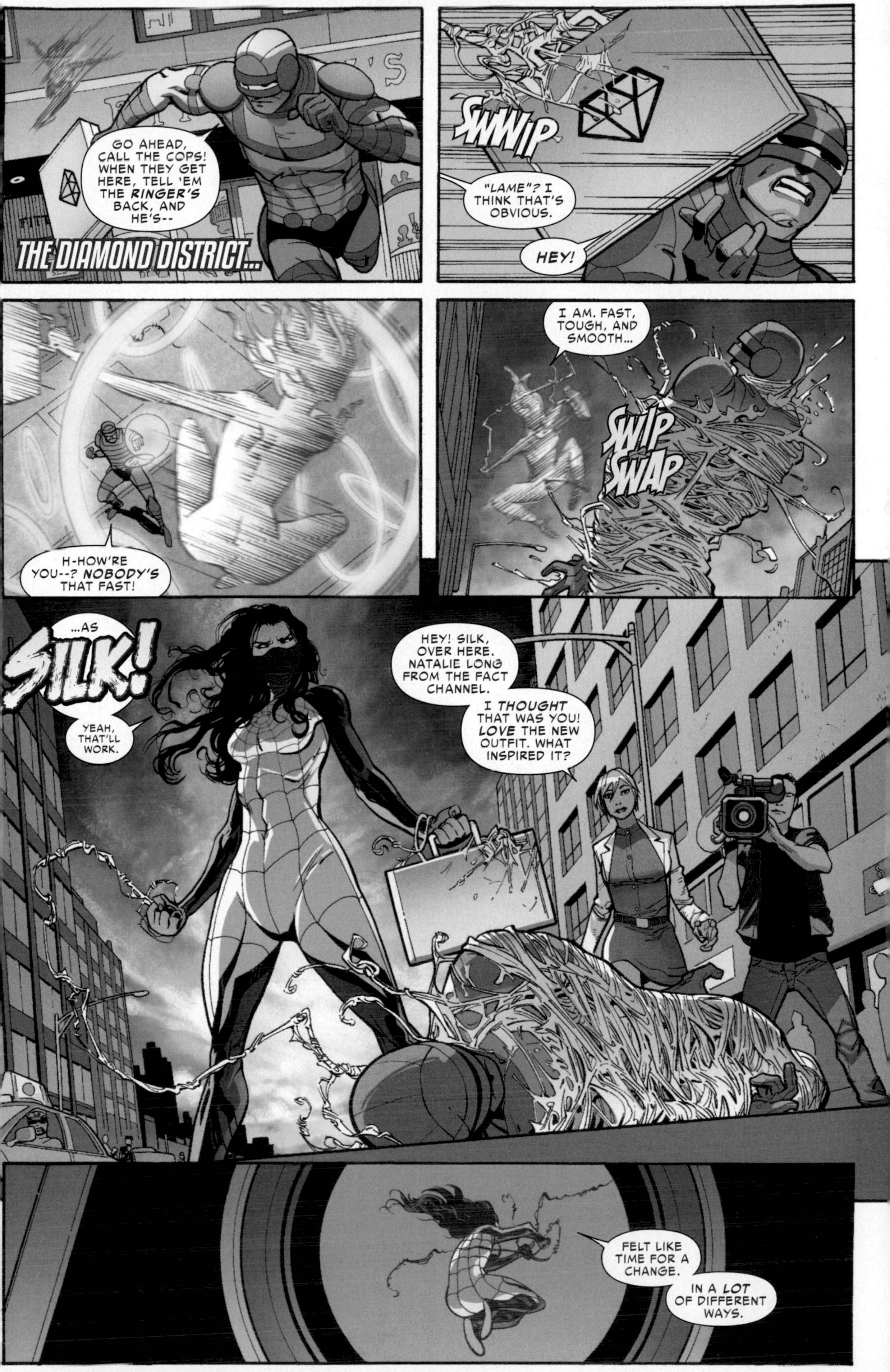

GO AHEAD, CALL THE COPS! WHEN THEY GET HERE, TELL 'EM THE RINGER'S BACK, AND HE'S--
THE DIAMOND DISTRICT...
SWWIP
"LAME"? I THINK THAT'S OBVIOUS.
HEY!
H-HOW'RE YOU--? NOBODY'S THAT FAST!
I AM. FAST, TOUGH, AND SMOOTH...
SWIP SWAP
...AS SILK!
YEAH, THAT'LL WORK.
HEY! SILK, OVER HERE. NATALIE LONG FROM THE FACT CHANNEL.
I THOUGHT THAT WAS YOU! LOVE THE NEW OUTFIT. WHAT INSPIRED IT?
FELT LIKE TIME FOR A CHANGE.
IN A LOT OF DIFFERENT WAYS.

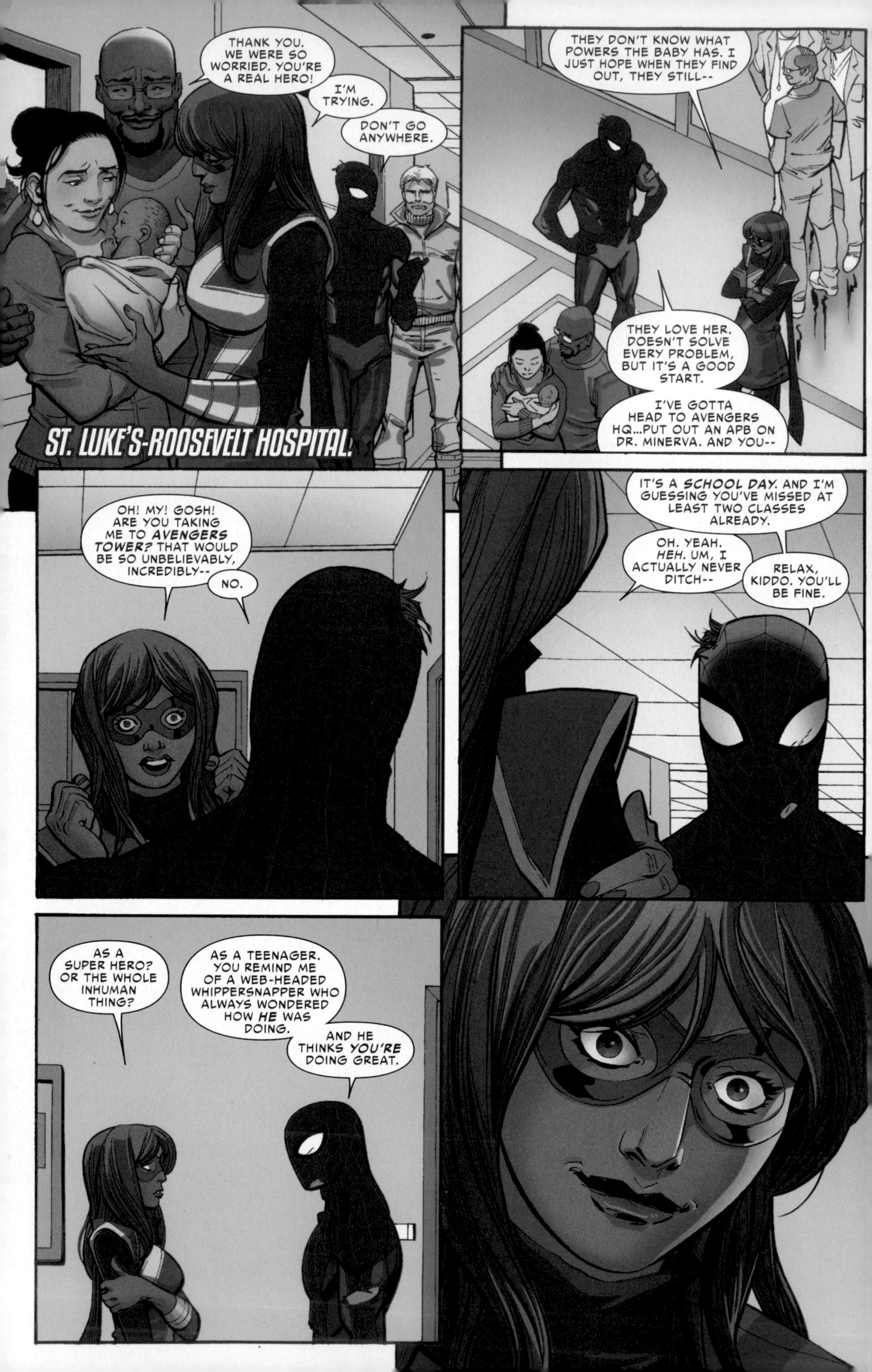
THANK YOU. WE WERE SO WORRIED. YOU'RE A REAL HERO!
I'M TRYING.
DON'T GO ANYWHERE.
ST. LUKE'S-ROOSEVELT HOSPITAL.
THEY DON'T KNOW WHAT POWERS THE BABY HAS. I JUST HOPE WHEN THEY FIND OUT, THEY STILL--
THEY LOVE HER. DOESN'T SOLVE EVERY PROBLEM, BUT IT'S A GOOD START.
I'VE GOTTA HEAD TO AVENGERS HQ...PUT OUT AN APB ON DR. MINERVA. AND YOU--
OH! MY! GOSH! ARE YOU TAKING ME TO AVENGERS TOWER? THAT WOULD BE SO UNBELIEVABLY, INCREDIBLY--
NO.
IT'S A SCHOOL DAY. AND I'M GUESSING YOU'VE MISSED AT LEAST TWO CLASSES ALREADY.
OH. YEAH. HEH. UM, I ACTUALLY NEVER DITCH--
RELAX, KIDDO. YOU'LL BE FINE.
AS A SUPER HERO? OR THE WHOLE INHUMAN THING?
AS A TEENAGER. YOU REMIND ME OF A WEB-HEADED WHIPPERSNAPPER WHO ALWAYS WONDERED HOW HE WAS DOING.
AND HE THINKS YOU'RE DOING GREAT.

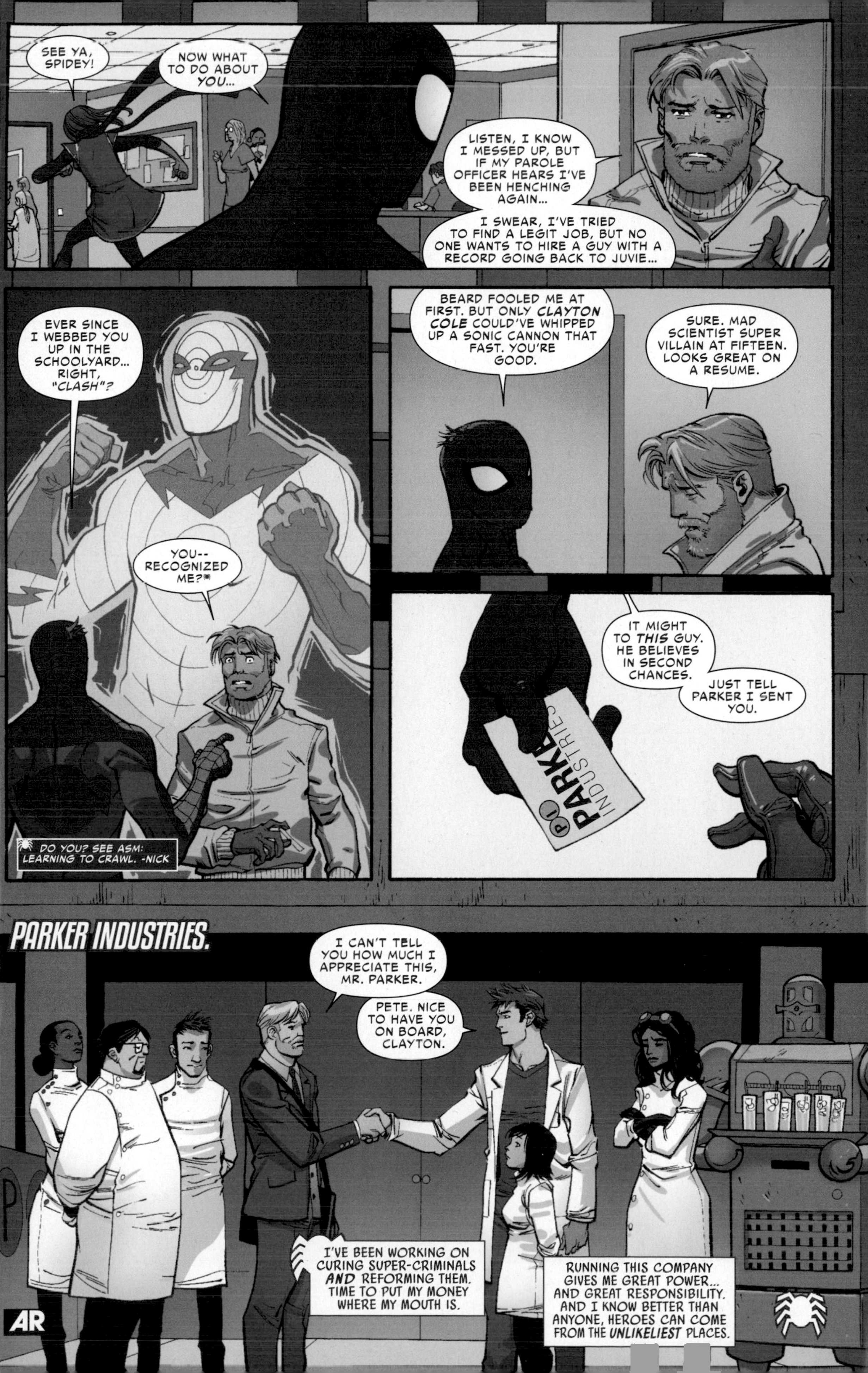
SEE YA, SPIDEY!
NOW WHAT TO DO ABOUT YOU...
LISTEN, I KNOW I MESSED UP, BUT IF MY PAROLE OFFICER HEARS I'VE BEEN HENCHING AGAIN...
I SWEAR, I'VE TRIED TO FIND A LEGIT JOB, BUT NO ONE WANTS TO HIRE A GUY WITH A RECORD GOING BACK TO JUVIE...
EVER SINCE I WEBBED YOU UP IN THE SCHOOLYARD... RIGHT, "CLASH"?
YOU--RECOGNIZED ME?*
*DO YOU? SEE ASM: LEARNING TO CRAWL. -NICK
BEARD FOOLED ME AT FIRST. BUT ONLY CLAYTON COLE COULD'VE WHIPPED UP A SONIC CANNON THAT FAST. YOU'RE GOOD.
SURE. MAD SCIENTIST SUPER VILLAIN AT FIFTEEN. LOOKS GREAT ON A RESUME.
IT MIGHT TO THIS GUY. HE BELIEVES IN SECOND CHANCES.
JUST TELL PARKER I SENT YOU.
PARKER INDUSTRIES
PARKER INDUSTRIES.
I CAN'T TELL YOU HOW MUCH I APPRECIATE THIS, MR. PARKER.
PETE. NICE TO HAVE YOU ON BOARD, CLAYTON.
I'VE BEEN WORKING ON CURING SUPER-CRIMINALS AND REFORMING THEM. TIME TO PUT MY MONEY WHERE MY MOUTH IS.
RUNNING THIS COMPANY GIVES ME GREAT POWER... AND GREAT RESPONSIBILITY. AND I KNOW BETTER THAN ANYONE, HEROES CAN COME FROM THE UNLIKELIEST PLACES.
AR

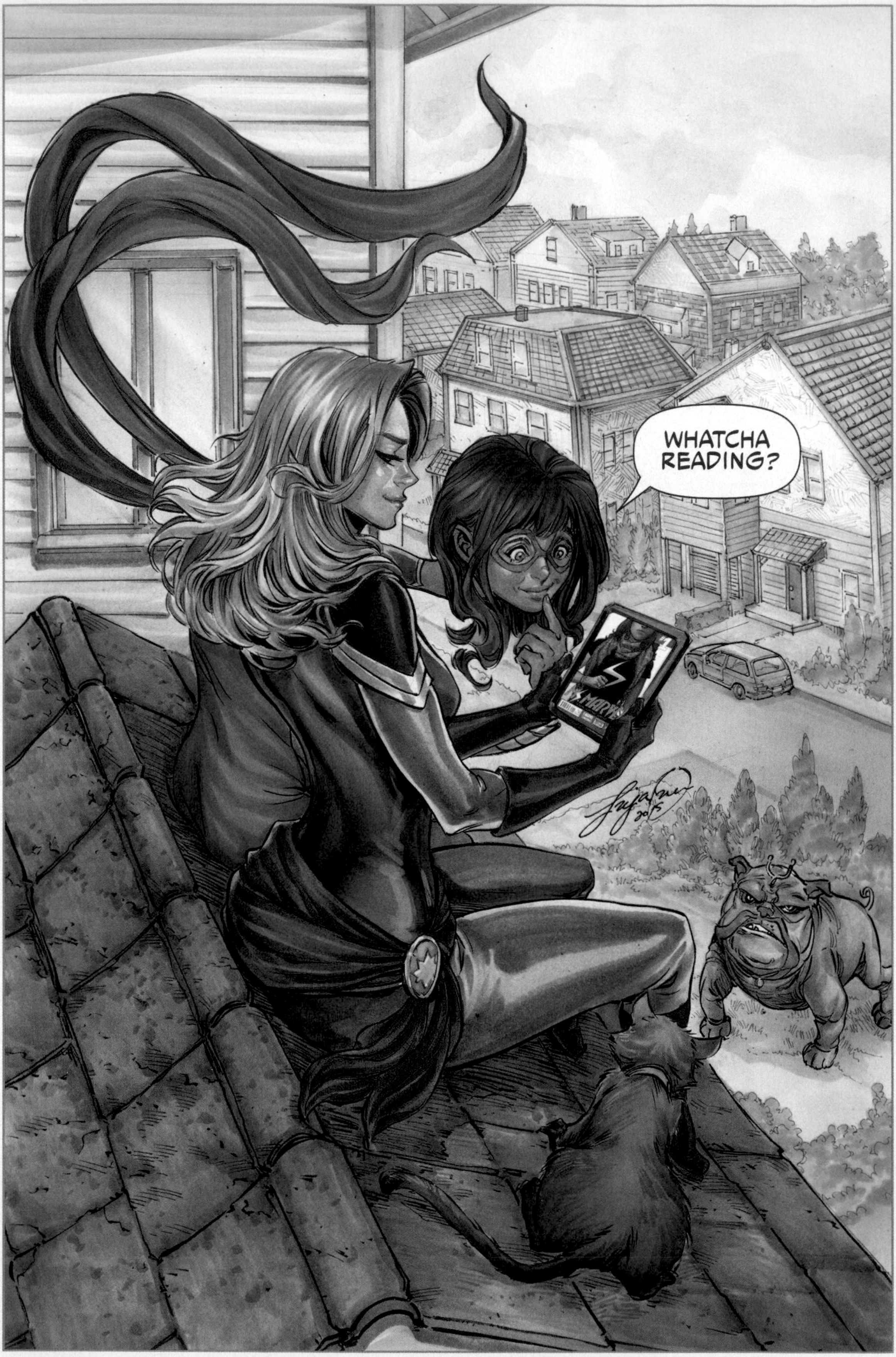
WHATCHA READING?

MS. MARVEL #17 VARIANT
BY SIYA OUM

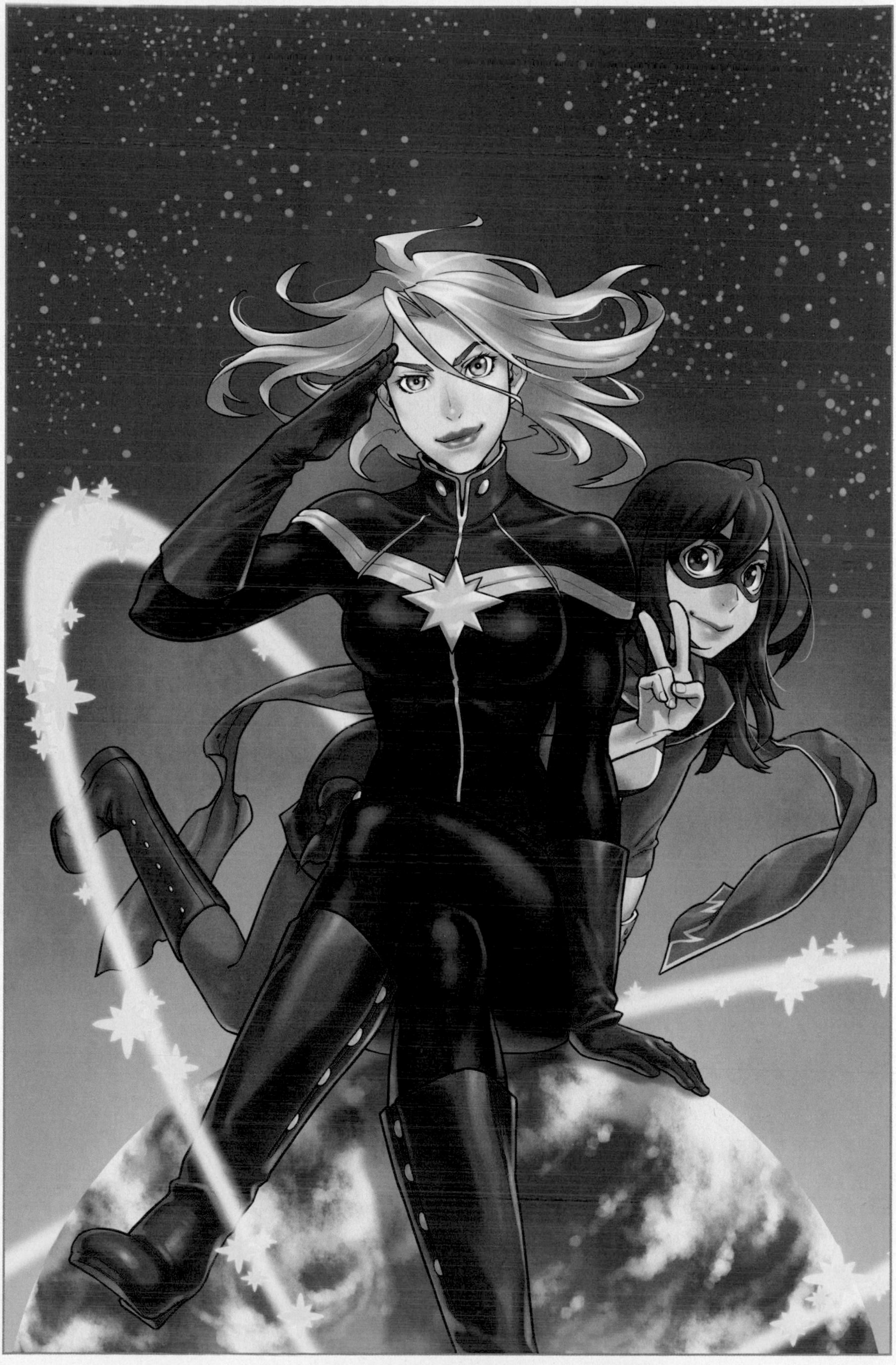

MS. MARVEL #18 MANGA VARIANT
BY RETSU TATEO

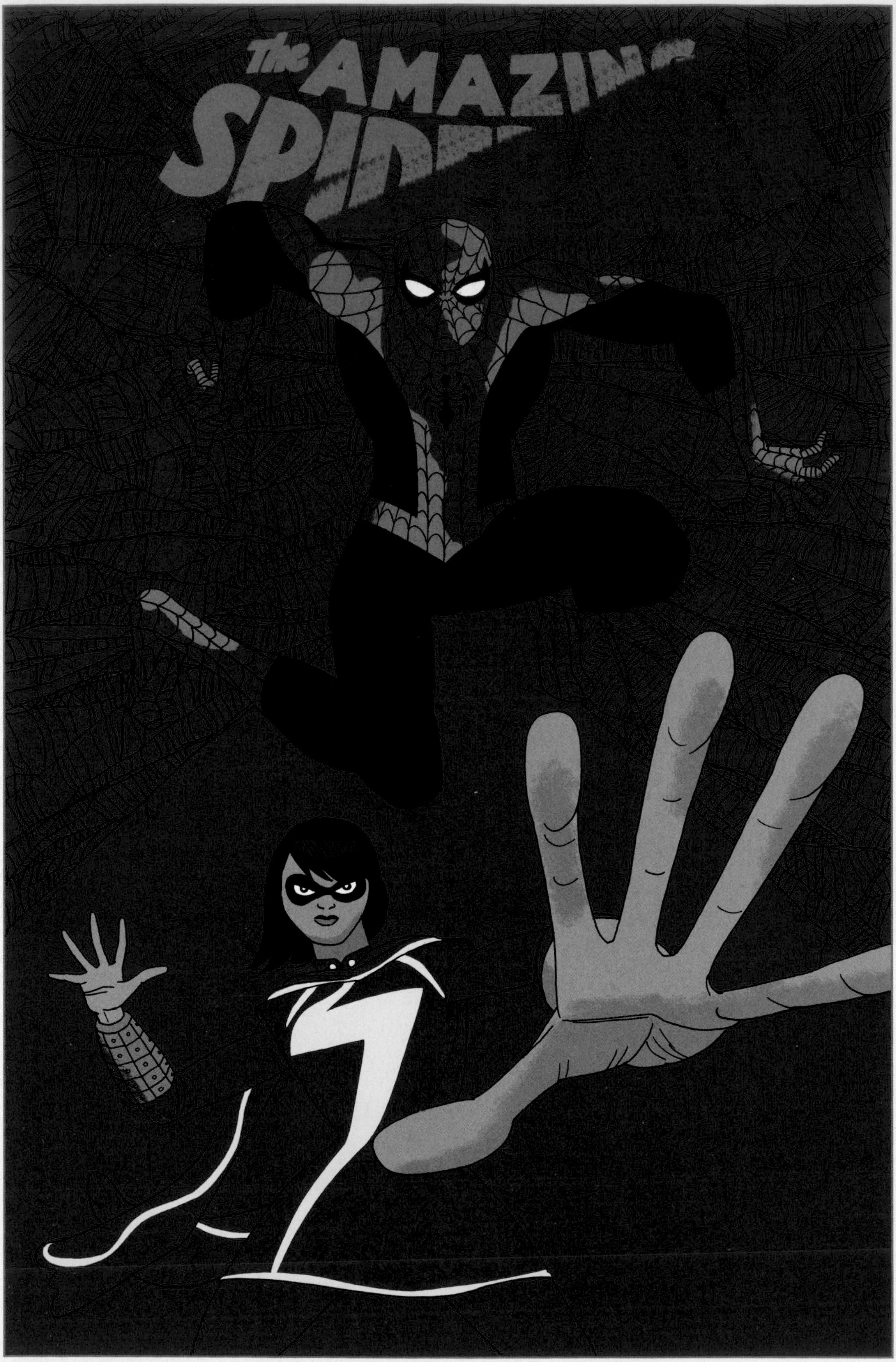
The AMAZIN

AMAZING SPIDER-MAN #7 VARIANT
BY JAVIER PULIDO